The ESL Miscellany

A treasury of cultural and linguistic information

Revised, Second Edition

Raymond C. Clark, Patrick R. Moran, Arthur A. Burrows

PRO LINGUA ☯ ASSOCIATES

Brattleboro, Vermont

Published by Pro Lingua Associates
15 Elm Street
Brattleboro, Vermont 05301

(802) 257-7779
San 216-0579

At
Pro Lingua,
our objective is to foster
an approach to learning and teaching
which we call Interplay, *the interaction of language*
learners and teachers with their materials,
with the language and the culture, and
with each other in active, creative,
and productive
play.

ISBN 0-086647-043-3

The ESL Miscellany was set in Century Schoolbook by Bill Martyn of TypeSet in Brattleboro, Vermont, and printed and bound by BookCrafters in Chelsea, Michigan. Designed by Arthur A. Burrows.

Printed in the United States of America.

Revised, second edition, third printing 1994
16,500 copies in print

Acknowledgements

"The first thing we should say is that a lot of people helped us and we appreciate their support." That is the way we began the acknowledgements in the first edition, and it is still true as we go to press on the Revised, Second Edition, only more so. For ten years people have been coming to us with raves about this section or that, with suggestions about improvements, corrections, and additions, and with complaints. The complaint we have heard many times over is "I can't hold on to this book. Someone keeps stealing it. This is the fourth copy I've had to buy!" We have tried to take all the other suggestions for improvements into account in this complete revision, but we haven't got a solution to that most common problem.

Our acknowledgement for all this help must be made in a very general way. Of the hundred or so teachers who have made recommendations, three sat down and wrote us a letter. First and foremost of these has been Richard Yorkey, most recently of Saint Michael's College in Vermont. Dick has sent us very useful ideas and resources on several occasions over the last ten years; we've used many and those we didn't have room or time for, we will save for the next edition. Both he and Terri Rapoport of the ELS Language Center at Wagner College, N.Y., recommended that we add the section on "Common Idioms and Collocations" based on specific words (page 40). Terri made several other good suggestions which we have included. Ding K. Lau of the Dekalb, Georgia, public schools wrote to tell us the proper term for a person from Singapore, and several other people gave us "nationality and regional words (page 18) more informally over the years. We decided that in revising

we should make our resource list "complete," so we included every member country of the United Nations in our list and may regions (Middle East, Scotland) as well. We accepted the terms used by the U.S. State Department when we could. In some cases, we called embassies in Washington and U.N. Missions in New York. To all the teachers who have used *The Miscellany* and helped us with suggestions, thank you. Keep the ideas coming for the third edition.

The original idea for this book came out of a project initiated at the School for International Training in 1977 for the U.S. Peace Corps. A graduate student in the MAT program, Eleanor Boone, with assistance from Rick Gildea and with support and advice from Mike Jerald, Mary Clark, and Ray Clark was contracted by the Peace Corps to develop a manual of practical suggestions for Peace Corps volunteers teaching English as a foreign language. Toward the end of the project Eleanor was joined by Pat Moran who, at Ray Clark's suggestion, compiled an appendix of information about the English language. The appendix was intended to be useful to the Peace Corps English teacher lost deep in the back country with no professional library to speak of, and nowhere to turn for such things as punctuation guidelines and metric conversion charts.

Two years later as Pro Lingua was being started, Ray, Pat, and Andy Burrows along with Mike Jerald, Peg Clement, Marilyn Funk, and John Croes began developing additional resource materials that might be useful to the ESL teacher. Pat's appendix has now become a book in its own right - a book that represents a collective effort by its three authors.

Peg Clement must be singled out among all those who added to the project for allowing us to use the pictures and classifications from her MAT thesis as the basis for the photographic study of American Gestures (page 273). She in turn would like to acknowledge the help of George McFadden, who took the original pictures, and of Mike Jerald, who processed them and has since added three pictures and provided the basis for the intrepretations.

Mike Jerald has also contributed numerous editorial suggestions in all parts of the book.

Susannah Clark has been our chief editorial assistant from the beginning. For the first edition, she spent hours in the Brooks Memorial Library producing the first draft of many of the Topics. For the second edition, she has edited and added to the topics in the Cultural Aspect and put that section on her computer.

Mary Clark suggested the title for our wild array of infromation. We think its a good one. She also gave permission to use and adapt her chart on modal verbs.

Diane Larsen-Freeman looked over the final draft of the Lingusitic Aspect in the first edition and made several suggestions that improved that section. Bonnie Mennell reviewed our list of communicative topics, added several words, and raised several good questions. Marty Fleischer, who with help from Lisa Cook typed the first edition on one of the world's first word processors (just ten years ago!), pointed out that our law topic didn't adequately cover crime and police work. So Topic # 49 came into being. Karen Kale also reviewed and made suggestions for some of the present topics. Susan McBean helped type some of the original manuscript.

And so we come back to ourselves for a final pat on the back. Pat contributed the illustrations including the Atlas in the new edition. He, Ray, and Andy wrote, edited, and revised the many lists so cooperatively that even they don't know who wrote what.

TABLE OF CONTENTS

THE COMMUNICATIVE ASPECT

THE CULTURAL ASPECT

The Metalinguistic Aspect and Miscellaneous Materials

The Paralinguistic Aspect

The ESL Miscellany

Introduction

The Purpose and Contents
of the Miscellany

This book is a compendium of useful and interesting information for the teacher and student of English as a Second Language. Although the book will be of greatest interest to teachers and students of American English, it will also be useful to teachers and students who are involved with other varieties of English.

The teacher will find this book helpful as a resource for developing material. Virtually every teacher at some time or another attempts to develop material of his/her own either to supplement a basic text, to expand upon some point, to replace or adapt inadequate material or develop a complete curriculum from scratch. This one book may not contain everything that the teacher/materials developer needs to know, but we believe it is the most comprehensive one-volume reference available to the lesson writer.

In addition to its usefulness in developing materials, this book offers another function: that of a guideline/checklist for the teacher who practices eclecticism. More and more teachers, rather than stick to one comprehensive program or one set method, find that in order to keep their classes relevant and interesting they need to teach "a little of this and a little of that." The problem with this kind of eclecticism, of course, is that it is not always easy to know if everything is being covered. This book, or for that matter, any book, will not be able to tell you everything you need to know about American English, but it can serve as a comprehensive outline. By consulting a list of Situations, for example, the teacher can rather quickly get a sense for which conversational situations have been covered and what remains to be covered.

A third use for this book is that many of the lists can be used just as they are as hand-outs. For example, the one-page summary of religions in America could be copied and given to the students as the point of reference for a question-answer practice or discussion of religion in America. For that reason we encourage copying of these lists for classroom use.

We suggested earlier that students of American English will also find this book useful, but it is likely that it will be especially valuable to advanced students of American English who are in need of a one-volume guide that will help them determine what they already know and what they should focus their study on. We think this book will be of particular interest to advanced students who are preparing to be teachers of English as a Second Language.

The Miscellany is divided into five parts. Parts I and II contain information about the language itself. This information is classified in two major aspects: Linguistic and Communicative. The linguistic aspect contains information that in some way deals with what is

1

commonly called the grammar of structure of the language. However, this linguistic aspect is not a grammar, but rather a series of lists of words and forms that exemplify some grammar point. For example, under two-word verbs, there will be no rules for the use of two-word verbs. Instead, there will be a list of separable and inseparable two-word verbs. In other words, it is assumed that the user will have some understanding of how two-word verbs function in English.

The communicative aspect does not deal with linguistic forms such as "go, went, gone" but outlines ways in which the language is used to send and receive messages. We have included lists of *functions* such as asking, introducing, telling, etc. We have also included in the communicative aspect vocabulary lists that outline potential *topics* of conversations, and we have compiled lists of *situations* in which communicative functions and topics of conversation are carried out.

In Part III we have compiled several lists that form an outline of American culture. Each list can be used as the basic data upon which can be based a discussion or controlled conversation about some facet of American culture. Part III can be used as the basis for an orientation to immigration and resettlement in the United States.

Part IV is a pot-pourri of information that is, in general, metalinguistic. In other words, the information in this part will help the teacher and the learner facilitate the teaching/learning process. But there is also information that does not fit neatly into any of the other categories and is best labeled as miscellaneous.

Part V needs little explanation. It contains some examples of communicative systems that parallel the language itself. Hence, we have called it the paralinguistic aspect. Of greatest interest is a photographic catalog of 50 gestures that are commonly recognized and understood in the United States. We have provided titles and minimal explanations for the gestures, but otherwise we leave it up to you, the user of this book, to discuss, compare, practice and even add to this listing.

We will be the first to admit that this volume represents an ambitious undertaking that probably contains inaccuracies, and that is far from complete. Furthermore, the nature of the information itself is such that it may need occasional updating. It is our hope and intention to produce a revision eventually, and to make the revised edition more useful and comprehensive. We ask you, the users, to help us in this effort with your suggestions. Send them to us at the address below and we will make every effort to use and acknowledge your contribution.

PRO LINGUA ASSOCIATES
Brattleboro, 1981

A Word about the Second Edition

The first edition of the Miscellany has been available, with only minor corrections made, for the last ten years. Over that time, seventy-five hundred copies have been sold and many of the teachers who bought them have let us know that our hopes for this teachers' resource were justified. However, over the last ten years much of the data in the section on the Cultural Aspect has become dated, and we have collected many suggestions for additions and other improvements to all the aspects of our book.

We feel that this edition of the Miscellany is richer than the first, but by the very nature of the book it can always be improved. So continue to send us your inspirations and corrections for the third edition.

PRO LINGUA ASSOCIATES, 1991
15 Elm Street
Brattleboro, Vermont 05301

The Linguistic Aspect

For years, the teaching and learning of English has focused on texts, techniques and exercises designed to enable students to manipulate the grammar of English with a minimum of grammatical errors, such as 'he go', and with clear pronunciation. Obviously, this is still an important part of teaching English; there will always be a time and place for the tried and true exercises and drills that help install grammatical accuracy. Practice still makes perfect.

On the following pages we have provided first a checklist of grammatical features that most teachers find it necessary to cover. This checklist is not intended to represent the best pedagogical sequence of what should be taught before what; it is only one possible sequence in which English grammar can be presented.

After the checklist are several selected lists that should prove helpful to the teacher or student who wants to work on a particular grammatical problem. It should be obvious that many syntactic features do not lend themselves to listing and so they will not be included in the lists.

Contents

5

A Grammar Sequence

The grammar sequence on the following pages is to be considered only a handy checklist for the person who wants to get a rough idea of what can or should be covered in an English course. We make no claims that it is complete or logical or carefully programmed in steps of equal difficulty or complexity. We have listed 139 steps, and we have placed them in a particular order. Some of the steps are big and some are small. Some steps can be omitted or placed elsewhere in the sequence, and some depend upon previous steps and should only be re-arranged with care. It will also be obvious that in some cases, two or more steps must be taken at the same time. In other words, please use this sequence with the understanding that it is not a grammar of English and it is not **the** best or **the** most natural sequence for proceeding through a grammatically-based English course.

The sequence does represent an attempt to proceed one step at a time through the grammar of English in a general progression of "easy and simple" points to "difficult and complex" points. It also represents a sequence that begins with useful and necessary points and leads to less useful and necessary points. At the very least, the sequence represents dozens of potential grammar lessons that nearly every teacher and student will need to struggle with in a basic English program. Mastery of what this sequence represents, along with commensurate progress in pronunciation and communicative skills, would probably mean that the student is capable of functioning independently in an English-speaking world.

☐	1.	Statement word order with **be**	*I am here.*
☐	2.	Forms of **be**	*Am; are; is*
☐	3.	Subject pronouns	*I, you, he, she, it, we, they*
☐	4.	Question word order with **be**	*Is he here?*
☐	5.	Negative of **be**	*I am not; you are not*
☐	6.	Plural of regular nouns	*We are students.*
☐	7.	Common irregular noun plurals	*They are women.*
☐	8.	Nationality words	*I am Swedish.* *They are Swedish.*
☐	9.	Indefinite article: **a/an**	*I am an American.*
☐	10.	Question word: **who**	*Who is she?*
☐	11.	**And** in compound sentences	*He is a teacher and she is a student.*
☐	12.	**But** in compound sentences	*He is a teacher but she is not.*
☐	13.	Contractions of **be** and **not**	*I'm not; he isn't*
☐	14.	Conjugation of verbs other than **be** (3rd person singular)	*I teach French.* *She teaches English.*

☐ 16.   *Have* and *have got*   *I have....*
           I have got....

☐ 17.   Contractions of *have*   *I've....; I've got....*

☐ 18.   Question word: *what*   *What do you have?*

☐ 19.   Short Answers.   *Yes, I do. No, he isn't.*

☐ 20.   Tag Questions   *You have..., don't you?*
           You don't have..., do you?

☐ 21.   Negative questions   *Don't you have...?*

☐ 22.   Stative verbs   *I want....*

☐ 23.   Positive imperative   *Take a....*

☐ 24.   Negative imperative   *Don't take a....*

☐ 25.   Colors   *Take a red....*

☐ 26.   Definite and indefinite articles   *...a yellow pencil.*
           ...the yellow pencil.

☐ 27.   Polite requests: *would, will, could, why don't you*   *Would you...?*

☐ 28.   Demonstratives: *this/that these/those*   *This is a ....*
           Those are ....

☐ 29.   Count and non-count nouns   *This is soup.*
           This is a spoon.

☐ 30.   Expletive *there is/are*   *There's a fly....*

☐ 31.   Expletive *here*   *Here's a....*

☐ 32.   Expletive **it**   *It's cold.*

☐ 33.   Form and position of modifiers   *...green shoes.*

☐ 34.   Order of modifiers   *...small green tennis shoes.*

☐ 35.   Past tense of *be*   *I was....*

☐ 36.   Past tense of regular verbs   *I studied....*

☐ 37.   Use of *did*   *Did you...?*
           No, I didn't....

☐ 38.   Irregular past tense forms   *I taught....*

☐ 39.   Question words as interrogative adjectives: *what, which*   *Which book...?*

☐ 40.   **Some,** *any* and **none**   *I don't have any,....*

☐ 41.   Quantity expressions **(how)**   *I have a few....*
         much/many, few, little

☐ 42.   Use of **quite** and **only**   *I have quite a few....*

☐ 43.   **One** as a pronoun   *...the green one.*

☐ 44.   **One of/none of**   *He needs one of the ....*

☐ 45.   **The other/another**   *She likes the other ....*

☐ 46.   **Each/every/all of**   *Each student has ....*

☐ 47.   Object pronouns   *...understand her.*

☐ 48.   Direct and indirect objects   *... give it to her.*

☐ 49.   Adverbs of frequency.   *He always ....*

☐ 50.   **Ever**   *Do you ever ...?*

☐ 51.   Question words: **how often,**   *How often do you ...?*
         when, where

☐ 52.   Cardinal and ordinal numbers   *The first five .... The fifth ....*

☐ 53.   Word order with place and time adverbials   *... here in the morning.*

☐ 54.   Prepositions with time expressions   *... at three o'clock on Monday.*

☐ 55.   Prepositions with places   *... on Main Street.*
                                                           In Brattleboro.

☐ 56.   **Do** vs. **make**   *Do the dishes and make the bed.*

☐ 57.   Form and position of adverbs of   *... speak slowly.*
         manner (**-ly**)

☐ 58.   Irregular adverbs of manner   *... talk fast.*

☐ 59.   Question word: **how**   *How does she ...?*

☐ 60.   **Say, tell, talk, speak**   *Tell me about ....*

☐ 61.   Indirect object after **ask**   *Ask her a question.*

☐ 62.   Indirect object with **to**   *Explain it to her.*

☐ 63.   Indirect object with **for**   *Do it for me.*

☐ 64.   Present progressive (continuous)   *I am ...ing.*

☐ 65.   **Going to** future   *I am going to ....*

8

☐ 66.	Question word: **why**	*Why are you ...?*
☐ 67.	Question word: **what ... for**	*What are you ... for?*
☐ 68.	Question word: **how come**	*How come you ...?*
☐ 69.	Anticipatory **it**	*It's easy to ....*
☐ 70.	**Let's**	*Let's ....*
		Let's not....
☐ 71.	Idioms with **go**	*Let's go swimming.*
☐ 72.	Indefinite **you**	*You can't go swimming there.*
☐ 73.	Question words: **who** vs. **who(m)**	*Who sees Mary?*
		Whom does Mary see?
☐ 74.	Question word: **whose**	*Whose ... is this?*
☐ 75.	Possessive adjectives	*That's my ....*
☐ 76.	Possessive **'s**	*Mary's ... is here.*
☐ 77.	Possessive **of**	*The leg of my table.*
☐ 78.	Possessive pronouns	*That's mine.*
☐ 79.	**Belongs to**	*That belongs to ....*
☐ 80.	**Be about to** future	*I am about to ....*
☐ 81.	Present tense for future time	*I am to ... next week.*
☐ 82.	Modals: **can, might should, must**	*We can go ....*
☐ 83.	Modals: **ought to**	*We ought to go ....*
☐ 84.	**Have to**	*We have to go ....*
☐ 85.	Modals in past tense with perfect aspect.	*We could have gone.*
		We had to go.
☐ 86.	Future tense with **will**	*We'll go ....*
☐ 87.	Contractions of **will not**	*We won't go ....*
☐ 88.	Future progressive	*We will be going.*
☐ 89.	**Had better**	*We'd better go ....*
☐ 90.	**Would rather**	*I'd rather be a ....*
☐ 91.	**Would like**	*I'd like to be a ....*

☐ 92. ***Was going to ... but***   *I was going to ... but ....*

☐ 93. ***And ... too/either***   *And she does too.*
                                               And I won't either.

☐ 94. Separable and inseparable   *Let's call on them.*
        two-word verbs   *Let's call them up.*

☐ 95. Adverbials of purpose: *He went for some books /*
        for and *(in order) to*   *to buy some books.*

☐ 96. Adverbials of means and instrument: *He went by bus.*
        by and ***with***   *He went with a suitcase.*

☐ 97. Verbs followed by an infinitive   *I want to go.*

☐ 98. Verbs followed by a gerund   *I enjoy singing.*

☐ 99. Verbs followed by an infinitive or a gerund   *I like reading / to read....*

☐ 100. Perception verbs followed by a   *I saw him go.*
         simple verb instead of *-ing*

☐ 101. ***Very, too, enough***   *That's too big.*

☐ 102. Comparison: **the same ... as,**   *This is the same as that.*
         different from and ***like***

☐ 103. Comparison: the same ... **as,**   *Mine is the same color as yours.*
         as ..., as

☐ 104. Comparison ***-er than,***   *It's bigger than his and more useful than hers.*
         more ... than

☐ 105. Superlative   *It's the biggest and most useful.*

☐ 106. Past habitual   *I used to ....*

☐ 107. ***Would* as past habitual**   *When we were young, we would ....*

☐ 108. ***Be used to***   *I'm used to ....*

☐ 109. Causatives: ***let, have, help,***   *We made him go.*
         make and ***get***

☐ 110. Reflexive pronouns   *He hurt himself.*

☐ 111. Emphatics   *He did it himself.*
                                               He himself did it.

10

☐ 112.   Embedded statements   *I know (that) he's here.*

☐ 113.   Embedded question-word statements   *I know where he is.*

☐ 114.   Relative clauses   *I know the man who did it.*

☐ 115.   **Who/whatever**   *Whoever has ....*

☐ 116.   **For** vs. **during**   *... during the afternoon for an hour.*

☐ 117.   Past Continuous   *He was studying ....*

☐ 118.   **While** and **then** in clauses   *... while I was sleeping.*

☐ 119.   **Before, until** and **after**   *He studied before you arrived.*

☐ 120.   Present perfect   *I have already studied.*

☐ 121.   Irregular past participles   *She has gone.*

☐ 122.   Participles as modifiers   *He is boring / bored.*

☐ 123.   **Still, anymore, already, yet**   *He hasn't studied yet.* ◄

☐ 124.   Present perfect progressive   *They have been playing.*

☐ 125.   Past perfect   *They had gone.*

☐ 126.   Reported speech   *He said she had gone.*

☐ 127.   Past perfect progressive   *They had been working.*

☐ 128.   Passive voice   *They were seen by ....*

☐ 129.   Adjective+preposition combinations   *She is interested in....*

☐ 130.   Subjunctive   *I suggested that she see....*

☐ 131.   **Wish** followed by a noun clause   *I wish (that) you were here.*

☐ 132.   **Wish** and noun clause in past time   *I wish (that) you had been here.*

☐ 133.   Conditionals   *If you were here ....*

☐ 134.   Subordinators: **unless, because**   *Unless I am mistaken ....*
          although, whether, whenever

☐ 135.   Future perfect   *They will have gone ....*

☐ 136.   Future perfect progressive   *They will have been working.*

☐ 137.   **So ... that** vs. **such ... that**   *He is so strong that ....*

☐ 138.   Nouns as complements   *We elected him president.*

☐ 139.   Verb+preposition combinations   *We agreed on that.*

Grammar Lists

Grammar Checklist

List 1: Minimal Pairs

Vowels

/iy/   /i/

sheep	ship
leave	live
seat	sit
green	grin

/iy/   /ey/

eat	ate
see	say
week	wake
creep	crepe

/iy/   /e/

meet	met
mean	men
seeks	sex
beast	best

/i/   /ey/

it	ate
kick	cake
chin	chain
give	gave

/i/   /e/

pick	peck
did	dead
sit	set
knit	net

/i/   /æ/

big	bag
it	at
sit	sat
zig	zag

/i/   /ə/

big	bug
live	love
sick	suck
rib	rub

/ey/   /e/

wait	wet
date	debt
pain	pen

/ey/   /æ/

snake	snack
ate	at
made	mad
hate	hat

/ey/   /ə/

ape	up
lake	luck
rain	run
came	come

/ey/   /ow/

taste	toast
say	so
break	broke
wake	woke

/e/   /æ/

dead	dad
said	sad
men	man
bed	bad

/e/   /ə/

beg	bug
ten	ton
many	money
net	nut

/e/   /a/

get	got
step	stop
red	rod
net	not

/æ/   /ə/

grab	grub
swam	swum
mad	mud
cap	cup

14

Vowels (Continued)

/æ/	/ɑ/
an	on
map	mop
cat	cot
lack	lock

/æ/	/ay/
am	I'm
sad	side
dad	died
back	bike

/ə/	/ɑ/
hug	hog
cup	cop
luck	lock
nut	not

/ə/	/u/
luck	look
buck	book
stud	stood
tuck	took

/ə/	/ow/
cut	coat
must	most
come	comb
but	boat

/ə/	/ɔ/
gun	gone
cut	caught
bus	boss
dug	dog

/ɑ/	/u/
lock	look
pot	put
cod	could
shock	shook

/ɑ/	/ow/
hop	hope
got	goat
want	won't
rod	road

/ɑ/	/ɔ/
cot	caught
sod	sawed
are	or
tock	talk

/ɑ/	/aw/
are	hour
shot	shout
dot	doubt
got	gout

/ɔ/	/oy/
all	oil
jaw	joy
ball	boil
bald	boiled

/u/	/uw/
full	fool
pull	pool
soot	suit
could	cooed

/u/	/ow/
bull	bowl
cook	coke
should	showed
brook	broke

/ow/	/oy/
toe	toy
old	oiled
bold	boiled
cone	coin

/aw/	/ay/
mouse	mice
tower	tire
proud	pride
found	find

/aw/	/oy/
owl	oil
vowed	void
sow	soy
bough	boy

/oy/	/ay/
toy	tie
boy	buy
voice	vice
alloy	ally

Consonants

/p/ /b/

pig	big
cap	cab
pie	buy
rapid	rabid

/b/ /v/

boat	vote
best	vest
curb	curve
cupboard	covered

/l/ /r/

light	right
bowl	boar
collect	correct
lead	read

/č/ /š/

cheap	sheep
catch	cash
watch	wash
cheese	she's

/ǰ/ /š/

jeep	sheep
jade	shade
jack	shack
gyp	ship

/ǰ/ /č/

gin	chin
joke	choke
jeer	cheer
junk	chunk

/ǰ/ /y/

juice	use
jet	yet
jam	yam
wage	weigh

/g/ /k/

bag	back
grape	crepe
glass	class
gap	cap

/θ/ /t/

death	debt
thigh	tie
thin	tin
three	tree

/θ/ /s/

think	sink
thing	sing
mouth	mouse
thin	sin

/ð/ /d/

they	day
lather	ladder
their	dare
breathe	breed

16

List 2: Irregular Noun Plurals (7)*

A.   Vowel change

man > men
woman > women

foot > feet
tooth > teeth

goose > geese
mouse > mice

B.   -en Suffix

child > children

ox > oxen

C.   f > v

thief > thieves
wife > wives
life > lives
knife > knives
calf > calves

half > halves
leaf > leaves
loaf > loaves
self > selves
sheaf > sheaves

shelf > shelves
wolf > wolves
hoof > hooves

D.   Same

sheep > sheep
deer > deer
moose > moose
fish > fish
trout > trout

salmon > salmon
bass > bass
series > series
means > means
species > species

Chinese > Chinese
Japanese > Japanese
Swiss > Swiss

E.   No singular

scissors
tweezers
tongs
trousers
slacks

shorts
pants
pajamas
(eye) glasses
spectacles

binoculars
clothes
people
Smithereens

F.   Borrowed Greek and Latin words

analysis > analyses
basis > bases
hypothesis > hypotheses
parenthesis > parentheses
synopsis > synopses
thesis > theses
crisis > crises

stimulus > stimuli
nucleus > nuclei
alumnus > alumni
radius > radii
syllabus > syllabi
medium > media
memorandum > memoranda

curriculum > curricula
phenomenon > phenomena
criterion > criteria
vortex > vortices
matrix > matrices
index > indices

*This number represents a step in the Grammar Sequence (p.6).

List 3: Nationality and Regional Words (8)*

Country	Person	Adjective
Afghanistan	Afghan(s), Afghanistani	Afghan, Afghani
Africa	African(s)	African,
North, West, East Africa	North, West, East African(s)	North, West, East African
Albania	Albanian(s)	Albanian
Algeria	Algerian(s)	Algerian
America	American(s)	American
Americas, The	South American(s), North American(s)	North, South American
Andora	Andorran(s)	Andorran
Angola	Angolan(s)	Angolan
Antigua and Barbuda	Antiguan(s), Barbudan(s)	Antiguan, Barbudan
Arabia (The Arab World)	Arab(s), Arabian(s)	Arab, Arabian
Argentina	Argentine(s), Argentinean(s)	Argentine, Argentinean
Armenia	Armenian(s)	Armenian
Asia	Asian(s)	Asian
Australia	Australian(s), Aussie(s) (colloq.)	Australian
Austria	Austrian(s)	Austrian
Azerbaijan	Azerbaijani(s)	Azerbaijan, Azerbaijani
Bahamas, The	Bahamian(s)	Bahamian
Bahrain	Bahrani(s)	Bahraini
Bangladesh	Bangladeshi(s)	Bangladeshi
Barbados	Barbadian(s)	Barbadian
Belgium	Belgian(s)	Belgian
Belize	Belizean(s)	Belizean
Benin	Beninese	Beninese
Bermuda	Bermudian(s)	Bermudian
Bhutan	Bhutanese, Bhutani(s)	Bhutanese, Bhutani
Bolivia	Bolivian(s)	Bolivian
Botswana	Motswana (sing.), Batswana (pl.)	Motswana (sing.), Batswana (pl.) Setswana (lang.)
Brazil	Brazilian(s)	Brazilian
Brunei	Bruneian(s)	Bruneian
Burkina Faso (Upper Volta)	Burkinabe (Voltan(s))	Burkinabe (Voltan(s))
Bulgaria	Bulgarian(s)	Bulgarian
Burma (Myanmar)	Burmese	Burmese
Burundi	Burundi(s)	Burundi, Kirundi (lang.)
Byelorussia (White Russia)	Byelorussian(s)	Byelorussian
Cambodia (Kampuchea)	Cambodian(s)	Cambodian
Cameroon	Cameroonian(s)	Cameroonian
Canada	Canadian(s)	Canadian
Cape Verde	Cape Verdean(s)	Cape Verdean
Central African Republic	Central African(s), Centrafrican(s)	Central African, Centrafrican
Central America	Central American(s)	Central American
Central Asia	Central Asian(s)	Central Asia

This list includes all to the members of the United Nations as of publication. It also includes a number of regions within nations (Wales, for example) and regions which contains several nations (such as Southeast Asia). No political comments are implied. These are all terms in common English usage. The list could, of course, be endless, but the editors will appreciate corrections and additions.

*This number represents a step in the Grammar Sequence (p.6).

Country	Person	Adjective
Chad	Chadian(s)	Chadian
Chile	Chilean(s)	Chilean
China, Peoples Republic of	Chinese	Chinese
Colombia	Colombian(s)	Colombian
Comoros	Comorian(s)	Comoran
Congo	Congolese	Congolese
Costa Rica	Costa Rican(s)	Costa Rican
Cuba	Cuban(s)	Cuban
Cyprus	Cypriot(s)	Cypriot
Czechoslovakia	Czechosolvak(s), Czech(s), Czechosolvakian(s), Slovak(s)	Czechoslovak, Czech, Czechoslovakian, Slovak
Denmark	Dane(s)	Danish
Djibouti	Djibouti(s)	Djibouti
Dominica	Dominican(s)	Dominican
Dominican Republic	Dominican(s)	Dominican
Ecuador	Ecuadorean(s)	Ecuadorean
Egypt	Egyptian(s)	Egyptian
El Salvador	Salvadoran(s)	Salvadoran
England	Englishman (men, women)	English
Equitorial Guinea	Equitorial Guinean(s), Euitoguinean(s)	Equitorial Guinean, Equitoguinean
Estonia	Estonian(s)	Estonian
Ethiopia	Ethiopian(s)	Ethiopian
Europe	European(s)	European
Far East, East Asia	East Asian(s), Far Easterner(s)	East Asian, Far Eastern
Fiji	Fijian(s), Fiji Islander(s)	Fijian
Finland	Finn(s)	Finnish
France	Frenchman (men, women)	French
French Antillies and Guiana Martinique, Guadeloupe	French Guianese, Martiniquais, Guadeloupean(s)	French Guianese, Martiniquais, Guadeloupean
Gabon	Gabonese	Gabonese
Gambia, The	Gambian	Gambian
Germany	German(s)	German
Georgia	Georgian(s)	Georgian
Ghana	Ghanaian(s)	Ghanaian
Greece	Greek(s)	Greek
Grenada	Grenadian(s)	Grenadian
Guatemala	Guatemalan(s)	Guatemalan
Guinea	Guinean(s)	Guinean
Guinea-Bissau	Guinea Bissauan(s), Bissau Guinean(s)	Guinea Bissauan, Bissau Guinean
Guyana	Guyanese	Guyanese
Haiti	Haitian(s)	Haitian
Honduras	Honduran(s)	Honduran
Hong Kong	Hong Kongese, Chinese	Hong Kong
Hungary	Hungarian(s)	Hungarian

Country	Person	Adjective
Iceland	Icelander(s)	Icelandic
India	Indian(s)	Indian
Indochina	Indochinese	Indochinese
Indonesia	Indonesian(s)	Indonesian
Iran	Iranian(s)	Iranian
Iraq	Iraqi(s)	Iraqi
Ireland	Irishman (men, women)	Irish
Israel	Israeli(s)	Israeli
Italy	Italian(s)	Italian
Ivory Coast (Côte d'Ivoire)	Ivorian(s)	Ivorian
Jamaica	Jamaican(s)	Jamaican
Japan	Japanese	Japanese
Jordan	Jordanian(s)	Jordanian
Kampuchea (Cambodia)	Kampuchean(s)	Kampuchean
Kazakhstan	Kazakh(s)	Kazakh
Kenya	Kenyan(s)	Kenyan
Kirghiz	Kirghiz(es)	Kirghiz
Kiribati (Gilbert Islands)	Kiribati(s)	Kiribati (Gilbertese)
Korea, North	North Korean(s)	NorthKorean
Korea, South	South Korean(s)	SouthKorean
Kurdistan	Kurd(s)	Kurdish
Kuwait	Kuwaiti(s)	Kuwaiti
Laos	Lao(s), Laotian(s)	Lao,Laotian
Latin America	Latin American(s), Hispanic(s)	LatinAmerican
Latvia	Latvian(s)	Latvian
Lebanon	Lebanese	Lebanese
Lesotho	Mosotho (sing.), Basotho (pl.)	Basotho, Sesotho (lang.)
Liberia	Liberian(s)	Liberian
Libya	Libyan(s)	Libyan
Liechtenstein	Liechtensteiner(s)	Liechtenstein
Lithuania	Lithuanian(s)	Lithuanian
Luxembourg	Luxembourger(s), Luxembourgian(s)	Luxembourgish, Luxembourgian
Madagascar	Malagasy(ies)	Malagasy
Malawi	Malawian(s)	Malawian
Malaysia	Malaysian	Malaysian
Maldives	Maldivian(s)	Maldivian
Mali	Malian(s)	Malian
Malta	Maltese	Maltese
Mauritania	Mauritanian(s)	Mauritanian
Mauritius	Mauritian(s)	Mauritian
Mexico	Mexican(s)	Mexican
Middle East, The (Mideast)	Middle Easterner(s)	Middle Eastern
Moldavia	Moldavian(s)	Moldavian
Monaco	Monegasque(s)	Monegasque
Mongolia	Mongolian(s)	Mongolian
Morocco	Moroccan(s)	Moroccan
Mozambique	Mozambican(s)	Mozambican

Country	Person	Adjective
Namibia	Namibian(s)	Namibian
Nauru	Nauruan(s)	Nauruan
Nepal	Nepalese	Nepalese, Nepali
Netherlands, The (Holland)	Dutchman (men, women)	Dutch
Netherlands Antilles and Aruba	Netherland Antillean(s) Aruban(s)	Netherland Antillean Aruban
New Zealand	New Zealander(s)	New Zealand
Nicaragua	Nicaraguan(s)	Nicaraguan
Niger	Nigerien(s)	Nigerien
Nigeria	Nigerian(s)	Nigerian
North America	North American(s), American(s)	North American, American
Norway	Norwegian(s)	Norwegian
Oman	Omani(s)	Omani
Orient	Oriental(s)	Oriental
Pakistan	Pakistani(s)	Pakistani
Palestine	Palestinian(s)	Palestinian
Panama	Panamanian(s)	Panamanian
Papua New Guinea	Papua New Guinean(s)	Papua New Guinean
Paraguay	Paraguayan(s)	Paraguayan
Peru	Peruvian(s)	Peruvian
Philippines	Filipino(s)	Filipino
Poland	Pole(s)	Polish
Polynesia	Polynesian(s)	Polynesian
Portugal	Portuguese	Portuguese
Puerto Rico	Puerto Rican(s)	Puerto Rican
Qatar	Qatari(s)	Qatari
Romania, Rumania	Romanian(s)	Romanian
Russia	Russian(s)	Russian
Rwanda	Rwandan(s)	Rwandan
St. Kitts and Nevis	Kittitian(s), Nevisian(s)	Kittitian, Nevisian
St. Lucia	St. Lucian(s)	St. Lucian
St. Vincent and the Grenadines	Vincentian(s)	Vincentian
San Marino	Sammarinese (sing.), Sammarinesi (pl.)	Sammarinese
Sao Tome and Principe	Sao Tomean(s)	Sao Tomean
Saudi Arabia	Saudi(s)	Saudi, Saudi Arabian
Scotland	Scot(s), Scotsman (men,women)	Scottish
Senegal	Senegalese	Senegalese
Seychelles	Seychellois	Seychellois
Sierra Leone	Sierra Leonean(s)	Sierra Leonean
Singapore	Singaporean(s)	Singaporean
Solomon Islands	Solomon Islander(s)	Solomon Island
Somalia	Somali(s)	Somali
South Africa	South African(s)	South African
South America	South American(s)	South American
Southeast Asia	Southeast Asian(s)	Southeast Asian
Spain	Spaniard(s)	Spanish
Sri Lanka (Ceylon)	Sri Lankan(s) (Ceylonese)	Sri Lankan (Ceylonese)
Sudan	Sudanese	Sudanese
Suriname	Surinamer(s)	Surinamese

Country	Person	Adjective
Swaziland	Swazi(s)	Swazi
Sweden	Swede(s)	Swedish
Switzerland	Swiss	Swiss
Syria	Syrian(s)	Syrian
Tadzhikistan	Tadzhik, Tajik	Tadzhik, Tadzhiki
Taiwan (Republic of China)	Taiwanese	Taiwanese
Tanzania	Tanzanian(s), Zanzabari(s)	Tanzanian, Zanzabari
Thailand	Thai(s)	Thai
Tibet	Tibetan(s)	Tibetan
Togo	Togolese	Togolese
Tonga	Tongan(s)	Tongan
Trinidad and Tobago	Trinidadian(s), Tobagonian(s)	Trinidadian, Tobagoan
Tunisia	Tunisian(s)	Tunisian
Turkey	Turk(s)	Turkish
Turkistan	Turkistani(s)	Turkistani
Turkmenistan	Turkoman(s)	Turkmen, Turkoman
Tuvalu (Ellice Islands)	Tuvaluan(s)	Tuvaluan
Uganda	Ugandan(s)	Ugandan
Ukraine, The	Ukrainian(s)	Ukrainian
United Arab Emirates	Emerian(s), Emeri(s)	U.A.E.
U.S.S.R. (Soviet Union)	Soviet(s), Russian(s)	Soviet, Russian
United Kingdom of Great Britain	Briton(s)	British
United States of America	American(s)	American
Uruguay	Uruguayan(s)	Uruguayan
Uzbekistan	Uzbeki(s), Uzbek(s)	Uzbeki, Uzbek
Vanuatu	ni-Vanuatu	ni-Vanuatu
Vatican City (The Holy See)	Roman Catholic(s)	Vatican
Venezuela	Venezuelan(s)	Venezuelan
Vietnam	Vietnamese	Vietnamese
Wales	Welshman (men, women)	Welsh
Western Samoa	Samoan(s)	Western Samoan
Yemen	Yemeni(s)	Yemeni
Yugoslavia	Yugoslav(s)	Yugoslav
Zaire	Zairian(s)	Zairian
Zambia	Zambian(s)	Zambian
Zimbabwe	Zimbabwean(s)	Zimbabwean

List 4: Prefixes and Suffixes

A. PREFIXES

Prefix	Meaning	Example
a-, an-	not	amoral, atypical, amorphous
ab-	away from	abnormal, abrupt, abstain
ad-	toward, to	administer, adhere, adapt
ante-	before, in front of	anteroom, antecedent, antedate
anti-	against, opposite	antidote, antipathy, antiseptic
arch-	chief, prime	archbishop, archangel, archenemy
auto-	self	automatic, automobile
be-	to cause, intensely	belittle, befriend, beware, bedecked, befuddled
bene-	well	benefactor, benefit, benevolent
bi-	two	bisect, bifocal, bigamy
circum-	around, on all sides	circumscribe, circumnavigate, circumvent
con-	with	conversation, confound, convoy
col-	with	collage, collateral, collapse
cor-	with	correlate, correspond, correct
co-	with	co-worker, co-exist, co-author
contra-	against, opposite	contradict, contraband, contravene
counter	against, opposite	counteract, counterbalance, countermand
de-	not, away from, down from	descend, deflate, deviate
di-	apart, away, not	diverge, diminish, dilute, divorce
di-	twice fold, double	dichotomy, diagraph, dilemma
dia-	through, completely	diameter, diaper, diaphanous, Diaspora
dif-	apart, away, not	diffuse, differ, difficult
dis-	apart, away, not	distrust, disinterested, disorder
en-	make, create	engage, enact, entrust
epi-	above, around, additional	epicenter, epidemic, epidermis
equi-	equal	equivalent, equinox, equilibrium
ex-, e-	out from, former	exit, excavate, ex-governor, egress, exhale
extra-	outside, beyond	extraordinary, extrasensory, extravagant
hetero-	different	heterogeneous, heterosexual
homo-	same	homogeneous, homosexual
hyper-	extremely	hyperactive, hyperventilate, hyperbole
hypo-	below, beneath	hypodermic, hypocrisy, hypotenuse
in-	into, not	inhale, inept, innocent,
im-	into, not	impel, imbalance, immoral,
il-	into, not	illuminate, illiterate, illegal, illegible
ir-	into, not	irradiate, irregular, irresponsible, irresolute,
inter-	between, at intervals	intersperse, intermittent, intervene,
intra-	within	intracellular, intramural
intro-	motion inward	introduce, introspective, introvert
macro-	large	macrocosm, macrobiotics, macro-organism
mal-	ill, badly, bad, wrong	malfunction, malnutrition, malevolent
mega-	big	megaphone, megaton, megalopolis
micro-	small	microscope, microphone, micro-organism
mini-	small, little	minivan, miniskirt, minimal
mis-	wrong, wrongly, not	misunderstanding, misuse, mistrust
mono-	single, one	monophonic, monologue, monomania
multi-	many	multisided, multiplex, multivitamin
neo-	new	neophyte, neoclassical, neonatal

Prefix	Meaning	Example
non-	not	nonexistent, nonpayment, nonconformist
ob-	against	obstinate, obscure, object
pan-	all, whole, completely	Pan African, panorama, pandemic
para-	beyond, outside, near	parabola, paramilitary, paradox, paramedic
pen-	almost	peninsula, penultimate
per-	motion through, thoroughly	percolate, perfect, perceive
peri-	around, about, enclosing	perimeter, periscope, periphery
poly-	many	polygamy, polyglot, polychrome
post-	behind, after	posterity, posthumous, postscript
pre-	before, earlier, in front of	preconceived, premonition, predict
pro-	forward, before, in favor of	propulsion, prologue, project
proto-	earliest, first, original	prototype, proto-American, protocol
re-	back, again	reappear, recapture, reclaim, return
retro-	backwards	retrospect, retroactive, retroflex,
se-	aside, apart	seclusion, secede, seduce
semi-	half, partly	semiannual, semicircle, semiprecious
simil-	like	similar, simile
sub-	under, below	subway, submarine, subnormal, submerge
super-	over, above, extra	superimpose, supernatural, superfluous
sur-	above, additional	survey, surtax, surface
syn-, sym-	together	synchronize, synthesis, sympathy
tele-	distant	telegraph, telepathy, television
trans-	across, over, through, beyond	transition, transcend, transgress
tri-	three	trimester, trilateral, trillion
ultra-	beyond, excessively	ultraliberal, ultramodern, ultraviolet
un-	not	unimportant, unflattering, unattractive
uni-	one	uniform, unicameral, unique
vice-	one who takes the place of another	vice-president, viceroy, vice-consul

NOUN SUFFIXES

Suffix	Meaning	Example
-ance, -ence	act of	attendance, precedence, reliance,
-ancy, -ency	state of	hesitancy, presidency, consistency
-age	action, condition collection	message, bondage, marriage, postage, baggage
-ant, -ent	one who, that which	stimulant, participant, student, president
-ar	one who	bursar, liar, beggar
-ary, -ory, -ery, -ry	one who, place where, study of	secretary, library, history, conservatory, winery, bakery, chemistry
-dom	domain, condition of	freedom, wisdom, kingdom
-ee	one who is	employee, refugee, absentee
-eer	one who	profiteer, racketeer, pamphleteer
-er	one who	painter, receiver, baker
-ess	one who (female)	actress, poetess, lioness
-hood	state of	boyhood, falsehood, manhood
-ian	one who	beautician, musician, librarian
-ics	science, art, or practice of	graphics, mathematics, athletics, dramatics
-ion, -ation, -sion, -tion	state, action, institution	fixation, exploration, starvation, foundation, organization, preservation, suspension, competition
-ism	doctrine, point of view	mannerism, idealism, realism
-ist	one who, believer	segregationist, realist, cyclist
-ity	state, quality	sanity, rapidity, elasticity

Suffix	Meaning	Example
-ment	state, quality, act of	amazement, payment, embodiment
-ness	state of	fullness, shyness, sickness
-ocracy	system style of government	democracy, autocracy, plutocracy
-or	one who	actor, governor, inspector
-ship	state, condition	friendship, dictatorship, membership

ADJECTIVE SUFFIXES

Suffix	Meaning	Example
-able, -ible	capable of	capable, edible, visible
-al	like, pertaining to	criminal, practical, musical
-ary, ory	connected with, engaged in	ordinary, budgetary, compensatory
-ed	covered with, affected by	wooded, clothed, blessed
-en	made of, resembling	wooden, ashen, silken
-ful	full of, having	useful, hopeful, successful
-ic	like, pertaining to	democratic, heroic, specific
-ish	like, pertaining to	foolish, childish, selfish
-ive	like, pertaining to	active, explosive, sensitive
-less	without	speechless, childless, harmless
-like	having the qualities of	childlike, cowlike, statesmanlike
-ly	having the qualities of	beastly, manly, worldly
-oid	like, resembling	spheroid, humanoid, paranoid
-ous	like, pertaining to	courageous, ambitious, grievous
-ward	manner, position	awkward, backward, forward

ADVERB SUFFIXES

Suffix	Meaning	Example
-ly	in a __ manner	happily, strangely, comically
-ward(s)	direction of movement	backward(s), earthward, homeward
-wise	in the manner of , as far as __ is concerned	crabwise, clockwise, corkscrew-wise education-wise, weather-wise

VERB SUFFIXES

Suffix	Meaning	Example
-ate	to cause, to make	placate, indicate, irritate
-en	to become, to make	deafen, ripen, widen
-ify	to cause, to make	beautify, diversify, simplify
-ize	to cause, to make	symbolize, hospitalize, publicize

List 5: Roots

Root	Meaning	Example
agr	field, farm	agriculture, agronomy
anthro	man	anthropoid, misanthrope
aqua	water	aquatic, aqueduct
astro	star	astrology, astronaut
aud	hear	auditorium, audience
biblio	book	bibliography, bibliophile
bio	life	biology, biography
celer	speed, hasten	accelerate, celerity
chronos	time	chronicle, chronology
cap, capt, cip	take	capture, reciprocate
cep, cept, ceive	take	reception, conceive
ced, cess, cede	go, move along	success, proceed
cid	kill	suicide, genocide
clud, clus	close, shut	seclusion, include
cosmo	world	cosmopolitan, cosmonaut
crat	power	democrat, autocrat
cred	believe, trust	credit, incredulous
cur, curr	run	incur, current
demo	people	democrat, demography
dict	say	diction, contradict
duc, duct	lead	induce, abduct, educate
fac, fact	make, do	manufacture, factory
fec, fect	make, do	infect, effect
fer	carry, bear	infer, conference
fic, fict	make, do	efficacious, fiction
flect	bend	inflection, deflect
frater	brother	fraternal, fratricide
fund, fus	pour	refund, effusive
gen, gener	birth, race	generation, regenerate
geo	earth	geology, geography
glot	tongue	polyglot, glottal
gram	written	telegram, grammar
graph	write	autograph, biography
gress, grad	go, step	progress, gradual
hydra	water	dehydrate, hydrant
ject, jact	throw	project, rejection
jud	judgement	judicial, judicious
lect, leg	read, choose	collect, legend, elect
logo, log, logy	study	anthropology, chronology
loq, loc	speak	eloquent, locution

Root	Meaning	Example
manu, mani	hand	manuscript, manicure
mar	sea	maritime, submarine
mater	mother	maternal, matriarch
med	middle	intermediary, medium
min	smaller, less	diminish, minute
mit, mis	send, let go	missile, missionary
mort	death	mortician, mortal
mot, mob, mo	move, start	motion, motivate
naut	sailor	astronaut, nautical
necro	death	necromancer , necropolis
neuro	nerve	neurology, neurotic
nom	name	nomenclature, nominal
nomo	knowledge, law	autonomy, astronomy
pater	father	paternal, patriotic
patho	suffering, ill	pathetic, pathology
ped, pod	foot	pedal, tripod
pend	hang, weigh	depend, ponderous
philo	love	philosophy, philanthropist
phobo	fear	hydrophobia, phobia
phone	sound, voice	phonology, telephone
photo	light	photography, photosynthesis
plex, pli, ply	fold	complexity, pliant, plywood
plic	fold	complicate, duplicate, implicate
poli	city	cosmopolitan, politician
port	carry	portable, import
pos, pon	place, put	postpone, position
psych	of the mind	psychic, psychology
reg, rect	rule, manage	direct, regulate
rupt	break	rupture, disrupt
scop	watch/look at	microscopic, telescope
scrib, scrip	write	inscribe, conscription
soph	wise	sophisticated, philosophy
spec, spic	see, watch	inspect, despicable
sta, stat	stand	stable, station
stit, sist	to set up, establish	constitution, insist
tact, tang	touch	tactile, tangible
ten, tain, tin	hold, keep	contain, tenacious
tend, tens, tent	stretch, weaken	extend, tenuous
typo	image	typical, typewriter
vacu	empty	vacuum, evacuate
ven	love	venerate, venereal
ven	come	prevent, convene, intervene
voca	call	vocal, invocation
vora	eat, devour	voracious, carnivorous

List 6: Verb Tenses

	SIMPLE	PROGRESSIVE	PERFECT	PERFECT PROGRESSIVE
FUTURE + ? −	I will walk. Will I walk? I won't walk.	You will be walking. Will you be walking? You won't be walking.	She will have walked. Will she have walked? She won't have walked.	We will have been walking. Will we have been walking? We won't have been walking.
PRESENT + ? −	I walk He walks. Do I walk? Does he walk? I do not walk He does not walk.	I am walking. You are walking. He is walking. Am I walking? Are you walking? Is he walking? I am not walking. You are not walking.	I have walked. He has walked. Have I walked? Has he walked? I have not walked. He has not walked.	I have been walking. He has been walking. Have I been walking? Has he been walking? I have not been walking. He has not been walking.
PAST + ? −	I walked. Did I walk? I didn't walk.	I was walking. You were walking. Was I walking? Were you walking? I was not walking. You were not walking.	I had walked. Had I walked? I had not walked.	I had been walking. Had I been walking? I hadn't been walking.

List 7: Stative Verbs (22)*

appear	hear	notice	smell
be	know	owe	taste
believe	like	own	think
cost	look like	prefer	understand
feel	love	remember	want
forget	mean	resemble	weigh
hate	need	see	wish
have	note	seem	

List 8: Frequency Adverbs (49)†

everlastingly	constantly	sometimes	rarely
eternally	frequently	regularly	hardly ever
forever	habitually	periodically	scarcely ever
perpetually	generally	every*day*	almost never
incessantly	commonly	occasionally	nearly never
always	normally	irregularly	never
almost always	usually	every so often	
nearly always	ordinarily	infrequently	ever
invariably	often	seldom	

*This number represents a step in the Grammar Sequence (p. 7).

†This number represents a step in the Grammar Sequence (p. 8).

List 9: Non-Countable (Mass) Nouns* (29)†

A. Abstract

advice
age
beauty
capitalism
communism
democracy
energy
fun
happiness
help
honesty
information
justice
kindness
knowledge
laughter
liberty
life
play
recreation
strength
trouble
truth
virtue
wisdom
work
youth
Percussion

B. Matter, material

air
beer
blood
bread
butter
cake
chalk
cheese
coal
coffee
electricity
fog
fish
gold
grass
hair
ice
ink
iron
juice
lumber
meat
milk
oil
oxygen
paper
rain
rice
smoke
snow
soap
soup
sugar
tea
water
wine
wood

C. Generic terms

business
change
equipment
fruit
furniture
jewelry
luggage
machinery
mail
money
news
propaganda
scenery
slang
stationery
traffic
vegetation
weather

†This list is far from complete; it is intended only to be suggestive. We have tried to include high-frequency nouns. Add your own to our lists.

*This number represents a step in the Grammatical Sequence (p. 7).

30

D. Subject matter

architecture
art
chemistry
civics
economics
engineering
English
geology
grammar
history
literature
mathematics
music
philosophy
physics
science
technology
vocabulary

E. Sports and recreation

baseball
basketball
bridge
camping
dancing
drinking
football
golf
hiking
hockey
homework
hunting
opera
sailing
singing
softball
swimming
television
traveling
volleyball

F. Countable and non- countable nouns*

age
baseball (and
    other balls)
beer (and
    other drinks)
business
change
company
dope
glass
iron
paper
play
room
smoke
tape
tea (party)
work
youth

*This list(F) contains words that can have dual meanings: one countable meaning and a different non-countable meaning. Example: *The game of American **football** is played with an oddly shaped ball called a **"football."***

Many non-count nouns, if used to refer to items or units, can also be used as count nouns. Example: *We work at home and do a lot of **business** there. I run one **business** here and my wife runs two others.*

List 10: Irregular Verbs

Past participle ends with *n*:

arise	arose	arisen	mow	mowed	mown
awake	awoke	awoken/awaked	prove	proved	proven
be	was/were	been	ride	rode	ridden
bear	bore	born	rise	rose	risen
beat	beat	beaten	run	ran	ran
begin	began	begun	see	saw	seen
bite	bit	bitten	sew	sewed	sewn/sewed
blow	blew	blown	shake	shook	shaken
break	broke	broken	shine	shone/shined	shone/shined
choose	chose	chosen	show	showed	shown
do	did	done	slay	slew	slain
draw	drew	drawn	sow	sowed	sown/sowed
drive	drove	driven	speak	spoke	spoken
eat	ate	eaten	spin	spun	spun
fall	fell	fallen	steal	stole	stolen
fly	flew	flown	stride	strode	stridden
forbid	forbid\forbade	forbidden	strike	struck	stricken/struck
forget	forgot	forgotten	strive	strove	striven
forgive	forgave	forgiven	swear	swore	sworn
forsake	forsook	forsaken	swell	swelled	swollen/swelled
freeze	froze	frozen	take	took	taken
get	got	gotten	tear	tore	torn
give	gave	given	throw	threw	thrown
go	went	gone	undertake	undertook	undertaken
grow	grew	grown	wake	woke	woken/waked
hide	hid	hidden	wear	wore	worn
know	knew	known	weave	wove	woven
lie	lay	lain	win	won	won
mistake	mistook	mistaken	write	wrote	written

Past participle ends with *d:*

bind	bound	bound	lead	led	led
bleed	bled	bled	make	made	made
breed	bred	bred	pay	paid	paid
dive	dove/dived	dived	read	read	read
feed	fed	fed	say	said	said
flee	fled	fled	sell	sold	sold
find	found	found	slide	slid	slid
grind	ground	ground	speed	sped	sped
have	had	had	stand	stood	stood
hear	heard	heard	tell	told	told
hold	held	held	understand	understood	understood
lay	laid	laid	wind	wound	wound

Past participle ends with *t:*

bend	bent	bent	lose	lost	lost
bring	brought	brought	mean	meant	meant
build	built	built	meet	met	met
buy	bought	bought	seek	sought	sought
catch	caught	caught	send	sent	sent
creep	crept	crept	shoot	shot	shot
deal	dealt	dealt	sit	sat	sat
fight	fought	fought	sleep	slept	slept
feel	felt	felt	spend	spent	spent
keep	kept	kept	spit	spat	spat
kneel	knelt	knelt	sweep	swept	swept
leave	left	left	teach	taught	taught
lend	lent	lent	think	thought	thought
light	lit	lit	weep	wept	wept

Past participle ends with *d* or *t,* but the verb does not change:

bet	bet	bet	quit	quit	quit
bid	bid	bid	rid	rid	rid
burst	burst	burst	set	set	set
cast	cast	cast	shed	shed	shed
cost	cost	cost	shut	shut	shut
cut	cut	cut	slit	slit	slit
fit	fit	fit	split	split	split
hit	hit	hit	spread	spread	spread
hurt	hurt	hurt	thrust	thrust	thrust
let	let	let	wet	wet	wet
put	put	put			

Past participle ends with *m, g,* or *k:*

become	became	become	sink	sank	sunk
come	came	come	sling	slung	slung
dig	dug	dug	spring	sprang	sprung
drink	drank	drunk	stink	stank/stunk	stunk
fling	flung	flung	strike	struck	struck
hang	hung/hanged*	hung/hanged*	swim	swam	swum
ring	rang	rung	swing	swung/swang	swung
shrink	shrank	shrunk	wring	wrung	wrung
sing	sang	sung			

*different meanings

33

List 11: Direct and Indirect Objects (48, 62, 63)*

A.   Verbs that require the direct object before the indirect object

Verbs that usually require **to**†

   Example: *He admitted his mistake to his father*

admit	explain	prove	report
announce	introduce	recommend	say
describe	mention	remember	speak
			suggest

Verbs that usually require **for**

   Example: *She answered the phone for me.*

answer	correct	keep	pronounce
cash	design	open	repeat
change	fill	prepare	sign
close	fix	prescribe	translate

B.   Verbs that can have the indirect object before the direct object‡

Verbs that usually require **to** or **Ø**

   Example: *He brought the apple to Eve.   He brought Eve the apple.*

bring	offer	sell	teach
deny	owe	send	tell
give	pass	show	throw
hand	pay	sign	write
lend	read	take	

Verbs that normally require **for** or **Ø**

   Example: *She built a cage for her pet snake. She built her snake a nice cage.*

build	cook	get	order
buy	do	hire	save
call	draw	leave	type
catch	find	make	

---

*This number represents a step in the Grammatical Sequence (p. 8).

†Some verbs can be used with either **to** or **for**, but note the difference in meaning.
   Example: *He brought the apple to Eve. He brought an apple for Eve.*

‡The direct object is usually not a pronoun when it comes after the indirect object.
   Example: *He brought her the apple,* but not: *He brought Eve it.*

List 12: *Go* with "Recreational" Gerunds and Prepositional Phrases (71, 98)*

Example: *He went to the beach.*

go biking	go for a bike ride	go birdwatching
go boating	go for a boat ride	go bowling
go canoeing	go for a canoe ride	go camping
go climbing	go for a climb	go to the beach
go diving	go for a dive	go to the movies
go picnicking	go for a picnic	go on a date
go riding	go for a ride	go cycling
go running	go for a run	go fishing
go sailing	go for a sail	go necking
go drinking	go for a drink	go shopping
go hiking	go for a hike	go singing
go jogging	go for a jog	go skating
go swimming	go for a swim	go skateboarding
go visiting	go for a visit	go skiing
go walking	go for a walk	go surfing
go dancing	go to a dance	go windsurfing
go partying	go to a party	

*These numbers represent steps in the Grammatical Sequence (pp. 9-10).

List 13: Modals

	Meaning	Modal	Pres	Fut	Past	Expression	Examples
Obligation	unavoidable	**must**	✓	✓	had to	need to, have to	We must pay our taxes by the 15th of April. You must be at school and at your desk before the bell rings.
	necessity	**must**	✓	✓	had to	need to, have to	We had to drink brackish water in order to survive. The crops must have water or they will die.
	prohibition	**must not**	✓	✓	it was prohib- ited	be forbidden to	You must not smoke in the arsenal. You must not play in the streets.
	no obligation	**not have to**	✓	✓	didn't have to		She doesn't have to be at home before 10:00 p.m. They don't have to come to class.
	avoidable obligation	**should**	✓	✓	should have	be supposed to	You should do your homework every day.
		ought to	✓	✓	out to have		We should return these books to the library today.
Advisability		**should**	✓	✓	should have		You look terrible, you should see a doctor.
		ought to	✓	✓	ought to have		You ought to have knocked before entering.
	obligation with implied consequences	**had better**	✓	✓	had better have		You had better pay me back before I leave. She'd better watch her language.
	strong advisability, recommen- dation	**must not**	✓	✓	✗	should not	You mustn't go out alone. It's dangerous. She mustn't drive so fast. She'll have an accident.
Preference		**would rather**	✓	✓	would rather have	would prefer, would sooner	I'd rather do it myself. He'd rather have read the book.

✓ indicates that the modal is used in this time reference with no change in its form.

✗ indicates that the modal is not found in this time reference in any form.

Where the modal changes its form, the new form is indicated

Ability	ability	**can**	✓	✓	could	be able to, know how to	I can speak Russian. He couldn't understand a word
	former ability	**could**	✗	✗	could	used to be able to	He could run a 4-minute mile in those days. I couldn't express myself then.
Possibility	theoretical and/or factual	**can**	✓	✓	can have	it is possible, maybe, perhaps	Any citizen can become a senator.
		could	✓	✓	could have		Could man have descended from apes? We could go to the movies tonight.
		may	✓	✓	may have		The road may be blocked. He may buy a new car next year.
		might	✓	✓	might have		He might have taken another road home.
Probability	expectation	**should**	✓	✓	should have	expect	He should be here any minute now.
		ought to	✓	✓	ought to have		They ought to have finished now.
	inference	**must**	✓	✗	must have	have to, have got to	It's very muddy; it must have rained a lot.
		can't	✓	✗	can't have	it is not possible	She can't be hungry; she just ate.
		couldn't	✓	✗	couldn't have		He couldn't have flown a plane; he died in 1512.
Willingness		**will**	✓	✓	✗	not mind	Stay there, I'll do the dishes.
Invitation	you	**could**	✓	✓	✗	would like, can, will	Could you go to the dance with me?
		would	✓	✓	✗		Would you come to dinner tonight?
Request	he, she we, they I	**may**	✓	✓	✗	can, might	May I leave the room?
		could	✓	✓	✗		Could Johnny stay overnight?
	you	**would**	✓	✓	✗	can, will	Would you open the window?
		could	✓	✓	✗		Could you please lower your voice?
Permission		**may**	✓	✓	was allowed to, was per-mitted to	be allowed to, be per-mitted to	You may leave the room. She may marry whomever she likes.
		can	✓	✓			Johnny can't stay over.

List 14: Two-Word Verbs

A. SEPARABLE

Example: beat up   *She beat up Freddy. She beat Freddy up.*

Verb	Meaning	Example
beat up	mix	First, beat the eggs up with the cream.
blow out	extinguish	The children wanted to blow the matches out.
break down	disassemble	Max broke his bike down into sixty parts.
bring up	raise children	Those parents brought their children up to respect the law.
call off	cancel	The umpire called the game off.
call up	telephone	Call me up tomorrow.
do over	do again	The teacher asked me to do the assignment over.
fill out	complete	Fill these forms out and come back tomorrow.
get up	to arouse from bed	Jane gets her husband up by six every morning.
give back	return	The teacher gave the papers back.
give up	abandon	We had to give the puppy up to its real owner.
hand in	submit	The students handed their exams in late.
hang up	place on hook	He always hangs the phone up when I'm speaking.
keep up	maintain	It costs a lot to keep that car up.
leave out	omit	I've published; don't leave that out on my resume.
let down	lower	Let your hair down.
look over	review, examine	Look the test over before beginning.
look up	search for	I spent hours looking those words up.
make out	distinguish	Her handwriting made it impossible to make her address out.
make up	compose, invent	They made a list up of people willing to contribute.
make up	use cosmetics	She made her daughter's face up for the party.
pack up	gather in a container	The carpenter packed his tools up at five o'clock sharp.
pass out	distribute	The captain passed aspirin tablets out to all of us.
pick out	choose	He picked a tie out to go with his shirt.
pick up	lift, collect	Someone picks the garbage up on Tuesday.
put away	put in the customary place	Put your toys away, children.
put off	postpone	Another meeting? Let's put it off.
put on	don	It's better to put your socks on before your shoes.
put out	extinguish	The fireman put the blaze out.
run over	hit by a car	The driver lost control and ran the old man over.
take back	return	This new radio doesn't work; I'm taking it back to the store.
take off	remove	They took their coats off when they entered.
take up	raise, discuss	Take that issue up with the manager.
talk over	discuss	The defendant talked his case over with lawyers.
throw away	discard	Don't throw those old magazines away.
try on	test the fit and appearance	She never tries clothes on when she shops.
try out	test	They tried the car out and decided not to buy it.
turn down	reject,	The boss turned my request for a raise down.
	lower the volume	Turn that television down! It's giving me a headache!
turn in	deliver, submit	The hub-cap thief turned himself in to the police.
turn off	stop power, shut off	Turn the lights off when you leave.
turn on	start power, put on	I turned the lights on to see better.
use up	finish	We've used all our sugar up.

B. NON-SEPARABLE

Example: break down   *Luckily the plane broke down before it took off.*

Verb	Meaning	Example
break down	stop functioning	My car broke down just as I passed the service station.
break up with	end a relationship with	Betsy breaks up with all her boy friends after a month
break into	enter forcibly	Sally broke into her piggy bank to get money for candy.
call on	ask to respond	That teacher enjoys calling on sleeping students.
come back	return	She never comes back from school on time.
come over	visit informally	Come over for lunch sometime.
come to	regain consciousness	She fainted from fright, but she soon came to.
find out	discover	I found out what was bothering her.
get along with	have a friendly relationship with	That fellow seems to get along with everyone.
get around	avoid	My daughter gets around every rule I set.
get by	succeed with a minimum effort	Do enough just to get by; that's his motto.
get over	recover	It took him weeks to get over the mumps.
get through	finish	I can never get through my exams in time.
get up	arise	He gets up early.
go along	agree	She goes along with every suggestion he makes.
go away	leave	Please go away; I'm busy now.
go over	review	Let's go over the battle plans again.
keep on	continue	He keeps on talking until everyone leaves.
keep up	continue	Keep up the good work, boys. You're doing fine!
look for	search for	They looked everywhere for the lost child.
look into	investigate	Detectives are looking into the mysterious death.
look like	resemble	She looks like her grandmother.
look out	beware	Look out! The roof's caving in.
look up	respect	Young boys often look up to famous athletes.
make out	to succeed	She made out well on these investments.
pass out	faint	The heat was so intense that many people passed out.
put up with	tolerate	He can't put up with dishonesty.
run into	meet accidentally	Two old friends ran into each other on the street.
run across	find accidentally	She ran across an old love letter and wept.
run out of	exhaust a supply	They ran out of gas in the middle of the Bay Bridge.
show up	appear	His ex-wife showed up at the marriage ceremony.
take after	resemble	He takes after his father in everything he does.
take off	leave	I can't stand this concert! Let's take off.
talk back	to answer rudely	My children never talk back to me.
wait on	serve	He waits on tables for a living.

List 15: Common Idioms and Collocations
with *give, take, have, get, make, do, tell, say, come,* and *go*

Give

give your best
give ground
give way
give up the ghost
give a lot
give the world
give 'em hell
give it to 'em
give an account of yourself
give rise to
give the benefit of a doubt

give authority
give permission
give offense
give a whipping
give confidence
give an idea
give time
give me the time
give promise
give a promise
give a damn

give notice
give as good as you get
give and take

give away – a giveaway
give back
give in
give into
give off
give out
give up

Take

take a nap
take a snooze
take a rap
take a fall
take a tumble
take the news
take messages
take notes
take dictation
take your medicine
take a crack at
take time
take care
take a try
take pains
take trouble
take under your wing
take home
take offense
take a back seat
take out food
take aback

take advantage of
take amiss
take someone's word
take me for a fool
take possession
take my hand
take unaware
take a drink
take the blame
take the train
take shelter
take a seat
take a picture
take a bet
take criticism
take to the cleaners
take to task
take place
take it from me
take it for granted
take it on the chin
take heart

take courage
take a break
take a breather
take ten minutes
take effect
take a shower
take a beating

take after
take along
take apart
take back
be taken by
take down
take for
take in
take off
take on
take out
take over
undertake
take up

Have

have a ball
have a good time
have a heart
have an advantage
have time
have the will
have a headache

have chicken pox
have an idea
have a seat
have a job
have an understanding
have an interest in
have a drink

have lots to do
have good weather
have a reason
have an excuse
had enough
have nots

Get

get thin	get pregnant	get after
get fat	get going	get ahead
get soft	get involved	get along
get hard	get under your skin	get around
get lost	get into a fight	get away – a getaway
get sick	get into trouble	get back
get well	get out of trouble	get back at
get tired	get busy	get back to
get rested	get down to business	get into
get some rest	get dressed, undressed	get off on
get to bed	get dressed up	get on
get to sleep	get together – a get-together	get on with
get some sleep	get up – a getup	get out
get nowhere		get over
get somewhere	get across	get through
get with it	get across to	get through to

Make (56)*

make do	make a decision	make a plane
make trouble	make a request	make room for
make peace	make an attempt	make progress
make war	make hay while the sun shines	make time
make love	make a bed	make up you mind
make a (phone) call	make a fire	on the make
make a copy	make a bet	clothes make the man
make friends	make book	
make money	make a date	make away with
make interest	make an appointment	make back
make a loan	make an agreement	make off with
make sense	make interesting	make out
make faces	make good	make over
make eyes at	make public	make up

Do (56)*

do your best	do the vacuuming	do or die
do your worst	do the cooking	do a drawing
do what's needed	do the shopping	do a portrait
do homework	do the cleaning	do a painting
do an assignment	do the laundry	do the artwork
do an excercise	do the chores	do the editing
do time	do housework	do away with
do a job	do rounds	do in
do a favor	do the driving	do up
do someone out of something	do evil	do over
do the dishes	do good	do out of
do the ironing	do the right thing	do unto

*This number represents a step in the Grammatical Sequence (p. 8).

41

Tell (60)*

tell the truth	tell time	time will tell
tell a lie	tell it like it is	tell about
tell a story	tell a fortune	tell apart
tell a secret		tell off
tell the weather	a telling detail	tell on
tell me what's on your mind	kiss and tell	all told

Say (60)*

say your piece	say your goodbyes	before you could say
say your prayers	goes without saying	Jack Robinson
say grace	I can't say	what do you have to say
say yes	say not a word	for yourself
say no	have a say in	say about
say what you have to say	that is to say	say against
say what's on your mind	say what you will	say of
say hello for me	never say die	say on
say goodbye	say it with flowers	say to

Come

come to an agreement	come along	come out
come by it naturally	come around	come out with
come to a stop	come away with	come over
come and see	come back - a comeback	overcome
come and get it	come between	come through
come and go	come in for	come to
come off it	come into	come upon
come about	come off	come up against
come across	come on - a come on	come up with
come ahead	come on to	

Go

go crazy	go AWOL (absent without	go ahead of
go mad	leave)	go around with
go nuts	food to go	go at
go insane	go one better	go away
go batty	go from bad to worse	go back on
go wild	from the word go	go beyond
go on a spree	so it goes	go for
go over the edge	go bald	go in for
go into debt	go blind	go into
go all the way	go deaf	go off
go for broke	go lame	go off with
go one-on-one	go soft	go on
go head-to-head		go on about
go over the top	go about	go over
go in over your head	go after	go through
go behind your back	go along	go up against
go about your own business	go against	go with
go through hell	go ahead	go without

*This number represents a step in the Gramatical Sequence (p. 8)

List 16: Verbs That Are Followed by an Infinitive (97)*

A. No object

Example: *He agrees to meet at noon.*

agree	deserve	learn	swear
appear	desire	manage	tend
arrange	fail	mean	volunteer
care	guarantee	offer	wait
claim	happen	promise	wish
consent	hesitate	refuse	
decide	hope	seem	
demand	know how	struggle	

B. With object

Example: *She advised the man to duck.*

advise	dare	instruct	request
allow	encourage	invite	require
authorize	forbid	oblige	teach
cause	force	order	tell
challenge	get	permit	train
command	help	persuade	urge
convince	hire	remind	warn

C. With or without object

Example: *He asks her to leave. He asks to be excused.*

ask	expect	prefer	want
beg	need	prepare	would like

*This number represents a step in the Grammatical Sequence (p.10).

List l7: Verbs Followed by Gerunds (98)*

Example: *She admits going to see the movie.*

admit	discuss	mention	resent
anticipate	dislike	mind	resist
appreciate	enjoy	miss	risk
avoid	finish	postpone	suggest
can't help	get through	practice	tolerate
complete	give up	quit	understand
consider	imagine	recall	
delay	keep	recollect	
deny	keep on	recommend	

List 18: Verbs Followed by Infinitives or Gerunds (99)*

Example: *He can afford to vacation in Italy.*   *He can afford vacationing in Italy.*

(can) afford	forget†	love	remember†
attempt	go	neglect	start
(can) bear	hate	plan	(can) stand
begin	hesitate	prefer	stop†
choose	intend	pretend	threaten
dread	like	regret†	try†

List 19: Perception Verbs Followed by Simple Verbs‡ (100)*

Example: *She felt him approach.*

feel	overhear	remark	smell
hear	perceive	see	watch
observe	notice	sense	witness

*These numbers represent steps in the Grammatical Sequence (p. 10).

†The meanings of these verbs are often slightly different when they are followed by an infinitive rather than a gerund. Example: *He stopped to listen to the speech. He stopped listening to the speech.*

‡These verbs may also be followed by a gerund. Example: *She felt him approaching.*

List 20: Participles As Modifiers†(122)*

Example: *She is amazing to him. He is amazed by her.*

absorbing	absorbed	fascinating	fascinated
amazing	amazed	frightening	frightened
amusing	amused	interesting	interested
annoying	annoyed	intriguing	intrigued
astonishing	astonished	irritating	irritated
boring	bored	pleasing	pleased
challenging	challenged	satisfying	satisfied
confusing	confused	shocking	shocked
convincing	convinced	surprising	surprised
disappointing	disappointed	terrifying	terrified
disgusting	disgusted	thrilling	thrilled
disturbing	disturbed	tiring	tired
embarrassing	embarrassed	touching	touched
exciting	excited		

*This number represents a step in the Grammar Sequence (p.11).

†This list is given because students are frequently confused by these confusing pairs, especially when they are used to describe people.

List 21: Intransitive and Transitive Verbs (128)*

Most English verbs can be used in either an intransitive or transitive way.

Example: (intransitive) *She writes everyday.* (transitive) *She is writing a book.*

The commonly-used verbs in the following lists generally are only intransitive or transitive.

Example: (intransitive) *He acted in Hamlet every night, and*
(transitive) *every night he accepted a standing ovation.*
(intransitive) *She agreed to plead guilty and* (transitive) *admit her crime.*

However, some of them may occasionally be used either way, especially when used with cognate objects (verb – *live,* cognate object – *life)*†

Example: (intransitive) *She lived on Manhattan, but* (transitive) *she lived a good life.*

A. Intransitive Verbs

act	dream	live	sit
agree	fall	look	sleep
appear	go	matter	stand
arrive	happen	occur	step
belong	laugh	rain	talk
care	lie	remain	think
come	listen	rise	wait

B. Transitive Verbs

accept	cost	have	pick
admit	cover	hear	put
allow	demand	hold	raise
beat	destroy	include	realize
bring	discover	join	say
build	enjoy	kill	send
buy	expect	know	suppose
carry	express	lay	take
catch	feed	let	tell
cause	find	like	wear
consider	force	make	
contain	give	mean	

*This number represents a step in the Grammatical Sequence (p. 11).

†An additional point: except when they are used transitively with cognate objects, intransitive verbs usually cannot be used in the passive voice.

Example: (intransitive-active) *Larry acted all over the world.* (no intransitive passive is possible)
(transitive-active with cog. obj.) *He acted the part of Hamlet well.*   (transitive-passive) *That part was acted well (by Larry).*
(intransitive-active) *She lived in New York.* (no intransitive passive is possible)
(transitive-active with cog. obj) *She lived her life to the fullest.*   (transitive-passive) *Her life was lived to the fullest.*

List 22: Adjective + Preposition Combinations (129)*

Example: *She is interested in becoming a judge.*

concerned about	slow at	conscious of	sure to
happy about	quick at	confident of	opposed to
angry about	lucky at	ashamed of	used to
enthusiastic about	surprised at	sure of	
careful about	amazed at	afraid of	bored with
excited about		certain of	impressed with
glad about	interested in	sick of	involved with
worried about	involved in		annoyed with
sorry about	disappointed in	upset over (about)	delighted with
disappointed about		disturbed over	satisfied with
pleased about	fond of		pleased with
	in favor of	accustomed to	disappointed with
good at	tired of	slow to	
clever at	capable of	quick to	
bad at	aware of	resigned to	

List 23: Verbs and Adjectives Taking Subjunctive (130)*

A. Verbs

Example: *He **advises** that you **watch** the stock market very carefully.*
Example: *It is **important** that you **do** this immediately.*

advise	propose	forbid	require
ask	recommend	desire	stipulate
beg	command	insist	suggest
demand	request	prefer	urge

Adjectives

advisable	essential	desirable	important
best	good	mandatory	urgent
better	imperative	necessary	vital
critical	crucial	required	requisite

*These numbers represent steps in the Grammar Sequence (p.11).

List 24: Verb + Preposition Combinations (139)*

A. Verb + preposition + object

Example: *They agree on everything.*

agree on	care for	hear about	succeed in
agree with	complain about	hear from	talk to
approve of	consent to	laugh at	talk about
argue with	comment on	listen to	think about
arrive at	consist of	look at	vote for
arrive in	count on	object to	wait for
belong to	decide on	pay for	wish for
believe in	depend on	rely on	work for

B. Verb + object + prepostion + object

Example: *She adds fertilizer to her garden soil.*

add __ to/with __	explain __ to __	prefer __ to __
blame __ for __	excuse __ for __	remind __ of __
compare __ with/to __	introduce __ to __	thank __ for __
congratulate __ on/for ___	keep __ for __	subtract __ from __

*This number represents a step in the Grammar Sequence (p. 11).

The Communicative Aspect

The communicative aspect does not deal with linguistic forms, the **medium**, such as *go, went, gone*. It outlines ways in which the language is used to send and receive **messages**. We have further analyzed this communicative aspect into three sub-aspects that are usually present when a message is being communicated. The **situation** is the context in which the message is exchanged, the *where*. The **topic** is the subject matter of the message, the *what*, and the **function** is the manner and purpose of the message, the *how* and *why*.

Contents

Situations

The situation is a frame for communication. In its simplest sense, it is a definite, identifiable place or setting where communication happens (*a bank*, for example). However, some of the situations in the following pages are not specific places. There are events or chains of events that are common and recurrent in everyday life (for example, *a wedding* or *asking for prices*). There are also contexts which are topics for discussion and cultural exploration (such as *planning nutritious meals*).

In order to communicate effectively in these situations, students need appropriate topical vocabulary, cultural information, and functional language. The materials in the following sections will be helpful.

This section amounts to a series of lists of suggested communicative contexts that could be used in presenting and practicing communicative language and cultural insights. In many cases, vocabulary topics relevant to these contexts are given in the next section. When they are, cross-references are given.

A teacher using this section as a planning guide selects a situation appropriate to the interests and needs of his or her students and then plans a lesson using any of the topics which seem relevant. For example, looking over the list, the teacher settles on *restaurant* from List 1. The reference is to topic number 28, *restaurants*, but a quick review of the Topic Checklist at the beginning of the section suggests that the topics on *food, cooking*, and *eating* might also be helpful. In reading the topic on *restaurants*, the teacher finds that the vocabulary list suggests both vocabulary and cultural information students will need in a restaurant. They will need to know about *reservations, menus, waiters, orders, checks*, and *tips*. After teaching the lesson, the teacher may handout photocopies of the relevant topic lists as further vocabulary enrichment.

Once the students have been given a handout, it can be used as the basis for peer teaching, writing assignments, situational role playing, and many other kinds of in-class and out-of-class activities.

The list of situations given in this section is in the form of an outline or checklist. It is intended to be suggestive rather than exhaustive. It is not intended as a situational sequence or syllabus, but it should help teachers develop sequences of their own appropriate for each class.

☐ 1. Basic Daily Needs
☐ 2. Transportation
☐ 3. Work
☐ 4. Health and Safety
☐ 5. Personal and Family Needs

☐ 6. Personal Finances
☐ 7. Education
☐ 8. Shopping & Service
☐ 9. Recreation
☐ 10. Citizenship

List 1: Basic Daily Needs

Food (Topics 1-4, 22, 28)
kitchen
dining room
cooking
restaurant
using a recipe
planning nutritious meals
storing food safely
grocery shopping
weights and measures
planning to save money
serving meals
eating and drinking

Clothing (Topics 5, 6, 29)
buying clothes, shoes
repairing clothes, sewing
using a washer, dryer
laundry/laundromat
cleaner

Shelter (Topic 4)
types of housing
rooms, including:
    living room
    bedroom
    bathroom
    kitchen
housekeeping
maintenance
yard work

List 2: Transportation*

asking directions
using maps
getting lost
walking—when,where
subway station, subway

bus stop, city bus
bus station, intercity bus
railway station, trains
airport, plane
taxis

commuting
buying tickets, tokens
travel agent
customs/immigration
hitchhiking

*(Topics 9 and 26)

List 3: Work*

the work place
    work shop
    factory
    store
    warehouse
    office
    studio
    farm
    hospital/clinic
    school
    restaurant
    out doors

work procedures
    using the telephone
    scheduling
    staff meeting
    safety regulations
    writing receipts
    making change
    placing/taking orders
    dictation
    typing
    filing
    taking messages

following instructions
getting paid
cashing pay checks
health insurance
social security
labor unions
changing jobs
employment office
applying for work
job training
asking for help
dealing with mistakes

*Topics 32, 43-47)

51

List 4: Health and Safety*

advice on a healthy diet
advice on getting exercise
gym, athletics
taking vitamins
taking medicine
drug store
doctor's office

dentist's office
emergency services
  police
  fire
  ambulance
medical center
health clinic

hospital
  emergency
  visiting
medical insurance
personal hygiene
sex and contraception
personal safety

*Topics 1-3, 24, 35, 38, 39 and 42)

List 5: Personal and Family Needs*

interpersonal relationships, roles
  work
  school
  sports
  friendship
  romance
family relationships
family planning
family counseling
children
  siblings
  discipline
  child care
  babysitting
  schooling
  afterschool activities
  birthdays/holidays
  camp

adult education, training
elderly people, relatives
spiritual
wedding
marriage
  anniversary
  counseling
  separation, divorce
living together
  as roommates
  out of wedlock
  commonlaw partners

family activities
family trips
record keeping
death, burial
places of worship
community organizations
  ethnic
  religious
  civic
  service
  political
  cultural
social life, entertaining
caring for pets
veterinarian

*(Topics 7, 8, 13, 14, 23, 33-36, 53-55, 60)

List 6: Personal Finances*

spending money
  cash
  checks
  charging
  charge accounts
  credit cards
  interest costs
  loan payments

bank
planning a family budget
getting/making a loan
getting a mortgage
getting a second mortgage
planning investments
  savings accounts
  savings bonds
  retirement accounts
  buying stock, bonds

insurance
social security
work benefits
taxes
gambling
retirement

*(Topic 32)

List 7: Education*

expectations, routines
classroom
schedules
being on time
assignments, homework
researching, writing papers
library
tests, quizzes
final exams
standardized tests
grades, records
tuition, room and board
scholarships
neatness
honesty/cheating

at school, on campus
registration
dean's office
adviser's office
  scheduling
  course change
teacher's office hours
  getting help
  planning a research paper
housing office
bursar's office
dormitory life
  rooms, roommates
  dorm rules
  laundry

off campus housing
campus post office
book store
student center
cafeteria, dining hall
fraternity, sorority
chapel, chaplain's office
student health services
foreign student adviser
other campus services
gymnasium
  team, coach
  team spirit
  locker room
drugs and sports

*(Topics 54 and 55)

List 8: Shopping and Service*

planning
making a shopping list
using the yellow pages
newspaper/magazine ads
junk mail
sales, come on's
coupons, bargains
finding products in big stores
kinds of stores
  department store
  supermarket
  mall
  specialty shops
  main street
  boutiques
  copy center
getting advice about products
  from consumer services
  in specialty shops
    bakery
    optician
    book store
    camera store, etc.
asking for prices
fixed prices/bargaining
unit pricing

ordering from catalogues
paying for purchases
  cash
  charge
  credit cards
  time payments
  layaway plans
  lease-purchase
  rental
  getting change
  tipping
returning merchandise
choosing and getting services
  mechanic
  barber/hair dresser
  plumber
  electrician
  carpenter
  doctor
  dentist
  lawyer
  accountant
  tax preparation service
  insurance agent
  pastor/priest
  real estate agent

getting help/public services
  police department
  court
  public defender/legal aid
  ambulance/emergency services
  hospital/emergency room
  fire department
  town offices/city hall
  local town officials
  extension agent
  post office
  state and congressional
    representatives
  school board
  IRS - internal revenue service
  INS - immigration and
    naturalization service
  public library
  adult center
  teen center
  YMCA, etc.

*(Topics 29 and 30)

List 9: Recreation*

athletics
local team sports - seasonal
  children's and adult leagues
  finding a team
  signing up
  schedules
exercising - running, swimming
games - tennis, golf
children's games
  capture the flag,
  jumping rope
  dodge ball
  marbles/jacks
hide and seek
tag
three legged races, etc.

social
dinner parties
cocktail/beer parties
dances
community events, socials
restaurants
entertainment
movies
theater
opera, musicals
popular music concerts
classical music concerts
rock concerts
professional sports events
night clubs
coffee houses

arts and crafts
art classes
music lessons
galleries
craft shows
gift shops
museums
at home
TV, radio
games - cards, board games
parties
  children's parties
  family parties
  holiday parties
special meals - barbecues, brunch
hobbies

*(Topics 33-37)

List 10: Citizenship*

town/city offices
police department
court
contacting government officials
  local and national
  getting help
  expressing opinions
election campaigns
voter registration
voting
discussing taxes
discussing immigration status
discussing work permits
discussing civil rights
discussing civil obligations
discussing national holidays
discussing historic landmarks
discussing corruption,
  bribery, protection,
  honor codes,
  organized crime
  codes of conduct
  truth in advertising
  civic responsibility

discussing
  national anthem
  other patriotic songs
  Gettysburg address
  Dr. King's "I have a dream,"
  other speeches and writings
American history
  explaining important events
  explaining important leaders
  explaining important movements
explaining the constitutions and
  functions of government
  local
  state
  national
  international

discussing the importance of
  dissent
  getting involved
  an informed electorate
  bill of rights
discussing what makes a
  community
    a good place to live
    a good place to work
    a good place to raise children
discussing the roles of
  organizations
    civic
    political
    special interest
    religious
    cultural

*(Topics 33,48,49,51,58,59)

Topics

The topics of human conversation are virtually endless, but it is possible to predict a general list of topics that virtually every language learner will encounter at some time or other. The following lists are an attempt at a comprehensive list of **basic** topics.

Each topic is outlined as a vocabulary list of the words, phrases, and idioms that might be encountered in a general conversation about the topic. In the case of the idioms, they are included not because they might appear in the context of a conversation, but rather because they have some semantic relationship to the topic.

It will again be obvious that the vocabulary collected under each topic is influenced by the cultural context of contemporary America.

Finally, please bear in mind that these lists are far from complete. They should be seen as basic words of fairly high frequency. You will want to add your own discoveries to our lists, and once again we welcome your additions and comments.

Topic checklist

☐ 1. Food
☐ 2. Cooking
☐ 3. Eating
☐ 4. Housing/Housekeeping
☐ 5. Clothes
☐ 6. Paraphernalia
☐ 7. Family
☐ 8. Human Relationships
☐ 9. Travel
☐ 10. Time
☐ 11. Weather and Climate
☐ 12. Geography
☐ 13. Animals
☐ 14. Birds
☐ 15. Plants and Trees
☐ 16. Language
☐ 17. Thinking
☐ 18. Numbers and Math
☐ 19. Colors
☐ 20. Shapes

☐ 21. Substances and Materials
☐ 22. Containers
☐ 23. Emotions
☐ 24. The Body and its Function
       and Vulgarities
☐ 25. Manipulations
☐ 26. Transportation
☐ 27. Hotels
☐ 28. Restaurants
☐ 29. Stores and Shops
☐ 30. Agencies and Services
☐ 31. Post office
☐ 32. Banks and Money
☐ 33. Community
☐ 34. Recreation
☐ 35. Sports and Games
☐ 36. Music
☐ 37. Photography
☐ 38. Medicine and Health
☐ 39. Dentistry

☐ 40. Barber and Beautician
☐ 41. Cosmetics and Toiletries
☐ 42. Hygiene and Contraception
☐ 43. Jobs and Work
☐ 44. Office
☐ 45. Business
☐ 46. Agriculture
☐ 47. Shops and Tools
☐ 48. Law
☐ 49. Police and Crime
☐ 50. Emergencies

☐ 51. Politics and Government
☐ 52. The Media
☐ 53. Religion
☐ 54. Elementary, Secondary Education
☐ 55. College Education
☐ 56. History
☐ 57. Disasters
☐ 58. The Military and War
☐ 59. Energy
☐ 60. Death

List 1: Food

Vegetables

bean	cucumber	radish
beet	lettuce	spinach
broccoli	onion	squash
cabbage	peas	tomato
carrot	pepper	turnip
celery	potato	
corn	pumpkin	

Fruit

apple	lemon	prune
banana	lime	raspberry
berry	melon	raisin
blueberry	orange	strawberry
cantaloupe	peach	tangerine
cherry	pear	watermelon
grape	pineapple	
grapefruit	plum	

Bread and Cereal

bread	grain	roll
biscuit	muffin	toast
cold	oatmeal	waffle
cereal	pancake	
doughnut	rice	

Meat

bacon	fish	meat loaf
beef	hamburger	pork
chicken	hot dog	turkey
duck	lamb	
egg	meatball	

Dairy

butter	cream	skim milk
cottage cheese	half and half	sour cream
cheese	margarine	yoghurt
ice cream	milk	

Desserts

brownie	ice cream	pudding
cake	pie	sundae
cupcake	cookies	

Spice and Flavoring

cinnamon	ginger	oregano
chili	herb	pepper
clove	honey	salt
cocoa	mustard	syrup
curry	nutmeg	sugar

Beverages

ale	lemonade	tea
beer	liquor	water
brandy	punch	whiskey
coffee	sanka	wine
coke	soda	
juice	soft drink	

Idioms and Expressions

baker's dozen	not know beans	egg on
baloney	pepper with questions	fishy
beef about	proof of the pudding	sour grapes
beef up	put one's eggs in one basket	spill the beans
bring home the bacon	food fit for the gods	square meal
corny	know which side your	take the cake
cream of the crop	bread is buttered on	upper crust
cry over spilled milk	like two peas in a pod	hot dog!
have one's cake and eat it	cup of tea	

List 2: Cooking

Equipment

baking pan	cover	mixer	saucepan
blender	double boiler	mixing spoon	sifter
bowl	eggbeater	oven	skillet
bread pan	food processor	pan	spatula
broiler	frying pan	pot	stove
burner	kettle	potato masher	strainer
casserole dish	ladle	pressure cooker	thermometer
cookbook	lid	recipe	whip
colander	measuring cup	rolling pin	

Processes

add	cover	measure	sift
bake	deep fry	melt	simmer
beat	dice	mince	slice
blend	drain	mix	spread
boil	fold in	parboil	sprinkle
braise	freeze	peel	stir
brown	fry	pour	stir-fry
chill	grate	refrigerate	toast
chop	grease	roast	toss
coat	grind	sauce	turn
combine	knead	season	whip
cook	mash	salt	

Ingredients, Dishes, Measures

baking soda	cup	molasses	steak
batter	dash	oil	stew
broth	dough	pinch	stick of butter
casserole	dressing	roast	stuffing
chops	filling	salad	syrup
cocktail	flavor	salad dressing	tablespoon
condiments	flour	sauce	teaspoon
corn meal	lard	seasoning	vinegar
cornstarch	loaf	shell	(egg) whites
crust	leftover	soup	(egg) yolks

Adjectives

boiled	fried	raw	steamed
broiled	ground	ripe	tender
crisp	medium	scalloped	thickened
curdled	moderate (oven)	slow (oven)	well-done
fresh	rare		

Idioms and Expressions

a flash in the pan	half-baked	pot calling the kettle black
take with a grain of salt	hard-boiled	watered down

List 3: Eating

Dishes and Utensils

carving knife	knife	serving dish
dessert dish	napkin	spoon
cup	plate	soup bowl
fork	platter	soup spoon
glass	salad bowl	tureen
goblet	saucer	
gravy boat	seconds	

Meals

appetizer	course	picnic
breakfast	dessert	smorgasbord
brunch	dinner	snack
buffet	lunch	supper

Verbs

chew	eat	sip
diet	gobble	stuff yourself
dine	munch	swallow
drink	nibble	taste

Adjectives

bitter	moist	tart
delicious	rich	thick
dry	sour	thin
famished	starved	thirsty
full	succulent	
hungry	sweet	

Misc

baker	cook	pot luck
chef	gourmet	

List 4: Housing/Housekeeping

General

building	farm	development	suburb
city	ghetto	neighborhood	town
community	home	quarter	village
country	house	residence	
development	housing	subdivision	

Types

adobe	high-rise	mobile home	tenement
A-frame	houseboat	palace	tent
apartment	hut	ranch house	tepee
cape	igloo	salt-box	trailer
condominium	log cabin	skyscraper	tree house
chalet	manor	split-level	wigwam
flat			

Construction Materials

brick	concrete	log	stone
cement	glass	shingles	wood
clapboard	linoleum	steel	

Parts

addition	drive	garage	walk
bay	electric sockets	light switch	wall
breezeway	ell	picture window	window
bulkhead	fireplace	plumbing	wiring
ceiling	floor	rafters	yard
chimney	foundation	sill	
door	frame	stairs	
dormer	fuse box	steps	

Rooms

attic	closet	kitchen	porch
basement	den	laundry room	store room
bath	dining room	living room	toilet
bed	family room	pantry	utility room
cellar	hall	play room	

Locations

kitchen	living room	den	yard
bedroom	laundry	study	sun porch
bathroom	cellar	nursery	hall
breakfast room/nook	attic	garage	

Events and Activities

visitors	guests	TV watching	light repair work
delivery men	cooking	doing the laundry	babysitting
mailman	house cleaning	yard work	home improvement

Furnishings and Equipment

ashtray	cupboard	iron	sheets
basin	curtains	ironing board	shower
bathtub	desk	kitchen table	sideboard
bed double	dining room table	lamp	sink
twin	dishwasher	light	sofa
bunk	draperies	linen	stereo
blanket	dresser	linoleum	stove
bookshelves/case	dryer	love seat	table
cabinet	easy chair	oven	television
carpet	end table	radio	TV/VCR stand
chair	electrical outlet	record player	toilet
coffee table	entertainment center	refrigerator	towel
corner cupboard	fireplace	rug	vacuum cleaner
cot	freezer	shades	washing machine
counter	furnace	shelf	water heater
crib	hutch		

Activities

change (the linen/sheets)	paint	vacuum	let
clean (up)	pick up	wash	mortgage
do the dishes	polish	wax	move
do the laundry	put away	buy	own
dust	repair	build	renovate
fix	scrub	furnish	re-model
hang out the laundry	straighten (up)	insure	rent
make the bed	sweep	lease	sub-let

Idioms and Expressions

hit home	handwriting on the wall	make a clean sweep of
on the house	keep up with the Joneses	up/down one's alley
raise the roof	pull up stakes	blind alley
wet blanket	hit the sack	new broom sweeps clean
on the carpet	spick and span	a house is not a home
turn the tables on	whitewash	

List 5: Clothes

General

bathing suit/trunks
bathrobe
belt
blazer
blouse
bow tie
boxer shorts
bra
briefs
buckle
cap
cape
cardigan
coat
cocktail dress
dinner jacket
dress
dungarees
earmuffs
garter
girdle
gloves
gown
hat
jacket

(blue)jeans
leotard
jumpsuit
mittens
muffler
nightgown
nylons
overalls
overcoat
pajamas
panties
pants
pantsuit
pantyhose
parka
raincoat
running shorts
scarf
shirt dress
  sport
shorts
ski jacket
  pants
skirt
slacks

slicker
slip
snowsuit
sport coat/jacket
stole
suit
suspenders
sweater
sweat pants
sweat suit
sweatshirt
(neck)tie
tank top
tights
trench coat
trousers
t-shirt
turtleneck
tuxedo
underclothes
underpants
undershirt
vest
wig

Footwear

boots
  cowboy
  dress
  riding
clogs
flats
high heels

gymshoes
moccasins
knee socks
overshoes
peds
rubbers
running shoes

shoes
shoelaces/strings
slippers
sneakers
socks
stockings

Sewing and Parts

bobbin
button
buttonhole
cloth
collar
cuff
darn
elastic
fabric
fringe

knit
hem
hemline
hood
material
mend
nap
neckline
needle
notch

patch
pattern
pins
pull
pocket
ruffle
scissors
seam
sewing machine

Sewing and Parts, continued

size	thimble	tape measure
sleeve	thread	tuck
snap	threader	yarn
stitch	tack down	zipper

Adjectives

brand new	large (sized)	silk
checkered	loose	small (sized)
corduroy	machine washable	striped
cotton	medium (sized)	tight
dress	nylon	torn
dry cleanable	permanent press	velvet
flannel	plaid	washable
frayed	polka dot	worn out
hand-me-down	polyester	wool
hand washable	rayon	woven
knit	second-hand	

Verbs

baste	hem	take in
cut (out)	knit	take off
darn	pin up	take up
dress	put on	tear (out)
fit	rip (out)	thread
gather	sew (up)	trace
get dressed	stitch	wear
grow out of (into)	tack	wear out

Idioms and Expressions

all dressed up	handle with kid gloves	on pins and needles
be in someone's shoes	hit below the belt	shoe on the other foot
burn a hole in one's pocket	if the shoe fits	spin a yarn
buttonhole someone	keep one's shirt on	spit and polish
collar someone	look for a needle in the haystack	stuffed shirt
clothes make the man	lose one's shirt	tied to someone's apron strings
dolled up	on a shoestring	wear and tear

List 6: Paraphernalia

Nouns

address book
bag
barrette
beads
billfold
bobby pin
bracelet
briefcase
brooch
calling card case
calculator
cane
change purse
checkbook
chewing tobacco
choker
cigar
cigarette
coin
coin purse
comb
contact lens
credit card case
crutches
date book
earring

(eye) glasses /spectacles
  bifocal
  driving
  reading
glasses case
hair pin
hair pull
handbag
handkerchief
hanging bag
identification
ID bracelet
jack knife
kerchief
key chain
key ring
keys
lighter
locket
matches
nail clippers
nail file
necklace
overnight bag
pen
pencil

penknife
pin
pipe
playing cards
pocketbook
pocket calendar
pocketknife
pocket watch
purse
ring
  engagement
  school
  signet
  wedding
shoulder bag
snuff
tie clip
tie pin
tissues
tobacco pouch
umbrella
wallet
walking stick
wristwatch

Idioms and Expression

draw matches
flip a coin
make head or tail
key to the city

little black book
pick pocket
pipe dream
purse snatcher

put that in your pipe
rose colored glasses
up to snuff
well groomed

List 7: Family

aunt
baby brother/sister
big brother/sister
bride
brother
cousin
dad
daddy
daughter
dependent
family dog
folks
father
fiancé(e)
first husband, etc.
foster parent
foster child
gram
gramp
granddaughter
grandfather

grandma
grandmother
grandpa
grandson
great aunt
great uncle
great grandson
groom
guardian
husband
in-laws
kin
kindred
ma
middle child
mom
mommy
mother
(mother)-in-law
niece
nephew

pa
pop
sibling
sis
sister
　half-
　step-
son
spouse
adopted
adoptive
maternal
paternal
orphan
uncle
widow
widower
wife
relation
relative

Idioms and Expressions

all in the family
better half
chip off the old block
come by it naturally
kissing cousins

family tree
favorite son
sibling rivalry
spitting image
take after

son of a gun
wicked stepmother
wife (to be)
your old (man)
like father, like son

List 8: Human Relationships

Nouns

admiration	cooperation	envy	intimacy	rivalry
affection	competition	hate	love	sex
antagonism	friendship	hatred	marriage	teamwork

Verbs

admire	compete	envy	ignore	make love
befriend	dislike	hate	like	share
cooperate	distrust	have sex	love	trust

People

acquaintance	company	enemy	host	partner
antagonist	comrade	fiancé/fiancée	leader	party
associate	counselor	follower	lover	playmate
boyfriend	crony	friend	mate	relative
buddy	crowd	gang	mistress	roommate
colleague	date	girlfriend	mob	team
companion	disciple	guest	pal	teammate

Human Qualities and Stages

aloof	cowardly	greedy	lovable	sentimental
artistic	crazy	handsome	plain	serious
attractive	cruel	hard-working	pleasant	sexy
bashful	dependable	helpful	polite	shy
beautiful	determined	humorous	pretty	stand-offish
brave	diligent	ill-mannered	quiet	strong
cheerful	disciplined	impolite	reserved	stuck up
conceited	dumb	insane	romantic	studious
cold	foolish	intelligent	rude	stupid
complacent	fresh	kind	sane	trustworthy
cooperative	friendly	lazy	self-conscious	ugly
courageous	funny	loud	selfish	up-tight
courteous	gorgeous	lovely	sensitive	well-mannered

Stages

adolescent	childhood	infant	middle-age	senile
age	childish	infantile	old	teenager
aged	elderly	kid	pre-teen	toddler
baby	grownup	juvenile	retired	young
child	immature	mature	senior citizen	young adult

Idioms and Expressions

have an affair	gang up on	side-kick	take down a peg
blind date	have a crush on	sponge off of	hang it up
breaking up	living together	steady date	pull no punches
fair sex	old man (lady)	sucker	flip one's lid
fall-guy	ringleader	Tom, Dick and Harry	through the motions

List 9: Travel

Places

airport	in flight	junction with
train station	on the bus	traffic light
bus station	in a train coach	hotel
travel agency	in a train club car	motel
ticket office	in a train dining car	restaurant
baggage office	in a train sleeping berth	tourist center
check-in counter	in a taxi	Chamber of Commerce
immigration	in a car	gas station
customs	on a ferry	auto rental agency
baggage claim	Interstate Highway	auto repair shop
waiting room	toll booth	

Some Events

arrival	hitch-hiking	packing
auto accident	hailing a cab	parking ticket
departure	hotel check-in	speeding ticket
flat tire	hotel check-out	traffic violation

Idioms and Expressions

bump into	hang around	go through customs
get a move on	hit the road	jet lag
let's split	catch the (bus)	hitch a ride
take off	take the (bus)	

List 10: Time

Daily

dawn	noon	dusk
sunrise	afternoon	evening
sunup	p.m.	night
morning	sunset	midnight
a.m.	sundown	
forenoon	twilight	

Instruments

almanac	clock	wristwatch
calendar	watch	

Measures

second	week	decade
minute	fortnight	century
half-hour	month	millennium
hour	year	
day	leap year	

General measures

instant	era	weekly
moment	eon	monthly
period	split-second	past
age	daily	present
epoch	every day	future

Seasons

spring	fall	winter
summer	autumn	

Idioms and Expressions

behind the times	on time	at no time
call it a day	keep time	time out
fly-by-night	make time	time honored
get along in years	the time is right	from the first
in the wink of an eye	lose time	in the beginning
for the time being	all the live long day	the crack of doom
in a jiffy	behind the times	ASAP - as soon as possible
in the nick of time	it's high time	PDQ - pretty darn (or damn) quick
in time	time zones	B.C. - before Christ
kill time	time-and-a-half	A.D. - *anno Domini* -
pass the time	the time of your life	in the year of our lord
all in good time	double time	C.E. - common era
make a night of it	two time	

List 11: Weather and Climate

Nouns

air	air mass	thunderstorm
breeze	front	cloud
cyclone	high	cumulus
gale	low	thunderhead
gust	bolt	humidity
hurricane	downpour	pressure
tornado	drought	temperature
wind	drizzle	velocity
blizzard	fog	barometer
drift	lightning	hygrometer
freezing rain	mist	thermometer
frost	ram	forecast
hail	shower	weather report
ice	smog	
sleet	squall	
snow	thunder	

Verbs

blow	hail	rain
cloud up	lift	shine
drift	mist	snow
drizzle	pour	thunder

Adjectives

breezy	frigid	rainy
chilly	frosty	severe
cloudy	hazardous	snowy
cold	hot	sunny
dreary	humid	temperate
dusty	inclement	tropical
dry	mild	wet
foggy	partly (sunny, etc)	
freezing	polar	

Idioms & Expressions

bolt from the blue	hot air	take the wind out of
break the ice	make hay while the	someone's sails
castles in the air	sun shines	three sheets to the wind
cats and dogs	rain on my parade	up in the air
cold snap	shoot the breeze	weather the storm
heat wave	silver lining	windfall

List 12: Geography

Space

comet	meteor	orbit	satellite	sun
constellation	meteorite	outer space	space	sun spot
falling star	moon	planet	solar wind	universe
galaxy	nebula	ring	star	

Solar System

Earth	Mars	Neptune	Saturn	Venus
Jupiter	Mercury	Pluto	Uranus	

Earth

Antarctic Circle	continent	glacier	mountain	sea
Arctic Circle	crater	globe	north	south
area	current	gorge	ocean	strait
atoll	dam	gulf	peak	stream
bay	dale	gully	peninsula	surf
beach	delta	hedge	plain	swamp
bog	desert	hill	plateau	tide
brook	ditch	island	pole	Tropic of Cancer
canal	east	isthmus	pond	Tropic of Capricorn
canyon	equator	lake	prairie	undertow
cape	estuary	lagoon	range	valley
cascade	fault	latitude	ravine	volcano
channel	field	ledge	reef	wave
chasm	fiord	longitude	reservoir	waterfall
cliff	forest	marsh	rift	west
coastline	geyser	meadow	river	woods

Material

dirt	mud	rock	soil	turf
earth	pebble	sod	stone	

Events

avalanche	ebb	eruption	landslide
earthquake	erosion	flow	

Idioms and Expressions

a stone's throw	high and dry	sell down the river
babes in the woods	leave no stone unturned	spaced out
bog down	make a mountain of a mole hill	stem the tide
dirt cheap	once in a blue moon	stick in the mud
down-to-earth	out of the woods	true grit
earthy	out of this world	under the sun
East is East and West is West	over hill and dale	win by a landslide

List 13: Animals

Rodents

bat	guinea pig	hamster	prairie dog	rat
gerbil	hare	mouse	rabbit	squirrel

Domestic animals

cat	donkey	horse	ox	pony
cow	goat	mule	pig	sheep
dog				

Wild Animals

badger	cougar	fox	porcupine	skunk
bear	coyote	moose	porpoise	squirrel
beaver	deer	mountain	possum	whale
bobcat	dolphin	lion	raccoon	wild cat
chipmunk	elk	otter	sea cow	wolf

Reptiles

frog	newt	snake	toad	turtle
lizard	salamander	tadpole	tortoise	

Fish

bass	cod	guppy	perch	sturgeon
bluegill	eel	herring	pike	sunfish
catfish	goldfish	monk	shark	trout

Shellfish, etc

clam	lobster	oyster	sea urchin	snail
crab	mussel	scallop	shrimp	starfish

Insects, etc

ant	butterfly	cricket	millipede	spider
aphid	caterpillar	dragonfly	praying mantis	termite
bee	centipede	grasshopper	scorpion	water strider
bug	cockroach	lady bug	silverfish	worm

Zoo animals

alligator	crocodile	gorilla	leopard	rhinoceros
bear	elephant	hippopotamus	lion	tiger
buffalo	giraffe	hyena	monkey	zebra

Body parts

abdomen	fur	legs	spine	thorax
antennae	hair	paw	spot	whiskers
claw	head	scale	stripe	wings
fangs	hoof	shell	tail	wool
feelers	horns	snout	teeth	

Dwellings

aquarium	cage	hutch	pasture	tank
barn	cave	nest	pen	trap
burrow				

Groupings

band (gorillas)	colony (ants)	herd (elephants)	pod (whales)	team (horses)
bed (clams)	flock (sheep)	herd (horses)	pride (lions)	tribe (goats)
brood (hens)	flock (birds)	nest (snakes)	school (fish)	troop (monkeys)
cloud (gnats)	gaggle (geese)	pack (dogs)	swarm (bees)	yoke (oxen)

Young Animals

bunny - rabbit	eaglet - eagle	gosling - goose
calf - cattle, elephant, whale	fawn - deer	kid - goat, man
chick - chicken, other fowl	filly - horse (female)	kitten - cat
colt - horse (male)	fingerling - fish	lamb - sheep
cub - fox, bear, lion, whale	fledgling - birds	piglet - pig
cygnet - swan	foal - horse, zebra	polliwog - frog
duckling - duck	fry - fish	puppy - dog

Comparative Expressions

big as a whale	proud as a peacock	wise as an owl
blind as a bat	quiet as a mouse	drinks like a fish
brave as a lion	silly as a goose	eats like a horse
busy as a bee	slippery as an eel	eats like a bird
crazy as a loon	slow as a turtle	runs like a deer
dumb as an ox	sly as a fox	swims like a fish
fast as a jackrabbit	strong as an ox	climbs like a monkey
happy as a clam	stubborn as a mule	chatters like a chipmunk

Idioms and Expressions

back the wrong horse	get one's goat	pig-headed
black sheep	gift horse in the mouth	play possum
bull session	go to the dogs	road hog
bum steer	hold one's horses	shooting fish in a barrel
let the cat out of the bag	horse around	smell a rat
cock and bull story	horse of another color	snake in the grass
copycat	in the doghouse	straight from the horse's mouth
crocodile tears	make a beeline for	take the bull by the horns
cry wolf	make a monkey out of	throw the bull
dark horse	monkey around with	white elephant
fish out of water	monkey business	wolf in sheep's clothing

List 14: Birds

albatross	grouse	raven
blackbird	gull	roadrunner
bluebird	hawk	robin
bobwhite	heron	sandpiper
cardinal	hummingbird	snipe
catbird	jay	sparrow
chickadee	kingbird	starling
chicken	kingfisher	swallow
condor	kite	swan
cowbird	lark	tern
crane	loon	thrush
crow	magpie	titmouse
cuckoo	meadowlark	turkey
duck	kingbird	vulture
eagle	oriole	warbler
egret	osprey	woodpecker
falcon	owl	wren
finch	parrot	beak
flamingo	partridge	claw
flycatcher	pelican	egg
goldfinch	pheasant	feather
goose	phoebe	tail
grackle	pigeon	talon
grosbeak	quail	

Idioms and Expressions

bird in the hand	eat crow	talk turkey
birds of a feather	feather in one's cap	ugly duckling
chicken	kill two birds with one stone	water off a duck's back
cook one's goose	nest egg	wild goose chase
early bird	swan song	

List 15: Plants and Trees

Types, etc.

arbor	forest	grove	orchard	woods
bush	garden	hedge	park	wilderness
field				

Trees

ash	cedar	elm	oak	spruce
beech	chestnut	lilac	palm	sumac
birch	dogwood	maple	pine	willow

Fruit trees

apple	cherry	lemon	orange	pear
apricot	grapefruit	lime	peach	plum

Parts

acorn	bud	pine cone	sap	trunk
bark	leaf	ring	seed	twig
branch	needle	root	stump	

Plants, Weeds, etc.

blueberry	cattails	fern	milkweed	reeds
burdock	crabgrass	grass	poison ivy	water lily

Wildflowers, etc.

clover	daisy	goldenrod	lady's slipper	sunflower
columbine	dandelion	Indian paintbrush	Queen Anne's lace	violets

Garden flowers

alyssum	daffodil	lily	poppy	sunflower
chrysanthemum	geranium	lily of the valley	rose	tulip
crocus	iris	marigold	snapdragon	zinnia

Flower parts

anther	petal	pollen	stamen	stigma
ovary	pistil	seed	stem	style

Idioms and Expressions

Adam's apple	hit the hay	rest on one's laurels
against the grain	in a nutshell	reap what you sow
beat around the bush	that's just peachy	sow one's wild oats
bed of roses	the last straw	turn over a new leaf
grapevine	out on a limb	wallflower

List 16: Language

Nouns

adjective	etymology	noun	sentence
adverb	fiction	paragraph	signature
article	grammar	paraphrase	slang
autograph	idiom	period	speech
comma	interview	phonology	spiel
comprehension	jargon	poetry	style
conversation	journalism	prayer	syntax
definition	linguistics	pronoun	title
dialect	literature	pronunciation	usage
dialogue	meaning	punctuation	verb
diction	monologue	quotation	verbiage
drama	narration	recitation	
essay	narrative	semantics	

Verbs

abridge	edit	pronounce	stutter
call	encode	punctuate	swear
censor	erase	quote	symbolize
chat	explain	read	talk
communicate	explicate	recite	tell
comprehend	express	relate	title
converse	gossip	report	transcribe
cry	interpret	respond	translate
curse	interview	say	transliterate
debate	mean	scrawl	type
decode	misspell	sign	utter
define	narrate	speak	vow
dictate	paraphrase	spell	write
discuss	pray	sputter	
drawl	print	stammer	

Idioms and Expressions

call a spade a spade	double talk	neither rhyme nor reason
call to order	read between the lines	talk of the town
a close call	sign on the dotted line	tall story
far cry	swear on a stack of Bibles	

List 17: Thinking

Nouns

analysis	fantasy	perception
attitude	feeling	rationale
belief	idea	realization
brains	image	reason
certainty	impression	reflection
comprehension	intellect	speculation
conception	intelligence	stupidity
conclusion	intention	thinking
contemplation	judgement	thought
conviction	knowledge	truth
decision	meditation	understanding
deduction	mind	view
deliberation	notion	wisdom
experience	observation	wit

Verbs

analyze	experience	perceive
appreciate	fantasize	ponder
apprehend	feel	realize
believe	figure out	reflect
brood	imagine	retain
comprehend	judge	ruminate
conceive	know	see
conclude	learn	sense
consider	meditate	speculate
contemplate	memorize	think
decide	note	trust
deliberate	notice	understand
distinguish	observe	view

Adjectives

analytical	decisive	pensive
appreciative	deliberate	rational
aware of	dull	reasonable
brainy	experiential	smart
brilliant	imaginative	stupid
certain	indecisive	thoughtful
clever	intellectual	trusting
conclusive	intelligent	truthful
cognitive	irrational	understanding
cognizant	knowing	vague
convinced	observant	wise
crafty	perceptive	witty

Idioms and Expressions

absent minded	level-headed	pipe dream
know the ropes	make head or tail	neither rhyme nor reason

List 18: Numbers and Math

Nouns

addition	equation	product
algebra	figure	proof
analysis	formula	radius
angle	fraction	rate
arithmetic	function	relativity
average	geometry	remainder
axiom	plane	root
calculation	solid	set
calculator	infinity	sequence
calculus	integral	solution
cipher	logarithm	square root
circumference	long division	statistics
computation	mathematics	straight line
computer	median	subtraction
cube	multiplication	sum
decimal	numeral	theorem
decimal point	percentage	theory
difference	pi	topology
diameter	postulate	trigonometry
dimension	probability	value
division	problem	variable

Verbs

add	divide	multiply
average	double	solve
calculate	equal	square
compute	figure	subtract
count	formulate	triple

Idioms and Expressions

face value	math facts	second-rate
fifty-fifty	multiplication tables	seeing double
lump sum	put two and two together	sixes and sevens

List 19: Colors

Primary

red	green	violet/purple
orange	blue	
yellow	indigo	

Secondary

beige	emerald	pink
black	gold	rose
bronze	gray	ruby
brown	ivory	silver
buff	khaki	slate
chestnut	lavender	tan
chocolate	maroon	turquoise
coffee	olive	white
copper	olive drab	

Adjectives

brilliant	glossy	mottled
dark	hot	pale
dull	light	pied
flat	lurid	vivid
fluorescent	metallic	

Miscellaneous

rainbow	camouflage	spectrum

Paints

acrylic	latex	tempera
enamel	oil	water
finger	pastel	

Idioms and Expressions

black and blue	in black and white	red herring
black hearted	in the pink	red letter day
blue, the blues	in the red	red tape
dyed in the wool	paint the town red	rose colored glasses
greenhorn	red carpet	silver lining
green with envy	red cent	yellow (cowardly)

List 20: Shapes

Adjectives

angular	globular	round
arched	hexagonal	rectangular
blunt	horizontal	regular
circular	irregular	sharp
concave	linear	slender
conical	long	slim
curved	narrow	square
crooked	octagonal	smooth
cylindrical	oval	straight
elliptical	parallel	triangular
elongated	perpendicular	twisted
flat	pointed	warped
flattened	ragged	wide

Nouns

arc	dome	pentagon
arch	globe	point
block	helix	pyramid
blob	heptagon	rectangle
circle	hexagon	sphere
cone	horseshoe	spiral
cube	mound	square
cylinder	octagon	surface
diamond	oval	tip
disc	peak	triangle

Idioms and Expressions

round peg in a square hole	odds and ends	straight as an arrow
domestic triangle	sharp as a tack	run circles around someone
vicious circle	square	the Pentagon
a crooked person		

List 21: Substances and Materials

Nouns

acid	flint	plastic
air	gas	plywood
aluminum	gasoline	powder
ashes	glue	rock
asphalt	goo	rubber
base	grease	sand
brass	gunk	sheet rock
bronze	kerosene	smoke
cement	lubricant	soil
cloth	moisture	steam
concrete	oil	steel
copper	ointment	stuff
dirt	paste	tar
dust	petroleum	water
earth	plaster	wood

Adjectives

abrasive	impermeable	slippery
corroded	invisible	slimy
corrosive	liquid	soft
crumbly	metallic	solid
dull	pliable	soluble
durable	resilient	spongy
dusty	rough	sticky
flammable	rubbery	strong
gaseous	rusty	thick
gooey	sharp	thin
gritty	shiny	tough
hard	slick	wet

Idioms and Expressions

blow off steam	go up in smoke	scratch the surface
brass tacks	lay it on thick	throw cold water on
fly in the ointment	take a powder	knock on wood
slick operator	greaseball	powder keg
grease the wheel	grease his palm	cement a deal
cast in concrete	to be plastered	dull as dishwater

81

List 22: Containers

bag	crate	pail
barrel	cup	pitcher
basket	demitasse	portfolio
bottle	demijohn	pot
bowl	dish	rack
box	file folder	sack
bucket	flask	snifter
can	glass	thermos
canister	jar	tin
canteen	jug	tray
carafe	keg	tub
carton	mug	tube
case	pack	vase
container	package	vessel

Idioms and Expressions

in the bag	boxed in	lock, stock and barrel
have someone over a barrel	drop in the bucket	soapbox
bottleneck	left holding the bag	windbag
barrel of monkeys	jug wine	ugly mug
bag lady	on the bottle	a real dish

List 23: Emotions

Nouns

affection	bravery	fatigue	joy	rage
aggravation	cheer	fear	joviality	regret
amusement	courage	feeling	laughter	restlessness
anger	craziness	fright	love	sadness
anguish	dejection	gladness	mood	sorrow
annoyance	delight	glee	nervousness	tears
anxiety	depression	greed	pain	temper
awe	disappointment	happiness	passion	terror
belligerence	disgust	hope	pity	tiredness
bitterness	embarrassment	horror	pleasure	trouble
bliss	enthusiasm	indifference	prejudice	weariness
boredom	envy	jealousy	pride	zest

Verbs

abhor	bother	disgust	hate	rejoice
aggravate	burn up	embarrass	hope	sadden
agitate	calm	envy	laugh	shake up
amuse	cheer up	excite	lament	stir
anger	console	fatigue	like	tire
annoy	cry	fear	love	tremble
antagonize	delight	feel	mope	trouble
bewilder	depress	frighten	mourn	weep
blush	detest	fume	pain	
bore	disappoint	gladden	please	

Adjectives

abhorrent	bitter	disgusted	happy	painful
abject	blissful	embarrassed	hopeful	passionate
affectionate	bored	enthusiastic	insane	pleased
afraid	bothered	envious	irritated	restless
aggravated	brave	excited	jealous	sad
amorous	calm	fatigued	jolly	sexy
amused	cheerful	fearful	joyful	shy
angry	cheery	flustered	jovial	sorrowful
annoyed	crazy	forlorn	loving	tearful
anxious	dejected	frightened	melancholy	timid
apprehensive	delighted	gay	merry	tired
belligerent	depressed	glad	moody	troubled
berserk	disappointed	gleeful	mournful	upset
bewildered	disconsolate	grouchy	nervous	weary

Idioms and Expressions

at wit's end	hot and bothered	out of sorts
blow one's top	in a dither	stand-offish
fit to be tied	make a scene	tear jerker
go to pieces	method in one's madness	troubled waters
happy as a clam	love will find a way	end of your rope

List 24: The Body and its Function

External

head	palm	stomach	thigh
hair	thumb	abdomen	calf
shoulders	finger	waist	shin
neck	index	hip	ankle
arm	middle	buttocks	heel
armpit	ring	penis	instep
forearm	little	testes	sole
elbow	fingernail	testicles	foot
wrist	chest	anus	toe
fist	breast	leg	big toe
hand	nipple	knee	little toe

Face

forehead	iris	nose	gums
eyebrow	white	nostril	lip
temple	eyeball	bridge	chin
eyelash	ear	mouth	dimple
eyelid	earlobe	jaw	mustache
eye	eardrum	tongue	beard
pupil	cheek	tooth	sideburns

Bones

skull	spine	ribs	thigh bone
backbone	collarbone	pelvis	kneecap
vertebrae	shoulder blade	hipbone	skeleton

Insides

brain	pancreas	vein	throat
windpipe	kidney	artery	tonsils
heart	intestines	muscle	larynx
lung	appendix	blood	vagina
liver	bladder	nerves	rectum

Body products

urine	saliva/spit	tears	sperm
feces	perspiration/sweat	oil	eggs

Adjectives

pregnant	skinny	robust	tight
tall, short	plump	weak	loose
thin, fat	healthy	strong	supple
muscular	sick	athletic	lithe

Verbs

sit	belch	spit	laugh
stand	burp	defecate	giggle
jump	breathe	urinate	titter
leap	gasp	swallow	cry
hop	see	taste	weep
skip	hear	digest	sob
run	smell	fornicate	sniffle
twist	eat	copulate	moan
bend	bite	menstruate	groan
flex	chew	smile	scowl
creep	nibble	grin	

Idioms and Expressions

after one's own heart
all ears
apple of one's eye
give one's right arm
at arm's length
with open arms
turn one's back on
bad blood
beat one's brains out
beat one's head against a
   stone wall
bend over backwards
bite off more than one can chew
in cold blood
brainstorm
waste one's breath
save one's breath
take away one's breath
breathe freely
cold feet
cool one's heels
cut off one's nose to spite
   one's face
eat one's heart out
eat one's words
rub elbows with
elbow grease
keep an eye on
see eye to eye
make eyes at
keep a straight face

keep one's fingers crossed
first-hand
foot the bill
put one's foot down
put one's best foot forward
put one's foot in one's mouth
on all fours
funny bone
get on one's nerves
get something off one's chest
guts
let down one's hair
split hairs
hard-hearted
hard headed
head and shoulders above all
over one's head
heart-to-heart
by heart
have a heart
a heel
keep a stiff upper lip
knock one's block off
lowbrow, highbrow
make no bones about
by word of mouth
shoot one's mouth off
narrow-minded
neck and neck
up to one's neck
nosey

pay lip service to
pay through the nose
pick a bone with
pull one's leg
pull the wool over someone's eyes
shake a leg
straight from the shoulder
a cold shoulder
a chip on one's shoulder
by the skin of one's teeth
get under one's skin
slap in the face
slip of the tongue
sweet tooth
take a load off one's feet
set one's teeth on edge
under one's thumb
all thumbs
toe the mark
be on one's toes
tooth and nail
tongue in cheek
tongue tied
tongue twister
on the tip of one's tongue
turn the other cheek
turn up one's nose
turn one's back on
watch one's step
make one's mouth water
wet one's whistle

Vulgarities*

"Proper" term	Acceptable euphemism	Vulgarity
anus		ass hole, bung hole
breasts		boobies, boobs, knockers, tits
buttocks	backsides	ass, buns, butt, tail, cheeks, fanny, rear end
copulate, (have) intercourse	make love	fuck, screw, lay
defecate	go to the bathroom go to the john	shit, (take a) dump (take a) crap
ejaculate		come
expectorate	spit	clam
(to be) flatulent	pass gas, break wind	cut the cheese, fart
masturbate		jack off, jerk off
menstruation	period, time of the month	on the rag
penis		cock, dick, dong, pecker, prick, shaft
testicles		balls, nuts
vagina, labia		cunt, pussy, snatch, twat
clitoris		clit
vomit	spit up	barf, throw up, up chuck toss (snap) your cookies

*To the teacher: These vulgarities should be taught, if at all, with warnings and care. They are included here because students often hear them and misuse them, and it is important that they know when and how to use them and when not to use them.

To the student: These vulgarities must be used very carefully since many Americans find them offensive. They are very rarely used between the sexes or with older people. If you are in doubt, don't use them.

List 25: Manipulations

aim	latch	stop
arrange	level	strike
assemble	light	strip
attach	load	take apart
bash	lock	take out
beat	loop	take up
bend	maneuver	take down
bolt	mix	tap
break	mold	tear
close	move	thread
cool off, down	open	throw
crack	pick up	thrust
crumble	pick out	tie
crush	pick over	tilt
cut	pluck	tip
deposit	plug in	trip
depress	plug up	turn
disassemble	pound	turn off
detach	press	turn on
drain	pull	turn over
drive	punch	turn under
empty	push	turn around
fill	put in reverse	twist
flatten	rap	undo
flex	rip	unfold
flick	roll	unhook
flip	rub	unplug
flop	sand	unlatch
fold	scrape	unlock
hammer	screw	unscrew
hang (up)	scratch	untie
heat	seal	unzip
hook	set	weave
ignite	set down	wipe
insert	slam	work
knead	start	zip

List 26: Transportation

Land

ATV (all-terrain vehicle)	jeep	stagecoach
automobile, auto	litter	subway
bus	locomotive	tanker
bicycle, bike	moped	tank truck
cable car	motorcycle	taxicab
camper	pick-up	train
car	rickshaw	tricycle
carriage	RV (recreational vehicle)	trolley
cart	sedan	truck
chariot	sled	van
coach	sleigh	wagon
convertible	sports car	

Animals

burro	dog (sled)	llama
camel	donkey	mule
cow	horse	oxen

People

bus driver	conductor	mechanic
chauffeur	engineer	teamster
coachman	guide	truck driver

General

alley	interstate	street
bridge	lane	thruway
burden	oil	timetable
cargo	path	trail
coal	rest area	tire
diesel engine	road	turnpike
gasoline	schedule	vehicle
highway	steam	wheel

Air

aircraft	aviator	gate
airliner	co-pilot	hangar
airplane	flight attendant	luggage
balloon (hot air)	pilot	propeller
glider	steward/stewardess	reservation
helicopter	airport	runway
jet	boarding pass	seat
light plane	baggage check	seat assignment
spacecraft, ship	concourse	ticket
spaceshuttle	control tower	window
rocket	engine	wings

Sea

ark	sailboat	lighthouse
barge	ship	mast
boat	steamship	oars
canoe	submarine	ocean
cruise ship	tugboat	paddlewheel
dinghy	vessel	pond
ferry	warship	port
freighter	yacht	propeller
galley	canal	rapids
hovercraft	channel	river
kayak	fleet	rudder
lifeboat	harbor	sail
motorboat	helm	sea
ocean liner	hull	steering wheel
raft	keel	stream
rowboat	lake	white water

Verbs

arrive	embark	sail
check in	fly	take off
depart	land	tow
disembark	paddle	travel
drive	ride	walk

Idioms and Expressions

back-fire	know the ropes	take a back seat to
get on the bandwagon	meet someone half-way	run around in circles
on the (water) wagon	pave the way for	slow boat to China
in the same boat	water under the bridge/	shipshape
off the beaten track	over the dam	up the creek without a paddle
burn one's bridges behind	fall asleep at the wheel	backseat driver

List 27: Hotels

airport limousine, limo
baggage
ball room
bar
bath
bed
bill
bureau
bed and breakfast
boarding house
chair
cashier
currency exchange
chambermaid
chauffeur
coffee shop
convention
desk clerk
dining room
doorman
elevator

elevator operator
flop house
guest house
information desk
hospitality center
travel desk
gardener
guest
housekeeper
hostel
hotel
inn
key
lobby
lounge
luggage
maid
manager
meeting
motel
operator

organization
party
reservation
residential hotel
resort
room
  single
  double
room clerk
room service
restaurant
safety deposit box
security guard
table
tourist
tourist cabins
tourist court
tour guide
travel desk

Verbs

call (wake-up)
check in
check out

disturb (do not)
pack
register

reserve
stay

Idioms and Expressions

bag and baggage
a place to hang your hat

room and board
it's the Ritz

stop for the night
overnight guest

List 28: Restaurants

Nouns

appetizer	cup	menu	salt
ashtray	dessert	mug	serving
bar	dish	napkin	spoon
bowl	fork	order	table
booth	glass	plate	tablecloth
buffet	gourmet	platter	tax
chair	gratuity	reservation	tip
check	knife	round (of drinks)	wine cellar
cocktail	main course	refill (of coffee)	wine list
course	meal	salad bar	

Verbs

dine	order	prepare	tip
eat out	pay	reserve	take out

Types

automat	diner	luncheonette	snack bar
cafe	drive-in	natural foods	soda fountain
cafeteria	fast-food	pizzeria/pizza	vending machine
coffee shop	gourmet	parlor	

Personnel

baker	chef	headwaiter	manager
bartender	cook	host	waiter
busboy	dishwasher	hostess	waitress
cashier	guest	maitre d'	

Adjectives

à la carte	dry	overdone	steamed
baked	fresh	rare	succulent
bland	fried	raw	take-out
boiled	grilled	salty	tasteless
broiled	hot	scrumptious	tasty
cold	mashed	sliced	to go
delicious	medium	spicy	well-done

Idioms and Expressions

wine and dine	doggy bag	go dutch	dine and dance
bill of fare	dutch treat	take the check	
bottomless cup	room and meals tax	foot the bill	

List 29: Stores and Shops

General

downtown
main street
window shopping
neighborhood

variety store
mall
specialty shops
browsing

shopping center
shopping district
one-stop shopping
outlet center

Specific

roadside vegetable stand
grocery store
supermarket
delicatessen
bakery
health food store
restaurant
cafeteria
snack bar
coffee shop
fast-food chain
pizza parlor
candy store
drug store
pharmacy
optician
department store
discount store

outlet store
department store
clothing store
shoe store
thrift shop
country store
mail-order
service center
flea market
furniture store
appliance store
hardware store
fabric store
sewing center
carpets & draperies store
paint store
stationery store
book store

art gallery
newsstand
tobacconist
music store
TV-radio store
sporting goods store
arts and crafts store
toy store
gift shop
pet shop
hobby shop
antique shop
jewelry store
photography store
"Green Stamp"
  redemption center
florist
car dealership

List 30: Agencies and Services

bank
post office
town/city offices
loan association
insurance agency
real estate agency
military recruiting office
travel agency
law firm
police department
fire department
Internal Revenue Service
certified public accountant office
stockbroker
telephone company
  business office
TV cable company office

advertising agency
auto rental agency
copy center
newspaper office
beauty parlor
barber shop
tanning salon
health center
martial arts studio
dance studio
funeral parlor
dry cleaners
laundry
laundromat
shoe repair service
radio-TV repair
appliance repair

auto parts store
electrician
plumber
welding shop
auto repair shop
service station
carpenter
moving company
storage warehouse
employment agency
day-care center
senior citizen's center
welfare office
Planned Parenthood
Hotline
Women's Crisis Center
charities

List 31: Post Office

Personnel

carrier	mail carrier	postmaster/mistress
clerk	postman	sorter

Nouns and Adjectives

address	first class, etc.	postage meter
aerogram	franking privileges	post card
airmail	general delivery	priority
book of stamps	insurance	rates
book rate	junk mail	registered mail
box	letter	return address
bulk mail	lobby	return receipt
cancellation	magazine	service window
certified mail	mail	special delivery
C.O.D.	money order	special handling
coil of stamps	next day	stamp
dead letter	newspaper	surface mail
envelope	overnight	U.P.S.
express mail	package	ZIP Code
fee	parcel post	Zone

Verbs

address	insure	register
cancel	lick	return
deliver	post	seal
fill out	pick up	send
forward	receive	stamp

List 32: Banks and Money

Verbs

apply for
authorize
balance
borrow
bounce a check
cancel
call a loan
cash
change
charge

close out
convert
count
credit
debit
deposit
endorse
insure
justify
loan

make change
overdraw
pay
put in
save
stop payment
take out
withdraw

Nouns

asset
automatic payment
ATM - automatic
  teller machine
balance
bank
bank account
bank book
bill
cash
certificate of deposit
check
checking account
check stub
coin
commercial loan
credit card
currency

deposit
deposit slip
deposit receipt
dime
dollar
half dollar
interest
invoice
frozen assets
line of credit
loan
loan agreement
loan payment
money
mortgage
nickel
paycheck
penny

piggy bank
principal
quarter
receipt
record book
safe deposit box
savings account
savings bond
second mortgage
secured loan
silver dollar
statement
traveler's check
total
vault
window
withdrawal
withdrawal slip

Personnel

drive-up teller
executive officer
loan officer

messenger
president
safe deposit clerk

secretary
security guard
teller

Idioms and Expressions

bank on something
bottom dollar
one's money's worth
pass the buck
pretty penny
queer as a three-dollar bill
rain check
rubber check

a run on the bank
bank holiday
flat broke
in the money
cheapskate
corner the market
make or break
make a buck

make both ends meet
I.O.U.
a man of means
penny wise and pound foolish
nickel and dime to death
waste not, want not
a penny saved is a penny earned

List 33: Community

Places and Organizations

city sidewalk	Protestant Church	Knights of Columbus	FFA
city park	Jewish Synagogue	Lions Clubs	American Legion
park bench	Grange	Shriners	fraternities/sororities
civic center	VFW	Masons	PTA
community house	DAR	IOOF	ASPCA
public library	Elks	Boy/Girl Scouts	garden club
Catholic Church	Eagles	4-H Club	arts council

Events

wedding	bingo	concert	tag, yard, lawn sale
reception	strike	county fair	Town Meeting
wake	picket line	hoedown	political rally
funeral	demonstration	rodeo	voting
memorial service	walk-a-thon	auction	rummage sales
church bazaar	parade	flea market	beauty contest
church supper	band		

List 34: Recreation

Games (also see 32)

backgammon	checkers	mahjong
board games	chess	Monopoly
bridge	cribbage	poker
canasta	crossword puzzle	rummy
cards	hearts	Scrabble
charades	jig saw puzzle	twenty questions

Hobbies

aquariums	gardening	pottery
butterfly collecting	gun collecting	rock collecting
coin collecting	miniatures	terrariums
collecting antiques, etc.	model building	stamp collecting
canning	model railroading	Sports (see List 35)
cooking	painting	Music (see List 36)

Amusements & Shows

amusement park	disco	night club
carnival	ice show	radio
circus	magic acts	television
concert hall	movies	theater
dinner theater	pool hall	video game arcade

Arts

ballet	exhibition	photography
concert	martial arts	recital
dance	music	sculpture
drama	painting	theater

Crafts

batik	embroidery	quilting
carpentry	knitting	sewing
crewel	needlepoint	weaving
crocheting	pottery	

Places

museum	sports stadium	nightclub
concert hall	health club	discotheque
historical site	country club	bar
zoo	racquet/racket club	cocktail lounge
aquarium	tennis club	marina
botanical garden	social club	swimming pool
circus	ski resort	teen center
campground	theatre	amusement park
bathing beach	movie theatre	national park, forest

Activities

concert	hunting	football
ballet	hiking	volleyball
opera	camping	croquet
board game	mountain climbing	tennis
playing cards	horseback riding	badminton
watching TV	bicycling	squash
listening to radio, stereo	roller skating	racquetball
reading	hockey	handball
gourmet cooking	skating	golf
gardening	skiing	minature golf
birdwatching	motor boating	gymnastics
jogging	canoeing	track and field
body building	sailing	bowling
weight lifting	swimming	frisbee
martial arts	diving	horse race
kite flying	surfing	dog race
sewing	soccer	car race
painting	baseball	long-distance running
pottery making	softball	
fishing	basketball	

Idioms and Expressions

put one's cards on the table	drawing card	steal the show
put your money on the line	go fly a kite	up one's sleeve
put up or shut up	a flop	do not pass Go
no dice	hit the jackpot	by a nose
ace up your sleeve	on the wrong track	nip and tuck

List 35: Sports and Games

archery	curling	jogging	soccer
badminton	diving	mountaineering	softball
baseball	fencing	pingpong	speedskating
basketball	figure skating	pool	surfing
billiards	fishing	polo	swimming
bowling	golf	racquetball	tennis
boxing	gymnastics	roller skating	track
bicycling	hiking	running	volleyball
bronco busting	hockey	skiing	water polo
canoeing	horseback riding	downhill	weight lifting
climbing	hunting	cross-country	wrestling

Equipment

arrow	flying rings	parallel bars	ski pole
balance beam	glove	ping pong ball	skis
baseball	golfball	pole	soccerball
bat	golf clubs	pool cue	softball
birdie	hockey stick	puck	surfboard
bow	horse	racket/racquet	target
bicycle	indian clubs	racquetball	tee
canoe	mat	reins	tennis ball
fishing lure	net	saddle	tennis racket
fishing rod	paddle	skates	trampoline

Areas

arena	court	lane	roller drome
coliseum	field	pool	stadium
country club	green	ring	track
course	gymnasium	rink	trail

Verbs

aim	hike	pitch	serve
attack	hit	place	tackle
catch	hurl	play	take part in
club	jog	punt	tie
coach	kick	run	throw
defeat	lose	save	win
defend	participate	score	

Idioms and Expressions

all part of the game	get to first base	right off the bat	long shot
batting average	go to bat for	pinch hit	pull one's punches
below par	have a lot on the ball	rain check	know what the score is
behind the eight ball	hook, line, and sinker	free-for-all	second wind
break the record	keep the ball rolling	hit or miss	have a score to settle
come-back	make a hit	jump the gun	seventh inning stretch
double-header	in the rough	last lap	shot in the dark
get on the ball	rate a ten	for keeps	win hands down

List 36: Music

Nouns

album	conductor	measure	solo
alto	concerto	melody	sonata
artist	disc	note	song
ballad	disc jockey (DJ)	piece	soprano
band	folk song	program	symphony
bar	group	recital	tenor
bass	hit	record, disc, tape	tune
beat	hymn	release	
composition	jazz	rhythm	
concert	lyrics	singer	

Verbs

accompany	harmonize	pluck	toot
compose	hum	read (music)	whistle
conduct	interpret	record	write
croon	pick	sing	
finger	play	strum	

Types

acoustic	country	modern	religious
Baroque	country & western	mood	rock and roll, rock
bluegrass	dance	muscial	rhythm and blues
chamber	electronic	opera	spirituals
classical	folk	operetta	soul
contemporary	jazz	popular, pop	symphonic

Instruments

banjo	drums	oboe	tambourine
bass	dulcimer	organ	trombone
bassoon	electric guitar	mandolin	trumpet
cello	fiddle	piano	tuba
clarinet	guitar	saxophone	viola
cornet	harp	strings	violin
cymbals	horn	synthesizer	

Idioms and Expressions

face the music	soft-pedal	music to one's ears
fiddle around with	song and dance	the blues
play second fiddle	for a song	to beat the band

List 37: Photography

Nouns

accessory	fixer	screen
album	flash	shutter
aperture	flashbulb	sitting
battery	lab	slide
developer	lens	snapshot
duplicate	light meter	speed
camera	mailer	strap
canister	movie	stop bath
cartridge	mug shot	studio
case	negative	telephoto
composition	photo	tripod
darkroom	photograph	VCR (video
developer	Polaroid	cassette recorder)
enlargement	portrait	video player
electronic flash	positive	video tape
exposure	projector	viewer
film	print	wide-angle
film setting	range finder	zoom lens
filter	roll (of film)	

Verbs

come out	expose	print
compose	focus	process
blow up	frame	reduce
develop	load	rewind
duplicate	mount	snap (a picture)
enlarge	pose	take (a picture)

Misc

automatic	flat, matte	self-focus
black and white	glossy	self-winding
color	out-of-focus	sound track
double exposure	over-exposed	under-exposed
double prints	reflex	washed-out

Standard print sizes:

3½ x 5	5 x 7	8 x 10

Standard film sizes:

Still Pictures:	Moving Pictures:
110	8mm
120	Super 8 mm
35 mm	16 mm
	35 mm

List 38: Medicine and Health

Places and Areas

ambulance	hospital	maternity ward	private room
birthing room	insane asylum	mental hospital	recovery room
clinic	intensive care unit	nursing home	sanitarium
delivery room	labor room	operating room	waiting room
emergency room	laboratory	pediatric ward	ward

Equipment

adhesive tape	crutches	sanitary napkins	toothpaste
band-aid	gauze	scalpel	tweezers
bandage	heating pad	stethoscope	vaporizer
bed	hot water bottle	thermometer	wheelchair
bed pan	operating table	oral	x-ray machine
cane	oxygen tent	rectal	
cast	Q-tip (swab)	tongue depressor	

Hospital

admittance	ICU (intensive care)	operating room	maternity ward
emergency room	out-patient clinic	ward/floor	private room

People

anesthetist	lab technician	pathologist	psychologist
candy striper	neurologist	patient	radiologist
chiropractor	nurse	pediatrician	receptionist
dermatologist	nurse practitioner	physician	registered nurse (R.N.)
doctor (M.D.)	obstetrician	podiatrist	specialist
general practitioner (G.P.)	ophthalmologist	practical nurse	surgeon
gynecologist	orthopedic surgeon	psychiatrist	undertaker
intern	out-patient	psychoanalyst	urologist

Verbs

ache	discharge	irritate	recuperate
admit	examine	nurse	relapse
bleed	faint	operate	set
cough	give birth	pain	swell
deliver	gargle	prescribe	throw up
diagnose	hurt	recover	vomit

Processes

appendectomy	EKG	intensive care	specimen
blood pressure	examination	observation	surgery
Caesarean section	heart beat	prognosis	temperature
D&C	hysterectomy	pulse	tonsillectomy
delivery (of a baby)	injection	sample	vaccination
diagnosis	inoculation	shot	x-ray

Medical & Misc

antacid	capsules	nasal spray	prescription
antidote	contraceptive	ointment	sedative
antihistamine	decongestant	penicillin	suppository
antiseptic	eyedrops	pill	tablet
aspirin	laxative	the Pill	vitamins

Problems

abscess	cough	fracture	runny nose
accident	cut	hemmorhoids (piles)	sore
ache	deaf	indigestion	sprain
allergy	diarrhea	injury	stiff
blind	dislocation	infection	strain
burn	dumb	inflammation	swollen
chills	exhaustion	nausea	virus
a cold	fever	pain	vomit
constipation	the flu	rash	wound

Diseases, etc.

AIDS	diabetes	influenza (flu)	psychosis
allergy	diarrhea	leukemia	rheumatic fever
alcoholism	drug addiction	malaria	rubella (German measles)
angina	emphysema	measles	scarlet fever
arteriosclerosis	fetal alcohol syndrome	meningitis	skin cancer
arthritis	gonorrhea	mental retardation	small pox
asthma	heart attack	mononucleosis (mono)	stroke
bronchitis	hepatitis	multiple sclerosis	syphilis
bursitis	hernia	mumps	tuberculosis (T.B.)
cancer	herpes	neurosis	tumor
chicken pox	high blood pressure	pneumonia	ulcer
cholera	HIV positive	polio	V.D. (venereal disease)

Idioms and Expressions

on call	hard of hearing	horrors (withdrawal)
office hours	over the hill	a shiner
say "ah"	kick the bucket	a black eye
turn your head and cough	a new lease on life	a shot in the arm
black and blue	give someone a dose	a sight for sore eyes
born with a silver spoon	of his own medicine	turn one's stomach
in one's mouth	take one's medicine	under the weather
cough up	nuts, nutty as a fruitcake	on the wagon
chain smoker	go off the deep end	"break a leg"
dead as a doornail	a bitter pill to swallow	an apple a day
dead to the world	in the pink	keeps the doctor away
over one's dead body	safe and sound	skin and bones
one foot in the grave	have a screw loose	to be sick and tired of something
croak	hooked on drugs	catch a cold
give up the ghost	monkey on your back	come down with

List 39: Dentistry

Places

clinic

office

waiting room

Equipment

air compressor
cleaning tools
dental floss

dentist's chair
drill
mirror

toothbrush
toothpaste
x-ray machine

People

dentist
dental assistant

dental hygienist
oral surgeon

orthodontist
receptionist

Verbs

ache
cap
clean
drill

extract
fill
hurt
pull out

repair.
seal
x-ray

Misc

abscess
bicuspid
braces
bridge
buck teeth
cavity
checkup
crown
canines

decay
dentures
dog tooth
eye tooth
false teeth
front tooth
filling
gap toothed
incisor

jaw
molar
nerve
novocaine
pain
root
root canal
wisdom tooth

Idioms and Expressions

baby teeth
his bark is worse than his bite
bite the hand that feeds you
bite off more
  than you can chew

cut one's teeth on
give one's eye tooth for
knock your teeth out
like pulling teeth

toothy grin
winning smile
the tooth fairy

List 40: Barber and Beautician

Nouns

Afro	conditioner	hair drier	ponytail
appointment	cosmetics	hair grease	razor
bangs	cream rinse	hairline	razor cut
barber	crew-cut	hair net	razor blade
barrette	curl	hair oil	receding hairline
beard	curler	hairpiece	redhead
full	DA (duck tail)	hairpins	rollers
scraggly	dandruff	hair style	scissors
beautician	depilatory	hair stylist	shampoo
blond,blonde	drier	highlight	shave
bobby pin	dye	manicure	setting lotion
bowl cut	fashion	manicurist	sideburns
braid	flat top	Mohawk	split ends
brunette	goatee (beard)	mousse	streak
brush	graybeard	moustache	tint
butch	hairbrush	handlebar	towhead
carrot top	haircut	page boy	toupee
clippers	hairdo	pedicure	wave
comb	hairdresser	permanent	whiskers
combs (decorative)	hairdressing	pigtails	wig

Verbs

bleach	curl	massage	tint
blow dry	cut	rinse	trim
brush	design	set	wave
clip	dry	shampoo	
comb	dye	shave	

Adjectives

bushy	frizzy	normal	thick
close	hairless	oily	thin
curly	hairy	over the ear	unisex
dry	kinky	short	wavy
dyed	long	straight	

Hair colors

auburn	brown	honey blonde	grey, gray
black	brunette	flaxen blond	red
blond, blonde	dishwater blonde	strawberry blond	white

Idioms and Expressions

get in one's hair	let one's hair down	put one's hair up	one's hair stands on end
hairbreadth escape	hairline crack	a hairy escape	throw it in one's teeth
hairpin turn	long hair	split hairs	not to turn a hair

List 41: Cosmetics and Toiletries

Nouns

after-shave lotion	eye drops	perfume
baby shampoo	eye-liner	powder
bath oil	eye-shadow	razor
bath salts	eye wash	disposable
bath soap	facial cleanser	one-track
beauty cream	facial mask	safety
beauty lotion	facial soap	two-track
blush	hand cream	razor blade
body lotion	hand cleanser	rouge
body cream	hand lotion	scent
bubble bath	hand soap	septic stick
cold cream	hair brush	shampoo
cologne	hair color	shaver (electric)
comb	hair dye	shaving brush
compact	hair remover	shaving cream
cosmetic base	hair rinse	shaving mug
cotton balls	lip balm	shaving soap
cotton swabs	lip gloss	skin cream
cuticle remover	lipstick	soap
deodorant	make up	sun block
roll-on	mascara	sun screen
soap	moisturizer	suntan lotion
solid	mouth wash	tissues
spray	mud pack	toilet water
stick	nail clippers	toothbrush
dental floss	nail file	tooth paste
depilatory	nail polish	tooth paste gel
ear drops	nail polish remover	tooth powder
emery board	ointment	tweezers
eyebrow pencil	oral rinse	witch hazel

Verbs

apply	cut	moisten
beautify	dab	perfume
brush	deodorize	put on
cleanse	diet	shave
clip	(give a) manicure	trim

Common Sayings

Beauty is in the eye of the beholder.	a close shave	painted woman
Beauty is only skin deep.	five o'clock shadow	not a hair out of place
B.O. (body odor)	great unwashed	smell of trouble
Cleanliness is next to Godliness.	Handsome is as handsome does.	wash one's mouth out with soap
	a little shaver	

105

List 42: Hygiene and Contraception

Hygiene

douche
  concentrate
  fluid
  powder
feminine syringe
fountain syringe
feminine napkins
sanitary napkins

mini (maxi) pads
panty liners
panty shields
sanitary belt
tampons
breast shield
nursing pads

feminine itching or
  irritation medication
feminine deodorant spray
tablets for cramps or
  menstrual pain
diuretic tablets
water pills

Contraception
contraceptive methods and information

vasectomy/tubal ligation
contraceptive implant
  norplant
oral contraceptives
  "the pill"
intrauterine device (IUD)
diaphragm with spermicide
cervical cap
condom
  bags
  balloons
  French letters

prophylactics
rubbers
safes
scum bags
sheaths
shields
skins
vaginal spermicides
contraceptive creams
foams
  gels
  inserts

jellies
  suppositories
  vaginal tablets
the rhythm method
withdrawal
  coitus interruptus
abstinence
  "just say no"
  self-constraint
  self-control

People

gynecologist

obstetrician

fertility counselor

Miscellaneous Organizations and Expressions

abortion
abortion clinic
abortion rights
anti-abortion

family planning
free choice
Planned Parenthood
population bomb

right to life
Roe versus Wade
women's rights
zero population growth

List 43: Jobs and Work

accountant
ad man, woman
advertising agent
artist
assembly line worker
automotive engineer
babysitter
baggage handler
baker
banker
bank teller
barber
beautician
bell man
bookkeeper
building contractor
bureaucrat
bus driver
business consultant
businessman, woman
butcher
carpenter
car washer
cashier
chambermaid
chef/cook
chiropractor
civil engineer
cleaning woman
cobbler
confidence man
commercial artist
computer programmer
construction worker
courier
cowboy
delivery person
dental hygienist
dentist
detective
diplomat
doctor
dog walker
door man
drug dealer
editor
electrical engineer
electrician

elevator operator
employment officer
entertainer
factory worker
farmer
farm hand
field hand
file clerk
fireman
fisherman
food handler
garbage man
gardener
glazier
guard
grounds man, keeper
heating contractor
hotel/motel clerk
house detective
housekeeper
housewife
insurance agent
insurance claims adjustor
insurance investigator
interpreter
illustrator
interior decorator
IRS agent
jack of all trades
janitor
jeweler
journalist
judge
junk dealer
lab technician
landscape architect
laundress
laundry worker
lawyer
legislator
librarian
lighting contractor
loan shark
lobbyist
logger
longshoreman
machine operator
mailman

maintenance worker
manager
mason
masseur, masseuse
mechanic (auto)
mechanic (shop)
medical lab technician
merchant marine
messenger
meter reader
mother/father
mover
musician
news reporter
nurse
office boy
ombudsman
optician
optometrist
painter (house)
parking lot attendant
pest exterminator
pharmacist
photographer
piano tuner
pilot
plumber
podiatrist
police officer
politician
pollster
post office clerk
potter
priest, minister,
   rabbi, evangelist
   nun, imam
priestess
press spokesman
printer
psychiatrist
psychologist
publicist
publisher
receptionist
real estate agent
red cap
repairman
roustabout

rubbish collector
sailor
sales clerk
scientist
school administrator
secretary
security officer
service station attendant
shipping clerk
shoemaker
soldier
spy
stenographer
steward(ess)
store clerk
street cleaner
student
surgeon
surveyor
swimming pool contractor
tailor
tax consultant
taxidermist
taxi driver
teacher, professor
telephone lineman
telephone operator
teller
thief
thug
translator
travel agent
traveling salesman
tree surgeon
trucker, truck driver
TV/radio repairman,
   -person
typesetter
typist
undertaker
upholsterer
veterinarian
volunteer
waiter, waitress
window washer
writer
zoo keeper

*Employment process, see Business, page 110.

List 44: Office

Nouns

adding machine
appointment
business
calculator
carbon copy
computer
hard disc
hardware
main frame
network
personal (PC)
program
software
conference
copier
department
desk
desk chair

dictaphone
dictation
disc storage
duplicate
envelope
equipment
FAX machine
file cabinet
files
information backup
intercom
letter
letterhead
mail
meeting
modem
paper clip
pencil sharpener

postage meter
postage scales
printer
records
shorthand
shredder
stapler
stationery
supplies
supply cabinet
switchboard
swivel chair
telephone
telephone answering machine
tape dispenser
typewriter
word processor
work station

Verbs

copy
dictate
input
FAX

file
manage
program
staple

take dictation
transmit
type

Personnel

accountant
assistant
boss
board of directors
bookkeeper
bursar
chairman
clerk
chief executive officer (CEO)

director
employee
employer
executive
executive secretary
manager
office manager
officer
personnel officer

president
receptionist
secretary
supervisor
treasurer
typist
vice-president (VP)

Idioms and Expressions

take a letter
secretarial/typing pool
girl Friday

to be called on the carpet
right-hand man
business is business

office politics

108

List 45: Business

Nouns

account
accounting software
accounts payable
accounts receivable
advertisement, ad
advertising
annual report
asset
audit
bad debt
balance
balance sheet
benefit
bid
bill
bond
books
bottom line
capital
capital gains
cash
cash flow
chief executive (CEO)
commercial
commission
common stock
computer
computer support
contract
corporate seal
corporate secretary
corporate officers
cost benefit analysis
cost of sales
credit
credit check
debit

debt
deduction
deficit
department
depletion
depreciation
(the) economy
equipment
equity
estimate
excise tax
expenditure
expense
expense account
fee
fiscal year
financial statement
fringe benefit
income
income tax
interest
inventory
investment
invoice
labor
labor union
labor contract
lease
ledger
liability
license
loss
maintenance
management
(the) market
merger
mortgage

negotiations
offer
operations
overhead
payroll
petty cash
president
profit
pro forma invoice
quotation (quote)
research and development (R&D)
receipt
rent
rental
retained earnings
royalty
sales
sales tax
secretary
securities
share of stock
social security
spread sheet
supplies
statement
stock
stock market
takeover
tax
treasurer
value added tax
vice president
wage
wage scale
Wall Street
worksheet
write off

People

accountant
administrative assistant
agent
bookkeeper
chairman of the board
clerk
consultant
certified public accountant (CPA)
dealer

director
employee
employer
executive
investor
lawyer
legal counsel
manager
operator

owner
partner
proprietor
salesman/woman
stockholder
trustee
worker

Types

agency	dealership	not for profit
chain	franchise	organization
company	holding company	partnership
conglomerate	industry	service
corporation	monopoly	trust

Verbs

balance	invest	loan
borrow	lend	merge
buy	liquidate	sell
finance	lease	tender an offer

Adjectives

commercial	industrial	non-commercial
fiscal	limited (Ltd.)	private
gross	net	public
incorporated (Inc.)		

Idioms and Expressions

in the black	in business to make money	good morale
bullish	profit motive	employee relations
in the red	good repute	industrial wasteland
bearish		

Employment: Getting a Job

apply for a job	probationary period	union membership, dues
application	wages, pay, salary	drug screening
employment forms	hours, work week	competency testing
employment record	payroll deduction	work evaluation
former employer	W-4 form	performance review
interview	I9 - eligibility verification	discrimination
reference	benefit packages	affirmative action
resumé	reimbursement	classified ads
skills	vacation	help wanted ads
training	child care	employment office, agency
work permit	civic duties (jury, etc.)	

List 46: Agriculture

Nouns

acreage	farmer	kitchen garden	shepherd
agronomy	farmers' market	manure	sheep farm
aqua culture	feed	market	silage
baler	fence	milking equipment	silo
barn	field	milk processing plant	spreader
bulk tank	fish farm	mowing	staple crops
combine	fodder	gardening	subsidy
commodity	garden	orchard	ranch
contour plowing	harrow	pasture	thresher
crop	harvest	pesticides	tiller
crop-dusting	herb garden	pitchfork	tractor
cultivation	horticulture	plow	truck
cultivator	horticulturist	produce	truck farming
dairy	hydroponics	product	veterinarian (vet)
earth	insecticide	rotation	wagon
fallow ground	irrigation	reaper	well
farm	implements	seed	yield

Verbs

breed	harvest	mow	reap
cultivate	harrow	mulch	sow
fertilize	hay	plant	water
graze	inseminate	plow	weed
grow	irrigate	raise	

Livestock

bull	duck	lamb	sheep
calf	goat	ox	steer
cattle	goose	pig	turkey
chicken	hog	poultry	
cow	horse	rabbits	

Crops and Products

berries	eggs	livestock	sugar beets
citrus	fruit	milk	vegetables
cotton	grains	peanuts	wool
dairy			

Idioms and Expressions

cut and dried	40 acres and a mule	you reap what you sow
farm out	the grass is always greener	sow wild oats
make hay while the sun shines	on the other side of the fence	separate the wheat from the chaff

List 47: Shops and Tools

Names of tools

ax, axe	hatchet	square
bit	level	straight edge
blow torch	mallet	staple gun
brace	plane	tape measure
calipers	pliers	tin snips
chisel	router	vise
clamp	sander	wedge
drill	saw	wire cutters
hammer	screwdriver	wrench

Verbs

bolt	nail	scribe
build	paint	solder
clamp	plane	staple
cut	pound	turn
glue	sand	varnish
hammer	saw	weld
measure	screw	wire

Misc

apprentice	plumber	staple
bolt	plywood	steel wool
brad	polyurethane	tack
carpenter	primer	tubing
coat (of paint)	sandpaper	varnish
electrician helper	screw	welder
nail	shellac	wire
nut	spike	
paint	stain	

Idioms and Expressions

get the axe	jack of all trades	handyman
have an axe to grind	live wire	on the level
hit the nail on the head	nuts and bolts	to measure up
many irons in the fire		

112

List 48: Law

People

attorney
bailiff
clerk
coroner
counsel
court
court reporter
defendant
district attorney
expert witness

Grand Jury
investigating officer
judge
juror
jury
jury foreman
law office
lawyer
minor
offender

parole officer
plaintiff
probation officer
prosecutor
prosecuting attorney
public defender
state's attorney
witness

Places and Things

bar
bench
civil court
courthouse
Court of Appeals
courtroom

Family Court
Federal District Court
gavel
jury box
judge's chambers
legal aid service

probate court
public defender
Small Claims Court
State District Court
Supreme Court
witness stand

Adjectives

alleged
hanged (criminal)
hung (jury)
guilty

innocent
judicial
legal
liable

no contest; *nolo contendre*
(objection) over-ruled
(objection) sustained
pre-trial

Verbs

accuse
acquit
allege
appeal
argue
award
charge
charge the jury
commute
convict

defend
deliberate
dissent
enter a plea
find
hear a case
indict
instruct
jump bail
plead

prosecute
reverse a decision
sentence
serve a sentence
sue
swear
testify
throw out a case
try
uphold

Events and Processes

accusation	deposition	parole
acquittal	evidence	perjury
alimony	exhibit	probation
allegation	findings	prosecution
appeal	fraud	recess
bail	grievance	retrial
case	hearing	right(s)
charge	indictment	ruling
claim	injunction	sentence
conviction	inquiry	sequester
court order	inquest	settlement
crime	law	suit
cross-examination	libel	summons
damages	litigation	testimony
death penalty	manslaughter	trial
decision	mistrial	verdict
defense	opinion	writ

Idioms and Expressions

bail out	lay down the law	take the fifth amendment
death row	of age	third degree
do time	open and shut case	throw the book at
get away with murder	take the law into one's own hands	under age
jailbird	take the stand	

List 49: Police and Crime

Good Guys

chief of police
constable
cop
detective
deputy
F. B. I.
game warden
investigator
meter maid

narcotics officer (narco)
patrolman
plainclothesman
policeman/woman
private eye
private investigator
riot police
sergeant
sheriff

state trooper
traffic cop
undercoverman/woman
U.S. Marshal
vice squad
victim
warden

Bad Guys

arsonist
burglar
call girl
con artist
con man
crook
felon
fence
gang
hit man
hood
juvenile delinquent
Ku Klux Klan (KKK)

killer
loan shark
lynch mob
madam
Mafia
mob
mobster
mole
mugger
petty thief
pickpocket
prostitute
pusher

rapist
rioters
robber
second-story man
serial killer
street walker
swindler
thief
thug
tough
underworld
vandal
whore

Crimes

armed robbery
arson
assault (and battery)
assassination
blackmail
breaking and entering
break in
bribery
burglary
con game
drunk driving
extortion
hold-up
homicide
embezzlement

forgery
fraud
gambling
gun running
kickback
kidnapping
larceny
laundering money
manslaughter
mugging
murder
narcotics smuggling
premeditated murder
prostitution
protection racket

purse snatching
pushing dope
rape
robbery
sexual molestation
skimming profits
smuggling
speeding
statutory rape
stick up
theft
treason
vandalism
wilding
white collar crime

Places

beat
betting parlor
cell

jail
lock-up
precinct

rounds
station
whore house

115

Events

apprehension	get away	raid
arrest	investigation	reading one's rights
chase	line up	round up
conviction	mug shot	speed trap
frame up	pay off	traffic violation

Things

badge	mace	police gazette
billy club	manacles	revolver
gun	night stick	siren
handcuffs	paddy wagon	squad car
knife	pistol	wanted posters

Idioms and Expressions

break in	decriminalization of narcotics	organized crime
cement overshoes	fuzz	police protection
cops and robbers	the godfather	the rackets
Cosa nostra	by hook or by crook	rub someone out
crime boss	inside job	Smoky the Bear
crime doesn't pay	in the name of the law	the syndicate
deadly weapon	the mob	victimless crime

List 50: Emergencies

accident
ambulance
blood bank
civil defense
clinic
CPR - cardiopulmonary
  resuscitation
dentist
doctor
doctor's office
drowning
drug overdose
drug store
Emergency Broadcasting System
emergency entrance
emergency room

emergency vehicle
evacuation
explosion
fire
fire department
fire drill
fire engine
fire horn
fireman
flashing lights
jaws of life
loud speaker
megaphone
monitor
mouth-to-mouth
natural disaster

neck brace
nuclear alert
pharmacist
pharmacy
public alarm signal
rescue
robbery
shock
siren
stretcher
tourniquet
training
transfusion
veterinarian's office

List 51: Politics and Government

see topics on Government in the Cultural Aspect section.

People

aide	congressman	secretary of state
alderman	delegate	selectman
assemblyman	governor	senator
attorney general	incumbent	sheriff
candidate	mayor	speaker
city councilman	pollster	vice president
columnist	president	voter
commentator	representative	

Places and Misc

apportionment	election	negotiation
bill	hearing	Pentagon
cabinet	inauguration	petition
capitol	independent investigation	polling place
congress	legislation	primary
Congressional Record	liberal	Republican
conservative	majority	State House
Democrat	minority	voter check list

Adjectives

city	judicial	state
county	legislative	town
executive	local	
federal	national	

Verbs

campaign	govern	re-elect
debate	lobby	reform
elect	pass	veto
enact	preside	vote
filibuster	propose	

Idioms, Expressions, and Issues

abortion rights	fiscal responsibility	one man, one vote
balanced budget	graft and corruption	pork barrel
civil rights	international security	rights and obligations
discrimination	military expenditures	terrorism
environmental protection	military-industrial complex	undue influence
equality before the law	minority representation	
equal rights	minority rights	

118

List 52: The Media

Nouns

ad, advertisement
AM
announcement
audience
broadcast
bulletin
cable TV
channel
classifieds
commercial
compact disc (CD)
coverage
edition

editorial
digital
FM
interview
journal
magazine
network
news
news flash
newspaper
pay TV
press
program

radio
ratings
reception
scandal sheet
scoop
space advertising
station
studio
tabloid
television transmitter
TV
UHF
VHF

Personnel

advertising manager
anchorman/woman
announcer
camera (man/woman) or operator
columnist
copy editor
commentator

correspondent
editor
journalist
listener
newscaster
printer
producer

publisher
reader
reporter
technician
typesetter
viewer
writer

Verbs

air
announce

broadcast
print

publish
televise

Misc

commercial
daily
entertainment
exclusive
illustrated
license
live

monthly
prime time
public
public interest
quarterly
recorded
review

special
taped
truth in advertising
videotaped
weekly

List 53: Religion

See the topic on Religion in the Cultural Aspect section.

Nouns

baptismal font	mosque	organ
cathedral	synagogue	pew
chapel	altar	steeple
church	belfry	transept
meeting house	confessional	parish

People

altar boy	imam	pastor
bishop	minister	Pope
choir	monk	priest
congregation	nun	rabbi
evangelist	organist	

Sacraments, Rituals, and Scriptures

baptism	Koran	ritual
Bible	last rites	scroll
catechism	marriage	sermon
christening	mass	Sunday school
confirmation	New Testament	Talmud
cross	offering	Torah
funeral	Old Testament	Tripitaka
Gospel	prayer	Veda
hymn	psalm	vestments

Verbs

believe	convert	preach
be saved	meditate	sing hymns
celebrate	pray	worship

Major Religions and Denominations

Baha'i Faith	Hinduism	Pentecostal Churches
Baptist Churches	Islam	Presbyterian
Brethren (German Baptist)	Jehovah's Witnesses	Protestant
Buddhism	Judaism	Quaker (Society of Friends)
(Roman) Catholic Church	Lutheran Churches	Seventh Day Adventist
Churches of God	Mennonite Churches	Shi'ah Moslem
Congregationalist Churches	Methodist Churches	Sufism (Islamic Mysticism)
Christianity	Mormon Churches	Sunni Moslem
Eastern Orthodox Churches	(Church of the Latter Day Saints)	Unitarian Universalist
Episcopal Church		

Adjectives

agnostic
atheist
Buddhist
Christian
Conservative
fundamentalist
Hindu

holy
Jewish
liberal
Moslem
Orthodox
Reform
religious

reverend
reverent
sacred
spiritual
strict

Important days

Ash Wednesday
Christmas
Easter Sunday
Good Friday

Lent
Palm Sunday
Passover
Rosh Hashana

Yom Kippur
Ramadan

Idioms, Expressions, and Concepts

act of God
Amen!
apocalypse
between the devil and the deep
  blue sea
Bible belt
damnation, damn
charity
crucifixion
end of the world is at hand
eye for an eye
faith
fire and brimstone

good heavens
goodness gracious
God bless you
God willing
go to hell
Hallelujah
heavens to Betsy
hell fire
Holy City
holy Moses!
judgment day
matter of faith
month of Sundays

next year in Jerusalem
pass the hat
pass the plate
redemption
resurrection
Revelation
raise Cain
salvation
seventh heaven
straight and narrow
vengeance

List 54 : Elementary, Secondary Education

Types of school

preschool programs	primary school	secondary school	parochial
day care	elementary	high school	specialized schools for:
nursery school	grade school	senior high	the blind, the deaf
toddler program	day school	preparatory (prep)	children with learning
head start program	middle school	school	disabilities
kindergarten	junior high school	public school	competitive athletes
		private school	Hollywood "brats"

Nouns

assignment	detention	language lab	semester
auditorium	exam	learning center	study hall
blackboard	grade	lunch room	teachers' room
bulletin board	grading period	photocopier	test
cafeteria	gymnasium, gym	playground	textbook
chalk	high honor roll	quiz	vacation
classroom	homework	recess	workbook
desk	honor roll	report card	
desk work	science laboratory	school	

People

instructor	pupil	student	teacher
principal	secretary	superintendent	teacher's aide

Verbs

cram	graduate	register	teach
enroll	learn	study	
fail, flunk	pass	take a course	

Subjects

Elementary	reading	*Secondary,*	history
art	science	* the above plus:*	home economics
arithmetic, math	social studies	chemistry	physics
geography	spelling	English	shop
music	writing	foreign language	

Classroom Activities

manipulating objects	using a tape recorder	spelling bee	games
moving furniture	using a typewriter	taking attendance	pencil and paper work
operating equipment	using a computer	operating a language lab	cutting and pasting
using the blackboard	taking dictation	body movements	map work

Idioms and Expressions

play hooky	teacher's pet	apple polishing	tardy

122

List 55: College Education

Types of schools

training schools
junior college
community college
college

university
graduate school
business school
medical school

law school
divinity school

Places

administration building
assembly hall
auditorium
boat house
book store
cafeteria
campus police
class room
chapel

dining hall
dormitory
field house
fraternity house
gym
housing office
lab
language lab
lecture hall

library
locker room
mail room
playing field
seminar room
sorority house
stadium
student union
theater

Offices

academic dean
academic departments
accounting
athletic department
bursar
campus dean

chancellor
counseling
dean
foreign student adviser
health
housing

physical education
president
registrar
R.O.T.C. headquarters
student activities
treasurer

Events

baccalaureate
convocation
examination
faculty tea
fraternity/sorority rush
games
away

championship
home
graduation
hell week
homecoming
open house

orientation
party
prom
registration
reunion
vacation

People

counselor
chaplain
dean
department head

dorm head
instructor
librarian

professor
psychologist
tutor

Academic activities

lecture	final exams	standardized test
lab	grades	thesis
class discussion	seminar	TOEFL
comprehensive exams	choosing a schedule	Graduate Record Exam
quiz, exam	research paper	Law Boards

Misc

academia	deadline	literary magazine
academic credit	diploma	marking period
academic freedom	disciplinary action	mortar board
academic gown	excuse	pass-fail grading
campus newspaper	expulsion	plagiarism
campus radio station	grading periods	social life
cheerleader	grind	suspension
co-education	humor magazine	student political organizations
co-ed	homecoming queen	undergraduate
co-habitation	liberal arts	year book

Idioms and Expressions

bone up on	burn the midnight oil	sheepskin

List 56: History

Periods

AD	CE	era	Stone Age
age	episode	geologic time	time
BC	epoch	period	
century	eon	pre-historic	

People

admiral	explorer	philosopher	scholar
adventurer	founder	political boss	secret agent
anthropologist	frontiersman	politician	senator
archaeologist	general	pope	slave
artist	geographer	president	spy
assassin	hero	prime minister	statesman
bishop	high priest	prince	teacher
builder	historian	princess	terrorist
businessman	innovator	promoter	trader
captive	inventor	prophet	tradesman
chief	judge	queen	traitor
common man	king	rabble rouser	tycoon
counselor	knight	rebel	usurper
creative genius	labor leader	representative	warlord
dictator	leader	saint	warrior
duke	orator	scout	
engineer	peasant	seer	
emperor	peon	serf	

Events

assassination	discovery	inflation	recession
coronation	election	invention	revolution
coup d'etat	epidemic	massacre	riot
battle	exploration	natural disasters	victory
breakthrough	famine	overthrow	war
defeat	genocide	plague	
depression	holocaust	rebellion	

Misc

agreement	constitution	historical research	social unrest
alliance	economic growth	mob	social upheaval
biography	enemy	pact	starvation
chronicle	historical novel	saga	treaty

Idioms and Expressions

chronicle of events	lessons of history	those who ignore history are
history is yesterday's news	milestone of history	condemned to repeat it
history is bunk	since the dawn of time	

List 57: Disasters

Nouns

accidents	explosion	relief
ambulance	famine	rescue
atomic, nuclear disaster	fire	riot
blizzard	fire storm	shelter
conflagration	first aid	storm
deforestation	flood	tidal wave
desertification	hurricane	tornado
drought	injury	twister
earthquake	loss of life	victim
emergency	nuclear meltdown	war
environmental destruction	plague	wild fire
epidemic	pollution	

Verbs

blow up	devastate	rescue
burn	explode	ruin
collapse	flatten	squash
crash	flood	starve
crush	freeze	
destroy	injure	

Idioms and Expressions

acts of God	calm before the storm	port in a storm
better safe than sorry	disaster relief	toll of human misery

List 58: The Military and War

Nouns

aircraft carrier
air force
airplane
air raid
alliance
allies
armed forces
armor
armored division
army
artillery
attack
battle
battleship
base
biological weapon
blackout
bomber
bomb
bomb blast
boot camp
briefing
brigade
bullet
bunker
cannon
cease fire
chain of command
coalition
coast guard
command
cruiser
defeat
defense
depot
destroyer

disinformation
division
draft
field of battle
field command
field hospital
field promotion
fighter
fire storm
fleet
foot soldier
foxhole
germ warfare
grenade
gun
headquarters
helicopter
information
infantry
jeep
jet
logistical support
map room
marines
materiel
morale
mine
mine sweeper
missile
national guard
navy
offense
offensive
officer
peace
personnel

planning session
platoon
poison gas
propaganda
promotion
reconnaissance
radioactive cloud
recruit
regiment
reserves
retreat
rocket
seabees (CB -
   Construction Battalion)
shell
squad
staff
strategy
submarine
superior officer
surrender
tactics
tank
target
target practice
torpedo
training camp
trench
victory
volunteer
volunteer army
warfare
war games
weapon
weaponry

People

admiral
bombardier
captain
cavalry
chaplain
chief of staff
colonel
corporal
deserter
draft dodger

foot soldier
general
G.I.(government issue)
guerrilla
gunner
hostage
lieutenant
liaison
major
marine

military adviser
navigator
officer
pilot
sailor
sergeant
soldier
terrorist

Events and actions

advance
ambush
battle
break through
bombardment
casualty
court marshal
cut off
defeat
deploy

dissent
infiltrate
interrogation
invasion
make war
offensive
order
over-run
retreat
shell(ing)

shoot
sink
sortie
skirmish
surround
strafe
torpedo
wound

Peace

appeasement
armistice
cease fire
concessions
conciliation
conscientious objector
defeat
disengagement

make peace
mediation
negotiation
pacification
peace conference
peace initiative
peacekeeping force
peacemaker

peace settlement
peace treaty
reconciliation
rest in peace
surrender
truce
United Nations
victory

Idioms and Expressions

all's fair in love and war
an army lives on its stomach
AWOL (absent without leave)
balance of power
balance or terror
battle hardened
bear arms
camp follower
concentration camp
cowards die twice
deterrence
Geneva Convention
isolationist
4F
a just and lasting peace
a just war
make love, not war

marked man
MIA (missing in action)
mutual assured destruction
Nobel Peace Prize
peace at any cost
"peace in our time"
peace with honor
POW (prisoner of war)
pull rank
point blank
on the warpath
R and R (rest and recreation)
scorched earth policy
shell shock
stick to one's guns
turncoat
turn tail

under the gun
USO
War and Peace
the war to end all war
win the war but lose the peace
world war
yeoman service
Symbols:
flags of all sorts
flags flown at half mast
flags in a graveyard
hands raised over the head
a white flag
a red cross
a red poppy
yellow ribbon

List 59: Energy

Nouns

acid rain	fire	oil well
atomic wastes	fission	ozone
barrel of oil	fossil fuel	petroleum
battery	fuel	pipeline
catalytic converter	fuel efficiency	pollution
coal	fusion	power
combustion	gas pump	propane
conservation	gasoline, gas	reactor
consumable resources	gasoline taxes	refinery
consumption	generator	regulations
dam	heat	renewable energy sources
depletion	hydro-electric power	resources
drilling rig	insulation	scrubbers
electricity	kinetic	smog
energy costs	light	smoke
energy efficiency	mass transit	solar power
energy (in)dependence	motor	source
energy loss	natural gas	steam
energy taxes	nuclear power	super conductors
engine	nuclear reactor	tidal
environmentalist	oil	turbine
environmental law	oil drilling	utilities
environmental policy	oil field	water power
environmental science	oil production	wildcat operator
ethanol	oil slick	windmill
filter	oil spill	wind power

Adjectives

active	mechanical	radioactive
chemical	nuclear	solar
electric(al)	off-shore	wood-burning
geothermal	petro-	
hydro-	passive	

Idioms and Expressions

burn the candle at both ends	gas guzzler	OPEC
carry coals to Newcastle	greenhouse effect	R factor
energy tzar	hold a candle to	unbridled consumption
environmental catastrophe	limits to growth	where there's smoke there's fire

List 60: Death

Nouns

ashes	demise	grave yard	necropolis
autopsy	dissection	inscription	obituary
body	effigy	lamentation	pall bearer
burial	elegy	last rites	pit
cadaver	epitaph	last words	plot
casket	eulogy	mausoleum	(the) remains
catacomb	euphemism	memorial	sepulcher
cemetery	euthanasia	memorial contribution	service
church yard	funeral	memorial service	tomb
coffin	funeral director	mercy killing	undertaker
coroner	funeral home	moaning	urn
corpse	funeral parlor	monument	vault
cremation	funeral procession	morgue	wake
crypt	grave	mortician	widow
(the) deceased	grave digger	mortuary	widower
(the) dead	grave side	mourner	
death	gravestone	mourning	

Verbs

bereave	die	expire	inter
bury	elegize	grieve	mourn
cremate	eulogize		

Idioms and Expressions

ashes to ashes, dust to dust	dearly departed	kick the bucket	open-casket funeral
	give up the ghost	pass	wake the dead
cash in one's chips	in deep mourning	pass away	RIP (rest in peace)
deader than a door nail	Irish wake	pass over	

Of the Living Dead

ashen	ghastly	horrible	shade
apparition	ghost	horror story	specter
appall	ghost story	loathsome	spell
banshee	ghoul	mummy	spider web
bat	gibbet	murmuring	spirit
body snatcher	glimmer	necromancer	spook
black magic	gloom	night walker	spooky
cadaverous	goblin	pact with devil	terrifying
conjure	gore	pallid	undead
demon	grave robber	phantom	vampire
devil	grisly	resurrectionist	voodoo
dreadful	hangman	revolting	werewolf
evil spirit	haunt	Satan	wolfman
fiend	hell fire	sorcery	wraith
frightful	hideous	seance	zombie
gallows			

130

Communicative Functions

Although the sub-aspect we have labeled as Communicative Functions is similar to the functions of a notional-functional syllabus, we would like to point out that what we have proposed below is not strictly a notional-functional syllabus as we understand that term. We have used the term communicative function to draw attention to the fact that the focus of this sub-aspect is on the how and why of the communicative exchange. To relate this sub-aspect to the Situations and Topics, we can say that the Situation is concerned with the "where" of the exchange, the Topic the "what" and the Function the "how" and "why."

To organize the various communicative functions in some useful way, we have presented them as a kind of syllabus/check list. We have used as a sequential basis four levels of language sophistication. These levels represent a transition from beginning language student to fully functioning bilingual person. These four levels are:

☐ Level 1 **Surviving** (Beginner)

☐ Level 2 **Adjusting;** settling in (Advanced beginner)

☐ Level 3 **Participating** (Intermediate)

☐ Level 4 **Integrating** (Advanced)

Within each level we have organized the functions into general types as described below:

A. **Basic Needs.** Using the language to satisfy basic physical requirements of food, shelter, and clothing.

B. **Socializing.** Using the language to forge social links with native speakers. At its lowest level it satisfies basic emotional needs.

C. **Metalinguistic.** Using the language to deal with the language. Also includes certain fundamental linguistic labels and functions.

D. **Professional.** Using the language to make a living.

E. **Cultural.** Using the language to deal with the social and cultural milieu.

Level 1: Surviving

(Beginner)

A. Basic Needs

☐ 1. Respond physically to simple instructions such as **give, take, stand, sit, open, close, pick up, put down, put on, take off,** etc.

☐ 2. Give another person simple instructions to perform the actions above.

☐ 3. Give and understand basic warnings such as **look out!**

☐ 4. State basic wants and needs.

☐ 5. Request and comprehend simple information.

☐ 6. Ask for and respond to simple street directions.

☐ 7. Interrupt someone to ask for assistance.

☐ 8. Get someone's attention and also use appropriate gestures.

☐ 9. Buy a small item.

☐ 10. Order something to eat and drink.

B. Socializing

☐ 1. Greet others.

☐ 2. Take leave of another person or a group of people.

☐ 3. Arrange to meet someone.

☐ 4. Introduce yourself.

☐ 5. Identify yourself. **(I'm a ___.)**

☐ 6. Use ritual apologies.

☐ 7. Reject unwanted attention firmly and simply.

☐ 8. Agree.

☐ 9. Express thanks.

☐ 10. State and comprehend simple biographical information.

C. Metalinguistic

☐ 1. Use and identify basic numbers.

☐ 2. Ask and tell time.

☐ 3. Use simple time expressions such as **today, yesterday, tomorrow morning, noon.**

☐ 4. Use and comprehend days of week, months, and ways of expressing dates.

☐ 5. Control a conversation with simple phrases such as **speak slowly, please,** or **please repeat that.**

☐ 6. Identify and label the environment. **(What's that? It's a ___.)**

☐ 7. Decipher simple signs and notices.

Level 2: Adjusting; Settling In

(Advanced Beginner)

A. Basic Needs

- ☐ 1. State plans for the future.
- ☐ 2. Request a loan.
- ☐ 3. Respond to a loan request.
- ☐ 4. Complain mildly.
- ☐ 5. Ask about the purpose of something.
- ☐ 6. Purchase household objects and equipment.
- ☐ 7. Make travel arrangements.
- ☐ 8. Describe a physical health problem.
- ☐ 9. Carry out a limited financial transaction such as cashing a check.
- ☐ 10. Fill out life forms such as a credit card application, a work permit, a school registration.

B. Socializing

- ☐ 1. Introduce another person.
- ☐ 2. Make small talk.
- ☐ 3. Share simple likes and dislikes.
- ☐ 4. Issue an invitation.
- ☐ 5. Decline an invitation.
- ☐ 6. Visit.
- ☐ 7. Entertain a visitor.
- ☐ 8. Play simple games/sports.
- ☐ 9. Recount past events.
- ☐ 10. Express basic emotions.
- ☐ 11. Apologize for a specific error.
- ☐ 12. Request and give permission to do something.
- ☐ 13. Compliment another person.
- ☐ 14. Accept a compliment.
- ☐ 15. Explain personal plans.
- ☐ 16. Express a personal opinion.
- ☐ 17. Express doubt.
- ☐ 18. Express irritation.
- ☐ 19. Express disappointment.

C. Metalinguistic

- ☐ 1. Clarify misunderstandings.
- ☐ 2. Use simple interjections.
- ☐ 3. Make a basic phone call.
- ☐ 4. Perform arithmetic operations aloud.
- ☐ 5. Spell words aloud.
- ☐ 6. Comprehend ads and announcements on radio and TV.
- ☐ 7. Read advertisements.
- ☐ 8. Read short notices, time tables, menus, etc.
- ☐ 9. Take simple dictation.
- ☐ 10. Write short informational notes.

D. Professional

- ☐ 1. Give simple instructions.
- ☐ 2. Explain professional objectives.
- ☐ 3. Express a professional opinion,
- ☐ 4. Explain how something functions.

E. Cultural

- ☐ 1. Follow or sing-along with popular songs and/or folk songs.
- ☐ 2. Identify folk tale characters and national heroes.

Make general cultural comparisons in these areas :

- ☐ 3. etiquette
- ☐ 4. mealtimes
- ☐ 5. kinship nomenclature
- ☐ 6. housing
- ☐ 7. cooking
- ☐ 8. gift-giving
- ☐ 9. holidays and festivals

Level 3: Participating

(Intermediate)

A. Basic Needs

- ☐ 1. Ask for favors.
- ☐ 2. Grant favors.
- ☐ 3. Sell a personal possession.
- ☐ 4. Make arrangements with household help.
- ☐ 5. Arrange for repairs and service (household; automotive).
- ☐ 6. Make substantial purchases such as a TV or refrigerator.
- ☐ 7. Apply for specific status (insurance, citizenship, etc.)
- ☐ 8. Retrieve a borrowed item.
- ☐ 9. Dispute a bill.

B. Socializing

- ☐ 1. Plan a social event.
- ☐ 2. Attend a recreational event.
- ☐ 3. Discuss current events.
- ☐ 4. Comment on sports events.
- ☐ 5. Avoid commitments.
- ☐ 6. Sympathize.
- ☐ 7. Share personal hopes and dreams.
- ☐ 8. Tell an anecdote.
- ☐ 9. Understand jokes.
- ☐ 10. Give personal advice.
- ☐ 11. Disagree tactfully.
- ☐ 12. Ask for forgiveness.
- ☐ 13. Make an excuse.

C. Metalinguistic

- ☐ 1. Understand radio and TV news.
- ☐ 2. Break social contact with appropriate mannerisms,
- ☐ 3. Summarize.
- ☐ 4. Ask for definitions.
- ☐ 5. Make a complicated telephone call.
- ☐ 6. Translate for a new-comer.
- ☐ 7. Swear.
- ☐ 8. Use verbal gestures such as **uh-uh, hm, well, huh?**
- ☐ 9. Read newspapers.
- ☐ 10. Read professional material.
- ☐ 11. Read magazine articles.
- ☐ 12. Write social notes and letters.
- ☐ 13. Write professional reports.

D. Professional

- ☐ 1. Allow or not allow another's requests.
- ☐ 2. Give professional advice.
- ☐ 3. Give detailed instructions and explanations.
- ☐ 4. Evaluate.
- ☐ 5. Give short talks/speeches on professional matters.

E. Cultural

- ☐ 1. Explain institutions of native country.
- ☐ 2. Compare major cultural differences.

Discuss major aspects of host culture, including:

- ☐ 3. courtship
- ☐ 4. marriage
- ☐ 5. sex
- ☐ 6. family
- ☐ 7. racial and ethnic groups
- ☐ 8. government
- ☐ 9. religion
- ☐ 10. death
- ☐ 11. mourning
- ☐ 12. funerals
- ☐ 13. education
- ☐ 14. superstitions
- ☐ 15. folklore
- ☐ 16. hospitality
- ☐ 17. humor

Level 4: Integrating

(Advanced)

A. Basic Needs

☐ 1. Act in emergencies.

B. Socializing

☐ 1. Share secrets.
☐ 2. Flirt.
☐ 3. Speak of personal accomplishments.
☐ 4. Tease.
☐ 5. Break off a relationship.
☐ 6. Counsel.
☐ 7. Praise.

☐ 8. Flatter.
☐ 9. Insult.
☐ 10. Plead.
☐ 11. Soften the truth.
☐ 12. Chastise another person.
☐ 13. Threaten.
☐ 14. Tell jokes.

C. Metalinguistic

☐ 1. Interpret and translate.
☐ 2. Paraphrase.
☐ 3. Play word games such as crossword puzzles.

☐ 4. Use source materials such as the Oxford English Dictionary.
☐ 5. Read books.
☐ 6. Write letters to the editor.

D. Professional

☐ 1. Debate ideas.
☐ 2. Negotiate.

☐ 3. Give professional direction.
☐ 4. Exercise leadership.

E. Cultural

☐ 1. Take and defend a stand on a current national issue.
Discuss, study, and critique the following aspects of the culture:
☐ 2. arts
☐ 3. law
☐ 4. attitudes toward animals and nature

☐ 5. community organization
☐ 6. residence rules
☐ 7. property rights
☐ 8. status differentiation
☐ 9. social mobility
☐ 10. ethics

The Cultural Aspect

Language and culture are intertwined. In the previous section on the communicative aspect, American culture makes its presence felt, especially in the lists of communicative situations and topics. To a lesser extent, communicative functions are also modified by culture. Ways of expressing thanks or extending invitations can be quite different in Boston English and Bombay English.

Because we have already listed communicative situations, topics, and functions in Part II, we will not repeat those lists here. Instead we will present cultural information that does not fit under these categories.

In other, paralinguistic ways, notably in body language and gestures, culture also impinges on communication, but we will deal with that in Part V.

And then there are all the cultural practices (customs) that can only be hinted at in a book such as this. Rather than attempt to describe American cultural practices, we will instead present a list of Cultural Common Denominators. This list can be used as a checklist by both teacher and student to see if these areas have been adequately explored in class.

In this part of **The ESL Miscellany,** we will attempt to deal with the huge body of information that is commonly known by most contemporary Americans. For example, the foreigner, unaware that the New York Yankees is a baseball team, could easily be mystified by overhearing one American ask another, "How did the Yankees do last night?"

Obviously, it takes years to learn everything there is to know about American culture—it is even possible that some natives of the U.S. do not know who Babe Ruth was. The capsule summaries of selected areas of American culture contained in this section are at best a starting point for discussion, research, explanation, and study. Once again our lists should be considered only guidelines.

Cultural Lists

Cultural Checklist

Cultural Common Denominators*

Every culture has customs, traditions, practices, and beliefs associated with the following cultural items. Each item in the list represents an essay, if not an entire book, but we will do no more here than suggest that the list can be used as a guideline for an orientation to American culture. Incidentally, the list can also serve as a checklist for a series of fascinating discussions of a cross-cultural nature.

- [ ] numerals
- [ ] calendar
- [ ] personal names
- [ ] greetings
- [ ] gestures
- [ ] etiquette
- [ ] mealtimes
- [ ] kinship nomenclature
- [ ] age-grading
- [ ] athletic sports
- [ ] games
- [ ] leisure activities
- [ ] music
- [ ] dancing
- [ ] feasting
- [ ] bodily adornment
- [ ] folklore
- [ ] luck superstitions
- [ ] cooking
- [ ] food and food taboos
- [ ] family
- [ ] marriage
- [ ] kin-groups
- [ ] housing
- [ ] hospitality
- [ ] visiting

- [ ] gift-giving
- [ ] friendship customs
- [ ] courting
- [ ] joking
- [ ] sexual restrictions
- [ ] incest taboos
- [ ] modesty in natural functions
- [ ] funeral rites
- [ ] mourning
- [ ] medicine
- [ ] education
- [ ] law
- [ ] land-use policies
- [ ] attitude toward animals
- [ ] community organization
- [ ] residence rules
- [ ] property rights
- [ ] status differentiation
- [ ] racial and ethnic groups
- [ ] mobility
- [ ] trade
- [ ] government
- [ ] patriotism
- [ ] religious practices

*Adapted from George P. Murdock, "The Common Denominators of Culture," in *The Science of Man in the World Crisis, ed. Ralph Linton, N.Y.: Columbia University Press, 1945.*

List 1: Immigration

IMMIGRATION BY COUNTRIES (1820-1989)

Country	1989	1820-1989
All countries	1,090,900	55,458,000
Europe	94,300	36,977,000
Austria	2,800	—
Belgium	700	210,000
Czechoslovakia	500	145,000
Denmark	600	370,000
Finland	300	37,000
France	4,100	783,000
Germany	10,400	7,071,000
Great Britain	17,000	5,100,000
Greece	4,600	700,000
Ireland	7,000	4,715,000
Italy	11,100	5,357,000
Netherlands	1,200	373,000
Norway	600	753,000
Poland	13,300	588,000
Portugal	3,900	497,000
Spain	2,200	282,000
Sweden	1,200	1,245,000
Switzerland	1,100	358,000
U.S.S.R.	4,600	3,429,000
Yugoslavia	2,500	133,000
Other Europe	4,700	290,000
Asia	296,400	5,697,000
China	39,300	874,000
Hong Kong	15,200	288,000
India	28,600	427,000
Iran	13,000	162,000
Israel	5,500	132,000
Japan	5,400	456,000
Jordan	3,800	70,000
Korea	33,000	611,000
Lebanon	3,800	91,000
Philippines	66,100	955,000
Turkey	2,500	409,000
Vietnam	13,300	444,000
Other Asia	66,700	779,000
America	672,600	12,017,000
Argentina	3,800	125,000
Brazil	3,700	93,000
Canada	18,300	4,271,000
Colombia	14,900	272,000
Cuba	9,500	739,000
Dominican Republic	26,700	468,000
Ecuador	7,600	143,000

IMMIGRATION (CONTINUED)

Country	1989	1820–1989
El Salvador	57,600	216,000
Guatemala	19,200	104,000
Haiti	13,300	215,000
Honduras	7,600	79,000
Mexico	405,600	3,208,000
Panama	3,900	90,000
Peru	10,000	106,000
West Indies	38,000	1,168,000
Other America	32,700	740,000
Africa	22,500	301,000
Australia and New Zealand	2,900	144,000
Other Oceania	2,000	54,000
Unknown or not reported	—	267,000

PERCENTAGE OF TOTAL IMMIGRANTS (1820-1989)

Years	Europe	Asia	America	Africa	Australia and New Zealand	Oceania
1820-1989	66.7	10.3	21.7	0.5	0.3	0.1
1961-1970	33.8	12.9	51.7	0.9	0.6	0.1
1971-1980	17.8	35.2	44.3	1.8	0.5	0.4

Sources: The World Almanac and Book of Facts 1991, New York © 1990
U.S. Immigration and Naturalization Service

List 2: Peoples of North America

AMERICAN INDIAN NATIONS

Eastern Woodlands
Abenaki
Algonquian
Conoy
Delaware
Erie
Fox
Huron
Illinois
Iroquois
   Cayuga
   Mohawk
   Onondaga
   Oneida
   Seneca
   Tuscarora
Kickapoo
Laurentian
Mahican
Malecite
Massachuset
Menominee
Miami
Micmac
Mohegan
Montauk
Nanticoke
Narraganset
Nauset
Neutral
Niantic
Nipmuc
Ojibwa
Pamlico
Passamaquoddy
Pennacook
Penobscot
Pequot
Pocomtuc
Potawatomi
Powhatan
Sauk
Susquehanna
Tionontati
Wampanoag
Wappinger
Wenrohronon
Winnebago
Wyandot

Southeast
Acolapissa
Acuera
Adai
Ais
Akokisa
Alabama
Apalachee
Atakapa
Avoyel
Bayogoula
Caddo
Calusa
Cape Fear
Chatot
Cheraw
Cherokee
Chiaha
Chickasaw
Chitimacha
Choctaw
Congaree
Coosa
Coweta
Creek
Cusabo
Dakota
   Biloxi
   Catawba
   Ofo
   Tutelo
Eno
Eufaula
Fresh Water
Guacata
Guale
Hasinai
Hitchiti
Houma
Jeaga
Kasihta
Koasati
Manahoac
Mobile
Mocoço
Monacan
Nahyssan
Naniaba
Natchez

Ocale
Occaneechi
Onatheaqua
Pascagoula
Pedee
Pensacola
Pohoy
Potano
Santee
Saponi
Saturiwa
Sewee
Sugeree
Surruque
Tacatacuru
Taensa
Tamathli
Tekesta
Timucua
Tocobaga
Tohome
Tunica
Tuskegee
Uamasee
Utina
Waccamaw
Wateree
Waxhau
Winyaw
Woccon
Yuchi
Yui
Yustaga

Plains
Arapaho
Arikara
Assiniboin
Atsina
Blackfoot
   Blood
   Northern
Blackfoot
   Piegan
Cheyenne
Comanche
Crow
Dakota
   Santee

Teton
   Yankton
Hidatsa
Iowa
Kansa
Kiowa Apache
Mandan
Missouri
Omaha
Osage
Ota
Oto
Pawnee
Plains Cree
Plains Ojibwa
Ponca
Quapaw
Scarcee
Wichita
   Dakota

Plains
Cayuse
Coeur D'Alene
Columbia
Cowlitz
Flathead
Kalispel
Klamath
Klickitat
Kutenai
Lake
Lillooet
Modoc
Molala
Nespelem
Nez Percé
Okanagon
Sanpoil
Shuswap
Sinkaietk
Spohan
Tenino
Thompson
Umatilla
Walla Walla
Wenatchee
Yakima

AMERICAN INDIAN NATIONS (CONTINUED)

Great Basin
Chemehuevi
Fish Lake
Gosiute
Kaibab
Kawaiisu
Las Vegas
Moapa
Mono
    Eastern Mono
    Western Mono
Numic
    Central Numic
    Southern Numic
    Western Numic
Pahvant
Paiute
    Northern Paiute
    Southern Paiute
    Owens Valley
Paiute
Red Lake
Shivwits
Shoshoni
    Bannock
    Eastern Shoshoni
    Lemhi
    Northern Shoshoni
    Panamint
    Sheep Eater
    Western Shoshoni
Tumpanogots
Uinkarets
Ute
    "Weber Ute"
    Northern Ute
    Southern Ute
    Eastern Mono
    Western Mono

Southwest
Apache
Central Pueblo
    Cochiti
    Jemez
    San Felipe
    Santa Ana
    Santo Domingo
    Zia

Eastern Puelo
    Isleta
    Nambe
    Picuris
    San Ildefonso
    San Juan
    Sandia
    Santa Clara
    Taos
    Tesuque
Papago
Pima
Western Pueblo
    Acoma
    Hano
    Hopi
    Laguna
    Zuni
Yuma
    Cocopa
    Havasupai
    Hualapai
    Maricopa
    Mojave
    Yavapai

Northwest Coast
Alsea
Chimakum
Chinook
Coos
Hupa
Kalapuya
Karok
Kwalhioqua
Makah
Quileute
Siuslaw
Tillmook
Tututni-Tolowa
Umpqua
Wiyot
Yurok

California
Achomawi
Akwa'ala
Atsugewi
Cahuilla
Chimariko
Chumash
Coast Miwok
Cocopa
Costanoan
Cupeño
East Diegueño
Esselen
Fernandeño
Gabrieleño
Halchidhoma
Juaneño
Kamia
Kawaiisu
Kitanemuk
Luiseño
Maidu
Miwok
Mojave
Mono
Nisenan
Patwin
Poma
Saboba
Salinan
Serrano
Shasta
Tubatulabal
Wappo
Washo
West Diegueño
Wintu
Wintun
Yana
Yokut
Yuki
Yuma

LARGEST INDIAN RESERVATIONS (1987)

Reservation	Nation	Location	Population
Navajo	Navajo	Arizona, New Mexico, Utah	173,018
Cherokee	Cherokee	Oklahoma	58,232
Creek	Creek	Oklahoma	54,606
Choctaw	Choctaw	Oklahoma	21,858
Pine Ridge	Dakota	South Dakota	19,246
Southern Pueblos		New Mexico	17,079
Chicksaw	Chicksaw	Oklahoma	11,780
Rosebud	Dakota	South Dakota	11,685 *
Gila River	Pima	Arizona	10,688
Papago-Sells	Papago	Arizona	10,138
Turtle Mountain	Ojibwa	North Dakota	9,889
Hopi	Hopi	Arizona	9,040
Standing Rock	Dakota	North Dakota, South Dakota	8,612
Fort Apache	Apache	Arizona	8,421
Zuni	Zuni	New Mexico	8,135
Pawnee	Pawnee	Oklahoma	7,657
Northern Pueblos		New Mexico	7,651
Shawnee	Shawnee	Oklahoma, Texas	7,263
Blackfoot	Blackfoot	Montana	7,193
Yakima	Yakima	Washington	6,846
Wind River	Shoshone, Arapaho	Wyoming	5,124

* 1984 data

NATIVE PEOPLES OF ALASKA

Eskimo
Aleut
American Indian
    Ingalik
    Kutchin
    Tanaina
    Tinneh
    Tlingit
    Tsimshian

Sources: The 1990 Information Please Almanac, Boston © 1989
The Encyclopaedia Brittanica, Chicago © 1990
North American Indians, Alice B. Kehoe

List 3: Population by Ethnic Identity

Note: The U.S. Census asks Americans to identify themselves by race, nationality and ethnic origin. The following information from the 1980 census shows how they identify themselves.

RACIAL AND NATIONAL ORIGIN

Origin	Population	Percentage
White	188,340,790	83.153
Black	26,488,218	11.693
American Indian	1,361,869	0.601
Chinese	806,027	0.356
Filipino	774,640	0.342
Japanese	700,747	0.309
Asian Indian	361,544	0.160
Korean	354,529	0.157
Vietnamese	261,714	0.116
Hawaiian	167,253	0.074
Eskimo	42,149	0.019
Samoan	42,050	0.019
Guamanian	32,132	0.014
Aleut	14,177	0.006
Other	6,756,989	2.983
Total	**226,504,828**	**100.002**

HISPANIC ORIGIN

Year	Population	Percentage
1970	9,072,602	4.464
1980	14,605,883	6.448

BLACK AND HISPANIC STATE POPULATIONS

	BLACK		HISPANIC	
Rank	State	Population	State	Population
1	New York	2,401,842	California	4,543,770
2	California	1,819,282	Texas	2,985,643
3	Texas	1,710,250	New York	1,609,245
4	Illinois	1,675,229	Florida	857,898
5	Georgia	1,465,457	Illinois	635,525
6	Florida	1,342,478	New Jersey	491,867
7	North Carolina	1,316,050	New Mexico	476,089
8	Louisiana	1,237,263	Arizona	440,915
9	Michigan	1,198,710	Colorado	337,300
10	Ohio	1,076,734	Michigan	162,388

BLACK PROPORTIONS OF STATE POPULATIONS

Note: During the Civil War (1860-1864), 11slave states seceded from the nation: Mississippi, South Carolina, Louisiana, Georgia, Alabama, North Carolina, Virginia, Arkansas, Tennessee, Florida and Texas; four slave states remained in the Union: Maryland, Delaware, Missouri and Kentucky.

Rank	State	Percentage
1	Mississippi	35.2
2	South Carolina	30.4
3	Louisiana	29.4
4	Georgia	26.8
5	Alabama	25.6
6	Maryland	22.7
7	North Carolina	22.4
8	Virginia	18.9
9	Arkansas	16.3
10	Delaware	16.1
11	Tennessee	15.8
12	Illinois	14.7
13	Florida	13.8
14	New York	13.7
15	Michigan	12.9
16	New Jersey	12.6
17	Texas	12.0
18	Missouri	10.5
19	Ohio	10.0
	United States	**11.7**

FOREIGN-BORN POPULATION

UNITED STATES		1980	
Year	Percentage	State	Percentage
1900	13.6	California	14.8
1920	13.2	Hawaii	14.0
1940	8.8	New York	13.4
1960	5.4	Florida	10.9
1970	4.7	New Jersey	10.3
1980	6.2	Rhode Island	8.8

Sources: The 1990 Information Please Almanac, Boston © 1989
The World Almanac and Book of Facts 1991, New York © 1990
U/S: A Statistical Portrait of the American People by Andrew Hacker. Viking Press, New York © 1983
U.S. Census Bureau

List 4: Major U.S. Cities

1990 Rank	City	State	Population 1990	Rank 1980
1	New York	New York	7,322,564	1
2	Los Angeles	California	3,485,398	3
3	Chicago	Illinois	2,783,726	2
4	Houston	Texas	1,630,553	5
5	Philadelphia	Pennsylvania	1,585,577	4
6	San Diego	California	1,110,549	8
7	Detroit	Michigan	1,027,974	6
8	Dallas	Texas	1,006,877	7
9	Phoenix	Arizona	983,403	9
10	San Antonio	Texas	935,933	11
11	San Jose	California	782,248	17
12	Indianapolis	Indiana	741,952	12
13	Baltimore	Maryland	736,014	10
14	San Francisco	California	723,959	13
15	Jacksonville	Florida	672,971	19
16	Columbus	Ohio	632,910	20
17	Milwaukee	Wisconsin	628,088	16
18	Memphis	Tennessee	610,337	14
19	Washington	District of Columbia	606,900	15
20	Boston	Massachusetts	574,283	21
21	Seattle	Washington	516,259	23
22	El Paso	Texas	515,342	28
23	Nashville-Davidson	Tennessee	510,784	25
24	Cleveland	Ohio	505,616	18
25	New Orleans	Louisiana	496,938	22
26	Denver	Colorado	467,610	24
27	Austin	Texas	465,622	42
28	Fort Worth	Texas	447,619	33
29	Oklahoma City	Oklahoma	444,719	31
30	Portland	Oregon	437,319	35
31	Kansas City	Missouri	435,146	27
32	Long Beach	California	429,433	37
33	Tucson	Arizona	405,390	45
34	St. Louis	Missouri	396,685	26
35	Charlotte	North Carolina	395,934	47
36	Atlanta	Georgia	394,017	29
37	Virginia Beach	Virginia	393,069	56
38	Albuquerque	New Mexico	384,736	44
39	Oakland	California	372,242	43
40	Pittsburgh	Pennsylvania	369,879	30
41	Sacramento	California	369,365	52
42	Minneapolis	Minnesota	368,383	34
43	Tulsa	Oklahoma	367,302	38
44	Honolulu	Hawaii	365,272	36
45	Cincinnati	Ohio	364,040	32

Source: U.S. Census

List 5: States of the U.S.

STATES

State	Date Entered Union	Capital	Electoral Vote	Congressional Seats
Alabama	1819	Montgomery	9	7
Alaska	1959	Juneau	3	1
Arizona	1912	Phoenix	8	6
Arkansas	1836	Little Rock	6	4
California	1850	Sacramento	54	52
Colorado	1876	Denver	8	6
* Connecticut	1788	Hartford	8	6
* Delaware	1787	Dover	3	1
Florida	1845	Tallahassee	25	23
* Georgia	1788	Atlanta	13	11
Hawaii	1959	Honolulu	3	1
Idaho	1890	Boise	4	2
Illinois	1818	Springfield	22	20
Indiana	1816	Indianapolis	12	10
Iowa	1846	Des Moines	7	5
Kansas	1861	Topeka	6	4
Kentucky	1792	Frankfort	8	6
Louisiana	1812	Baton Rouge	9	7
Maine	1820	Augusta	4	2
* Maryland	1788	Annapolis	10	8
* Massachusetts	1788	Boston	12	10
Michigan	1837	Lansing	18	16
Minnesota	1858	St. Paul	10	8
Mississippi	1817	Jackson	7	5
Missouri	1821	Jefferson City	6	4
Montana	1889	Helena	3	1
Nebraska	1867	Lincoln	5	3
Nevada	1864	Carson City	4	2
* New Hampshire	1788	Concord	4	2
* New Jersey	1787	Trenton	15	13
New Mexico	1912	Santa Fe	5	3
* New York	1788	Albany	33	31
* North Carolina	1789	Raleigh	14	12
North Dakota	1889	Bismarck	3	1
Ohio	1803	Columbus	21	19
Oklahoma	1907	Oklahoma City	8	6
Oregon	1859	Salem	7	5
* Pennsylvania	1787	Harrisburg	23	21
* Rhode Island	1790	Providence	4	2
* South Carolina	1788	Columbia	8	6
South Dakota	1889	Pierre	3	1
Tennessee	1796	Nashville	11	9
Texas	1845	Austin	32	30
Utah	1896	Salt Lake City	5	3
Vermont	1791	Montpelier	3	1
* Virginia	1788	Richmond	13	11
Washington	1889	Olympia	11	9

STATES (CONTINUED)

State	Date Entered Union	Capital	Electoral Vote	Congressional Seats
West Virginia	1863	Charleston	5	3
Wisconsin	1848	Madison	11	9
Wyoming	1890	Cheyenne	3	1
District of Columbia	1846		3	**1

* The 13 original colonies

** Delegate may vote in committee but not on the floor

STATE RANKING BY POPULATION (1990)

Rank	State	Population	1980 Rank
1	California	29,279,000	1
2	New York	17,627,000	2
3	Texas	16,825,000	3
4	Florida	12,775,000	7
5	Pennsylvania	11,764,000	4
6	Illinois	11,325,000	5
7	Ohio	10,778,000	6
8	Michigan	9,179,000	8
9	New Jersey	7,617,418	9
10	North Carolina	6,553,000	10
11	Georgia	6,387,000	13
12	Virginia	6,128,000	14
13	Massachusetts	5,928,000	11
14	Indiana	5,499,000	12
15	Missouri	5,079,385	15
16	Wisconsin	4,869,640	16
17	Washington	4,827,000	20
18	Tennessee	4,822,134	17
19	Maryland	4,733,000	18
20	Minnesota	4,358,864	21
21	Louisiana	4,180,831	19
22	Alabama	3,984,000	22
23	Kentucky	3,665,220	23
24	Arizona	3,619,000	29
25	South Carolina	3,407,000	24
26	Colorado	3,272,000	28
27	Connecticut	3,226,929	25
28	Oklahoma	3,124,000	26
29	Oregon	2,828,214	30
30	Iowa	2,766,658	27
31	Mississippi	2,534,814	31
32	Kansas	2,467,000	32
33	Arkansas	2,337,395	33
34	West Virginia	1,782,958	34
35	Utah	1,711,117	36
36	Nebraska	1,572,503	35
37	New Mexico	1,490,381	37
38	Maine	1,218,053	38
39	Nevada	1,193,000	43

STATE RANKING BY SIZE (CONTINUED)

Rank	State	Population	1980 Rank
40	New Hampshire	1,103,163	42
41	Hawaii	1,095,000	39
42	Idaho	1,003,558	41
43	Rhode Island	988,609	40
44	Montana	794,329	44
45	South Dakota	693,294	45
46	Delaware	658,031	48
47	North Dakota	634,223	46
48	District of Columbia	575,000	47
49	Vermont	560,029	49
50	Alaska	546,000	51
51	Wyoming	449,905	50

ASSOCIATED FREE STATES

Name	Capital	Congressional Representatives	Organization
Guam	Agana	*1	Self-governing territory
Puerto Rico	San Juan	*1	Commonwealth
Virgin Islands	Charlotte Amalie, St. Thomas	*1	Self-governing territory
American Samoa	Pago Pago	*1	Self-governing territory

* Delegate may vote in committee but not on the floor

NON SELF-GOVERNING POSSESSIONS

Name	Population
Baker, Howland and Jarvis Islands	Uninhabited
Johnston Atoll	Military personnel
Kingman Reef	Military personnel
Palmyra	Government personnel
Navassa	Uninhabited
Midway Islands	Military personnel
Wake Island	Military personnel

ISLANDS UNDER TRUSTEESHIP

Name	Capital	Population
Commonwealth of the Northern Mariana Islands	Saipan	21,777
Federated States of Micronesia	Pohnpei	111,500
Republic of Palau	Koror	14,000
Republic of the Marshall Islands	Majuro	43,000

Sources: The World Almanac and Book of Facts 1991, New York © 1990
U.S. Census

List 6: Government Structure of the U.S.

There are three basic levels of government: local, state, and federal or national. At each level, there are three, independent branches: the legislative, the executive, and the judicial. Because each branch is independent, it can check and balance (control) the authority of the other branches. This is called the balance of powers.

The United States is a democracy; it is controlled by its citizens. As Abraham Lincoln said, it is a "government of the people, by the people, and for the people." The United States is also a republic, to be specific, a democratic republic. This means that its laws are made and administered by representatives elected by the people. (In this sense, the President, senators, and even local mayors are representatives.)

The only governments in the U.S. run directly by the people (pure democracies) are those of small towns, like those in New England, which make all basic decisions in Town Meetings, and even in those towns elected volunteers (selectmen) run the town between Town Meetings.

FEDERAL GOVERNMENT

The structure and function of the federal government are established and limited by the Constitution of the United States and its twenty-six amendments. The responsibilities of the federal government are for the common defense and the general welfare of the citizens, for the regulation of interstate commerce, and for relations with other countries and between the states. All powers not specifically given to the federal government by the Constitution or prohibited by the Bill of Rights (the first ten amendments) are left to the states.

How laws are made and used: The executive branch can suggest laws to the congress (the legislative branch) or the congress can originate laws. Laws authorizing the government to tax or spend money are written by the House of Representatives. All laws must be passed by both houses of congress and signed by the President. If the President will not sign (vetoes) a law, the congress can vote to override the veto.

The executive branch uses the laws made by congress; it spends the government's money and runs most of the functions of government following the instructions (laws) passed by congress, and it makes the people obey the law (enforces the law).

When people or the government are accused of breaking the law, the courts (the judiciary branch) judge whether the law has been broken and what the government should do if it has been. The courts interpret the laws made by congress, but they also base their decisions on previous decisions made by the courts. Under this system (called "common law"), the courts make decisions which function as new laws.

LEGISLATIVE BRANCH

The Congress of the U.S. has two houses (a bicameral structure). The congress makes laws, advises the President, and must consent (agree with) his appointments and certain of his decisions such as treaties with other countries and declarations of war.

U.S. Senate: There are 100 senators, two from each state, elected directly by popular vote to serve six-year terms.

Each senator has his or her own office and staff.

Officers: President of the Senate (the Vice President of the U.S.), President Pro Tempore, Majority Leader and Whip, Minority Leader and Whip.

Annual salary of a senator: $89,500.

U.S. House of Representatives: There are 435 Representatives, apportioned to the states based on the size of each state's population, elected directly by popular vote to serve two-year terms.

Each representative has his or her own office and staff.

Officers: Speaker of the House, Majority Leader and Whip, Minority Leader and Whip.

Annual salary of a representative: $89,500

Major Offices of the Congress:
• General Accounting Office
• Government Printing Office
• Office of Technology Assessment
• Congressional Budget Office
• Library of Congress

See List 5 for information on the States, their electoral votes, and number of congressional representatives.

EXECUTIVE BRANCH

President: The President is the Chief Executive Officer of the federal government and Commander-in-Chief of the Armed Forces. He or she serves a four-year term. No president can be elected for more than two four-year terms.

Annual salary of the President: $200,000 plus expenses.

See list 8 for information on the Presidents of the U.S.

The President is the head of the administration. The administration runs the government. The White House staff and the President's Cabinet work directly for the President. They are all political appointees; most of these appointments are then sent to the congress for its advice and consent (approval). The staff advises the President and does his planning and office work. The cabinet advises the President and runs the many departments and agencies of the federal government.

See list 7 for information on these departments and agencies.

Election of the President: People who want to become President usually try to become the nominees of one of the two major political parties. They run in the primary elections held in some of the states. In these primaries, delegates to each party's national convention are elected by direct popular vote. In some states, the parties choose their delegates in political caucuses. At the national conventions, the delegates elect the man or woman who will be the nominee of their party.

During the presidential campaign, the two major party candidates and sometimes candidates representing minor, third parties or independent candidates try to win the support of the majority of voters in each state. No third party has won the presidency since the new Republican Party won its first election under Abraham Lincoln in 1860.

In the general election in November, the voters in each state elect electors to represent their state in the electoral college; these electors vote for the candidate who won the election in their state. Each state has as many electors (the electoral vote) as it has senators and representatives, which gives smaller states some extra influence. The candidate who wins the greatest number of electoral votes becomes president; this is not necessarily the candidate who gets the greatest number of popular votes nationwide. The winner of the popular vote has failed to become president three times, in 1824, 1876, and 1888.

Order of presidential succession: When a President dies or leaves office for any reason during his or her term, he or she is succeeded by the Vice President, Speaker of the House, President Pro Tempore of the Senate, Secretary of State.

The President (or Vice President) can be removed from office only by being impeached by the House of Representatives and convicted by the Senate presided over by the Chief Justice of the Supreme Court. The congress also has the power to impeach, convict, and remove from office federal judges and other civil officers.

Vice President: The Vice President is the successor to the President if he or she leaves office, a member of the President's Cabinet, and the President of the Senate. Recently, he has also been an adviser on most of the President's decisions.

Annual salary of the Vice President: $115,000 plus expenses.

Election of the Vice President: After he or she is elected by the national convention of his or her party, each presidential candidate chooses a running mate, a nominee for Vice President. After he or she is elected by the convention, the candidate joins the presidential ticket for the election campaign. The President and Vice President win the election together.

Other parts of the executive branch:

The Civil Service: most employees of the federal government are not political appointees but civil servants who stay in the government from one administration to the next.

The Diplomatic Corps: The ambassador and delegation to the United Nations, other ambassadors, their staffs, and the rest of the diplomatic service are directed by the Secretary and Department of State.

Legal Services: All the departments and agencies of the federal government have lawyers. The Department of Justice under the Attorney General reviews and coordinates all laws proposed to the congress, enforces the law, and represents the executive branch in the courts. The FBI (Federal Bureau of Investigation) is part of this department.

The Military: The Army, the Navy and Marines, and the Air Force are under the direct command of the President through the Secretary of Defense and then the Chairman of the Joint Chiefs of Staff, who is the nation's top military officer.

JUDICIAL BRANCH

General The legal system in the U.S. is Common Law rather than Civil Law. Laws are written and enacted by the legislatures of the states and by congress, but the decisions of the courts in interpreting these laws are based on precedents (earlier court decisions). Court decisions function as new laws; the courts have a powerful influence on all levels of government.

Some judges at the state and local levels are elected for specific terms in some states. Federal judges are appointed by the President and confirmed with the advice and consent of the Senate. They all serve for life or until they chose to resign, which protects them from political influence.

Criminal Law: All people accused of breaking criminal law before the state or federal courts have the right to be tried by a jury of either six or twelve citizens who will decide if they are guilty or innocent. They are indicted (formally accused) by the government, sometimes by a grand jury of citizens. In court they are prosecuted by a government prosecutor and defended by their own lawyer or a public defender. If they are found guilty, they can appeal the decision of the jury or the judge to a higher court, a court of appeals. If the verdict is innocent, the government cannot appeal. The constitution says nobody can be tried twice for the same crime.

If a defendant does not appeal a guilty verdict, punishment is decided on by the judge following the penal code (penalty law). Sometimes the judge is advised by the jury; sometimes his or her choice of judgments is limited by a uniform sentencing law enacted by the legislature. The punishment is then administered by the justice department of the executive branch (the police and prison system). Punishments may be appealed to the Supreme Court if they may be cruel or unusual because such punishments are forbidden by the Constitution's Bill of Rights.

Civil Law: All forms of business and relations between people, companies, and states are regulated (ruled) by either criminal or civil law. Conflicts between people, etc., which do not involve criminal activity, are resolved by the courts using civil law. Juries are used in some cases; others are decided by a judge or a panel of judges.

Federal and State Jurisdictions: The federal courts have authority (jurisdiction) in all criminal and civil cases involving the federal government or law, federal officers, and other countries, their officers or their citizens. The federal courts also have authority in cases between states, between any state and a citizen of another state, or between citizens of different states. This includes most cases involving big businesses. All other cases are tried in the state courts.

The U.S. District Courts: These courts are the lowest level of the federal court system. Most cases involving federal law, both civil and criminal, begin at this level.

There are 91 district courts, at least one and sometimes several in each state and in the territories of Guam, Puerto Rico, and the Virgin Islands.

The U.S. Courts of Appeals: There are eleven Circuit Courts, each covering a multistate region, plus two special courts, one for the District of Columbia and one for temporary emergencies. Each court holds court in several places which make up a circuit.

These Circuit Courts hear appeals brought to them from the lower district courts and cases involving federal regulatory agencies.

The U.S. Supreme Court: There are nine justices of the Supreme Court, one Chief Justice and eight Associate Justices. They are appointed by the President and confirmed with the advice and consent of the Senate. The justices serve for life unless they choose to retire or they are impeached by the House and convicted by the Senate.

Annual salary of the Chief Justice: $115,000;
Annual salary of the Associates Justices: $110,000.

The Supreme Court is the highest court of appeals; its main function is to decide whether decisions of the lower courts and laws passed by the states or federal government are constitutional (in accord or agreement with the Constitution and the Bill of Rights.) The Supreme Court also decides cases when there is a conflict between the laws of one state and another or the federal government. It chooses the cases it will hear from among cases appealed to it from the lower courts and cases involving challenges to state and federal laws.

Because the Supreme Court interprets the Constitution and either cancels or defines the meaning of laws based on its interpretations of the Constitution, it has a great influence on the way the laws of the country are used. From the beginning of U.S. history, the Supreme Court has often used its power to change the political and social development of the country.

154

STATE GOVERNMENTS

There are 50 states in the U.S. and 13 associated states and possessions in the Caribbean and Pacific. Each has its own government. Although their structures vary in many ways, each of these governments has three branches like the federal government and the following explanations are generally true.

LEGISLATIVE BRANCH: The legislative branch of each state has a bicameral (two-house) structure like the federal government. There is an upper house called the the senate and a lower house called the house or assembly of representatives. The state legislatures make both civil and criminal laws for their states.

EXECUTIVE BRANCH: Each state has a governor and a lieutenant governor, who are elected by the people of the state. The structure and functions of the executive branch differ from state to state. Most states have a secretary of state, a treasurer, a comptroller and an attorney general.

JUDICIAL BRANCH: The highest court is called the appellate court, the court of appeals, or the supreme court. Below it are the superior and inferior courts, which in some states include all local and municipal courts.

LOCAL GOVERNMENTS

There are many variations in the structures of local governments. The smallest government structures are villages. Towns are generally larger, and cities are larger still. The whole state is divided into counties. In some states, each county is divided into several townships, each containing several towns and villages. In other states, each county is divided into towns, which may have several villages, town centers, or hamlets in them. The open (unincorporated) countryside between villages is governed by the township (town) or the county.

LEGISLATIVE BRANCH Villages, towns, and cities (municipalities) always have some form of legislative board, which is directly elected by the local citizens. In cities and large towns it is called the town or city council or the board of aldermen. In smaller towns and villages, the town council is sometimes called the board of selectmen. The local legislatures make regulations and spend local tax money. To help them plan for changes, they often appoint local zoning and planning boards.

In most municipalities, the school system is run by a local school board, which is also directly elected by the people. Sometimes there is a township school board.

EXECUTIVE BRANCH The smallest towns are run by the selectmen with the help of an elected town clerk or manager. In larger towns and cities there is always an independent town or city manager or mayor.

JUDICIAL BRANCH Villages and small towns have elected justices of the peace or local town magistrates. Larger towns and cities have municipal courts. In some states, these are part of the state court system; in others, they are independent.

OTHER ORGANIZATIONS

There are other organizations which govern life in the United States, usually through political and financial influence.

POLITICAL PARTIES: There are two major political parties, the Democratic Party and the Republican Party. There are also many minor, special interest, and regional and local parties including the Libertarian Party, Socialist Party, Socialist Labor Party, Communist Party, and Socialist Workers Party. Individuals may also run for political office as independents (without party support).

Other Groups With Political Influence:
- Business and trade associations
- Chambers of commerce
- Professional organizations
- Labor unions
- Public service boards
- Civil rights organizations
- Political action committees
- Veteran's and Fraternal organizations
- Alumni associations
- Consumer and public interest groups
- Churches
- Other special interest groups

List 7: U.S. Departments and Agencies

DEPARTMENTS AND THE CABINET

Note: Each department is headed by a member of the president's Cabinet, who is given the title of secretary, with the exception of the Department of Justice, which is headed by the attorney general. The vice president is also a member of the Cabinet.

Department of Agriculture
Department of Commerce
Department of Defense
Department of Education
Department of Energy
Department of Health and Human Services
Department of Housing and Urban Development
Department of Justice
Department of Labor
Department of State
Department of the Interior
Department of the Treasury
Department of Transportation
Department of Verterans' Affairs

WHITE HOUSE STAFF

Chief of staff
Assistant to the president
Deputy to the chief of staff
Assistants to the president
Cabinet secretary
Communications
Counsel to the president
Economic and domestic affairs
Legislative affairs
Management and administration
National security
Presidential personnel
Press secretary
Public events amd initiatives
Science and technology
Secretary for domestic affairs

EXECUTIVE AGENCIES

Central Intelligence Agency (CIA)
Council of Economic Advisers (CEA)
Council on Environmental Quality
Office of Management and Budget
Office of National Drug Control Policy
Office of the U.S. Trade Representative

MAJOR INDEPENDENT AGENCIES

ACTION
Consumer Product Safety Commission
Environmental Protection Agency (EPA)
Equal Employment Opportunity Commission (EEOC)
Farm Credit Administration (FCA)
Federal Communications Commission (FCC)
Federal Deposit Insurance Corporation (FDIC)
Federal Election Commission (FEC)
Federal Maritime Commission
Federal Mediation and Conciliation Service (FMCS)
Federal Reserve System
Federal Trade Commission (FTC)
General Services Administration (GSA)
Interstate Commerce Commission (ICC)
National Aeronautics and Space Administration (NASA)
National Foundation on the Arts and Humanities
National Labor Relations Board (NLRB)
National Mediation Board
National Science Foundation (NSF)
National Transportation Safety Board
Nuclear Regulatory Commission (NRC)
Office of Personnel Management
Peace Corps
Securities and Exchange Commission (SEC)
Selective Service System (SSS)
Small Business Administration (SBA)
Tennessee Valley Authority (TVA)
U.S. Agency of International Development
U.S. Arms Control and Disarmament Agency
U.S. Commission on Civil Rights
U.S. Information Agency
U.S. International Trade Commission
U.S. Postal Service

Sources: The 1990 Information Please Almanac, Boston © 1989
The World Almanac and Book of Facts 1991, New York © 1990
The Encyclopaedia Brittanica, Chicago © 1990

List 8: U.S. Presidents

1. **George Washington**
   (1732-1799)
   Party: Federalist
   Term: 1789-1797
   Birthplace: Virginia

2. **John Adams**
   (1735-1826)
   Party: Federalist
   Term: 1797-1801
   Birthplace: Massachusetts

3. **Thomas Jefferson**
   (1743-1826)
   Party: Democratic-Republican
   Term: 1801-1809
   Birthplace: Virginia

4. **James Madison**
   (1751-1836)
   Party: Democratic-Republican
   Term: 1809-1817
   Birthplace: Virginia

5. **James Monroe**
   (1758-1831)
   Party: Democratic-Republican
   Term: 1817-1825
   Birthplace: Virginia

6. **John Quincy Adams**
   (1767-1848)
   Party: Democratic-Republican
   Term: 1825-1829
   Birthplace: Massachusetts

7. **Andrew Jackson**
   (1767-1845)
   Party: Democratic
   Term: 1829-1837
   Birthplace: South Carolina

8. **Martin Van Buren**
   (1782-1862)
   Party: Democratic
   Term: 1837-1841
   Birthplace: New York

9. **William Harrison**
   (1773-1841)
   Party: Whig
   Term: 1841 *
   Birthplace: Virginia

10. **John Tyler**
(1790-1862)
Party: Whig
Term: 1841-1845
Birthplace: Virginia

11. **James Polk**
(1795-1849)
Party: Democratic
Term: 1845-1849
Birthplace: North Carolina

12. **Zachary Taylor**
(1784-1850)
Party: Whig
Term: 1849-1850 *
Birthplace: Virginia

13. **Millard Fillmore**
(1800-1874)
Party: Whig
Term: 1850-1853
Birthplace: New York

14. **Franklin Pierce**
(1804-1869)
Party: Democratic
Term: 1853-1857
Birthplace: New Hampshire

15. **James Buchanan**
(1791-1868)
Party: Democratic
Term: 1857-1861
Birthplace: Pennsylvania

16. **Abraham Lincoln**
(1809-1865)
Party: Republican
Term: 1861-1865 **
Birthplace: Kentucky

17. **Andrew Johnson**
(1808-1875)
Party: Union
Term: 1865-1869
Birthplace: North Carolina

18. **Ulysses S. Grant**
(1822-1885)
Party: Republican
Term: 1869-1877
Birthplace: Ohio

19. Rutherford B. Hayes
(1822-1893)
Party: Republican
Term: 1877-1881
Birthplace: Ohio

20. James Garfield
(1831-1881)
Party: Republican
Term: 1881 **
Birthplace: Ohio

21. Chester Arthur
(1829-1886)
Party: Republican
Term: 1881-1885
Birthplace: Vermont

22. Grover Cleveland
(1837-1908)
Party: Democratic
Term: 1885-1889
Birthplace: New Jersey

23. Benjamin Harrison
(1833-1901)
Party: Republican
Term: 1889-1893
Birthplace: Ohio

24. Grover Cleveland
(second nonconsecutive term)
Term: 1893-1897

25. William McKinley
(1843-1901)
Party: Republican
Term: 1897-1901 **
Birthplace: Ohio

26. Theodore Roosevelt
(1858-1919)
Party: Republican
Term: 1901-1909
Birthplace: New York

27. William Taft
(1857-1930)
Party: Republican
Term: 1909-1913
Birthplace: Ohio

28. Woodrow Wilson
(1856-1924)
Party: Democratic
Term: 1913-1921
Birthplace: Virginia

29. Warren Harding
(1865-1923)
Party: Republican
Term: 1921-1923 *
Birthplace: Ohio

30. Calvin Coolidge
(1872-1933)
Party: Republican
Term: 1923-1929
Birthplace: Vermont

31. Herbert Hoover
(1874-1964)
Party: Republican
Term: 1929-1933
Birthplace: Iowa

32. Franklin D. Roosevelt
(1882-1945)
Party: Democratic
Term: 1933-1945 *
Birthplace: New York

33. Harry S. Truman
(1884-1972)
Party: Democratic
Term: 1945-1953
Birthplace: Missouri

34. Dwight D. Eisenhower
(1890-1969)
Party: Republican
Term: 1953-1961
Birthplace: Texas

35. John F. Kennedy
(1917-1963)
Party: Democratic
Term: 1961-1963 **
Birthplace: Massachusetts

36. Lyndon B. Johnson
(1908-1973)
Party: Democratic
Term: 1963-1969
Birthplace: Texas

37. Richard Nixon
(1913-   )
Party: Republican
Term: 1969-1974 §
Birthplace: California

38. Gerald Ford
(1913-   )
Party: Republican
Term: 1974-1977
Birthplace: Nebraska

39. Jimmy Carter
(1924-   )
Party: Democratic
Term: 1977-1981
Birthplace: Georgia

40. Ronald Reagan
(1911-   )
Party: Republican
Term: 1981-1989
Birthplace: Illinois

41. George Bush
(1924-   )
Party: Republican
Term: 1989-
Birthplace: Massachusetts

* Died in office
** Assassinated in office
§ Resigned from office

Source: The World Almanac and Book of Facts 1991, New York © 1990

List 9: U.S. Industries

LARGEST U.S. INDUSTRIAL CORPORATIONS (1989)

Rank	Company	Sales
1	General Motors	$ 127,000,000,000
2	Ford Motor Company	96,900,000,000
3	Exxon	86,600,000,000
4	IBM	63,400,000,000
5	Mobil	60,000,000,000
6	General Electric	55,300,000,000
7	Philip Morris	39,100,000,000
8	Chrysler	36,100,000,000
9	Du Pont	35,200,000,000
10	Texaco	32,400,000,000
11	Chevron	29,400,000,000
12	Amoco	24,200,000,000
13	Shell Oil	21,700,000,000
14	Procter & Gamble	21,700,000,000
15	Boeing	20,300,000,000
16	Occidental Petroleum	20,100,000,000
17	United Technologies	19,800,000,000
18	Eastman Kodak	18,400,000,000
19	USX	17,700,000,000
20	Dow Chemical	17,700,000,000
21	Xerox	17,600,000,000
22	Atlantic Richfield	15,900,000,000
23	Pepsico	15,400,000,000
24	RJR Nabisco	15,200,000,000
25	McDonnell Douglas	15,000,000,000

TEN LARGEST INDUSTRY GROUPS (1987)

Rank	Industry	Employees	Payroll (in millions)	Value Added by Manufacturing (in millions)
1	Machinery, except electric	1,870,600	$ 51,156.8	$ 117,538.0
2	Transportation equipment	1,834,500	59,557.5	139,090.8
3	Electric, electronic equipment	1,599,800	39,295.3	98,332.2
4	Printing and publishing	1,500,200	33,594.6	90,204.3
5	Fabricated metal products	1,473,600	35,435.4	76,054.7
6	Food and kindred products	1,449,600	30,247.5	124,186.6
7	Apparel and other textile products	1,076,600	13,915.5	33,126.5
8	Instruments and related products	964,900	28,165.9	70,939.8
9	Rubber and miscellaneous plastic products	857,700	18,060.4	45,562.0
10	Chemicals and allied products	817,700	24,978.0	120,866.5

Sources: The World Almanac and Book of Facts 1991, New York © 1990
FORTUNE Magazine

List 10: Some Famous Americans

-1812

Adams, Samuel	(1722-1803)	Patriot, Boston Tea Party firebrand
Allen, Ethan	(1738-1789)	Leader of the Green Mountain Boys
Arnold, Benedict	(1741-1801)	Treasonous Revolutionary War general
Attucks, Crispus	(c.1723-1770)	Led group that began the Boston Massacre in 1770
Boone, Daniel	(1734-1820)	Frontiersman
Clark, William	(1770-1838)	Explored the northwest with Lewis in 1804
Crockett, Davy	(1786-1836)	Frontiersman, died at the Alamo
Franklin, Benjamin	(1706-1790)	Writer, statesman, scientist
Hale, Nathan	(1755-1776)	Revolutionary War officer
Hamilton, Alexander	(1755-1894)	Statesman, author, first secretary of the treasury
Hancock, John	(1737-1793)	Statesman, Declaration of Independence signer
Henry, Patrick	(1736-1799)	Revolutionary war figure, orator
Jones, John Paul	(1747-1792)	Naval hero
LaSalle, Sieur de (R.C.)	(1643-1687)	Explored and claimed Mississippi Basin for France
Lewis, Meriwether	(1774-1809)	Explored the northwest with Clark in 1804
Pilgrims		Founded Plymouth Plantation Colony in 1720
Pocahontas	(c. 1595-1617)	Indian princess, saved explorer John Smith's life
Revere, Paul	(1735-1818)	Silversmith, hero of famous ride in 1775
Ross, Betsy	(1752-1836)	Designed and sewed first American flag
Sacagawea	(1784-1884)	Guided Lewis and Clark
Smith, Capt. John	(c. 1580-1631)	Led first colony (1607-9) in Jamestown, Virginia
Thomas Paine	(1737-1809)	Political philosopher
Turnbull, John	(1756-1843)	Historical themes painter
Whitney, Eli	(1765-1825)	Invented cotton gin and manufacture

1812-1865

Audubon, John James	(1785-1851)	Artist, ornithologist
Brown, John	(1800-1859)	Abolitionist
Carson, Kit	(1809-1868)	Scout
Clay, Henry	(1777-1852)	Political leader
Custer, George	(1839-1876)	Union general in Civil War, killed by Indians
Davis, Jefferson	(1808-1889)	President of the Confederacy
Douglass, Frederick	(1817-1895)	Author, diplomat, abolitionist
Emerson, Ralph Waldo	(1803-1882)	Philosopher, author, lecturer
Geronimo	(1829-1909)	Apache chieftain
Jackson, Thomas (Stonewall)	(1824-1863)	Confederate general in Civil War
Key, Francis Scott	(1779-1843)	Author of national anthem
Lee, Robert E.	(1807-1870)	Confederate general in Civil War
Sherman, William T.	(1820-1891)	Union general in Civil War
Sitting Bull	(1835-1890)	Dakota chief
Thoreau, Henry David	(1817-1862)	Philosopher, author, naturalist
Truth, Sojourner	(1797-1883)	Suffragette, abolitionist
Tubman, Harriet	(1820-1913)	Abolitionist, liberator
Webster, Daniel	(1782-1852)	Statesman
Webster, Noah	(1759-1843)	Lexicographer
Young, Brigham	(1801-1877)	Mormon leader, colonized Utah

1866-1916

Anthony, Susan B.	(1820-1906)	Suffragette
Barton, Clara	(1821-1906)	Organizer of American Red Cross
Bell, Alexander Graham	(1847-1922)	Inventor of telephone, teacher of deaf
Buffalo Bill (William Cody)	(1846-1917)	Scout, showman
Carver, George Washington	(1861-1943)	Educator, botanist
Cassatt, Mary	(1845-1926)	Impressionist painter
Crazy Horse	(1849-1877)	Dakota war chief victorious at Little Bighorn
DuBois, W. E. B.	(1868-1963)	Historian, sociologist, founded NAACP
Edison, Thomas	(1847-1931)	Inventor of lightbulb, practical electric power
Ford, Henry	(1863-1947)	Industrialist, built first assembly-line cars
Homer, Winslow	(1836-1910)	Painter of marine themes
Liliuokalani, Lydia Kamekeha	(1838-1917)	Last monarch of Hawaii
Long, Huey	(1893-1935)	Politician
Peary, Adm. Robert E.	(1856-1920)	Explorer, first to reach North Pole 1909
Rockefeller, John D.	(1839-1937)	Established Standard Oil, philanthropist
Sargent, John Singer	(1856-1925)	Portait artist
Washington, Booker T.	(1856-1915)	Educator
Wright, Orville	(1871-1948)	Built first powered airplane with brother Wilbur

1917-1970

Bethune, Mary McLeod	(1875-1955)	Educator
Copland, Aaron	(1900-1990)	Composer
Cronkite, Walter	(1916-)	Television journalist
Disney, Walt	(1901-1966)	Film animator and producer
Earhart, Amelia	(1898-1937)	Aviatrix
Freidan, Betty	(1921-)	Feminist
Glenn, John	(1921-)	Astronaut, politician
Goddard, Robert	(1882-1945)	Physicist, father of modern rocketry
Hearst, William Randolph	(1863-1951)	Publisher
Hopper, Edward	(1882-1967)	Painter of realistic urban scenes
Keller, Helen	(1880-1968)	Educator and writer
King Jr., The Rev. Dr. Martin Luther	(1929-1968)	Civil rights leader
MacArthur, Douglas	(1880-1964)	General in WW II, Korean War
Malcolm X	(1925-1965)	Civil rights leader
Marshall, Thurgood	(1980-)	Supreme Court justice, appointed 1967
McCarthy, Joseph	(1908-1957)	Anti-communist, politician
Moses, Grandma	(1860-1961)	Folk painter
O'Keeffe, Georgia	(1887-1986)	Painter of southwestern motifs
Oppenheimer, J. Robert	(1904-1967)	Physicist, father of atomic bomb
Patton, George S.	(1885-1945)	General in WW II
Pollock, Jackson	(1912-1956)	Abstract expressionist painter
Rockwell, Norman	(1894-1978)	Illustrator
Roosevelt, Eleanor	(1884-1962)	Humanitarian, UN delegate
Spock, Benjamin	(1903-)	Pediatrician
Steinem, Gloria	(1934-)	Feminist
Stevenson, Adlai	(1900-1965)	Statesman
Warhol, Andy	(1928-1989)	Pop artist
Wright, Frank Lloyd	(1867-1959)	Architect

1970-

Baker, James A.	(1930-	)	Secretary of state for President Bush
Bombeck, Erma	(1927-	)	Humorist
Brokaw, Tom	(1940-	)	Television news anchor
Brothers, Joyce	(1928-	)	Psychologist
Brown, Helen Gurley	(1922-	)	Publisher
Child, Julia	(1912-	)	Chef
Chung, Connie	(1946-	)	Television journalist, anchor
Cosell, Howard	(1920-	)	Sports announcer
Donaldson, Sam	(1934-	)	Television journalist
Eisner, Michael	(1942-	)	Chairman of Walt Disney
Falwell, Jerry	(1933-	)	Televangelist
Ferraro, Geraldine	(1935-	)	Politician
Graham, Billy	(1918-	)	Televangelist
Graham, Katherine	(1917-	)	Publisher of *Washington Post*
Harvey, Paul	(1918-	)	Radio personality
Hefner, Hugh	(1926-	)	Publisher, philanthropist
Iacocca, Lee	(1924-	)	Businessman, chairman of Chrysler
Jackson, The Rev. Jesse	(1941-	)	Civil rights leader, politician, reverend
Jennings, Peter	(1938-	)	Television news anchor
Karan, Donna	(1948-	)	Fashion designer
Klein, Calvin	(1942-	)	Fashion designer
Landers, Ann	(1918-	)	Advice columnist
Lauren, Ralph	(1939-	)	Fashion designer
Nader, Ralph	(1934-	)	Public advocate
Nunn, Sam	(1938-	)	Politician
O'Connor, Sandra Day	(1930-	)	Supreme Court justice
Onassis, Jacqueline	(1929-	)	Widow of John F. Kennedy
O'Neill, Thomas P. (Tip)	(1912-	)	Former speaker of the House
Pauley, Jane	(1950-	)	Television journalist, anchor
Pei, I.M.	(1917-	)	Architect
Quinn, Jane Bryant	(1939-	)	Economist
Rather, Dan	(1931-	)	Television anchor
Ride, Sally K.	(1952-	)	Astronaut
Sagan, Carl	(1934-	)	Astronomer, author
Sawyer, Diane	(1945-	)	Television journalist
Schroeder, Patricia	(1940-	)	Politician
Steinbrenner, George	(1930-	)	Owner of the New York Yankees
Van Buren, Abigail	(1918-	)	Advice columnist
Westheimer, Ruth	(1928-	)	Sex therapist

Sources: The World Almanac and Book of Facts 1991, New York © 1990
The 1990 Information Please Almanac, Boston © 1989

List 11: Entertainers

Name	Occupation	
Allen, Woody	Actor, director, screenwriter	(1935-)
Andrews, Julie	Actress	(1935-)
Armstrong, Louis	Jazz musician	(1900-1971)
Astaire, Fred	Actor, dancer	(1904-1983)
Avalon, Frankie	Actor, singer	(1940-)
Balanchine, George	Choreographer	(1904-1983)
Ball, Lucille	Actress, comedienne	(1911-1989)
Barnum, P. T.	Circus master	(1810-1891)
Baryshnikov, Mikhail	Dancer, actor	(1948-)
Bernstein, Leonard	Conductor, composer	(1918-1990)
Blanc, Mel	Cartoonist	(1908-1989)
Bogart, Humphrey	Actor	(1899-1957)
Brando, Marlon	Actor	(1924-)
Burnett, Carol	Actress, comedienne	(1933-)
Capra, Frank	Director	(1897-)
Carson, Johnny	Comedian, TV entertainer	(1925-)
Cash, Johnny	Country musician	(1932-)
Charles, Ray	Blues & rock musician	(1930-)
Cher	Actress	(1946-)
Clark, Dick	TV entertainer	(1929-)
Close, Glenn	Actress	(1947-)
Cody, Buffalo Bill	Creator of wild west show	(1846-1917)
Como, Perry	Musician	(1912-)
Coppola, Francis Ford	Director	(1939-)
Cosby, Bill	Actor, comedian	(1937-)
Costner, Kevin	Actor, director	(1855-)
Crosby, Bing	Actor, singer	(1904-1977)
Cronyn, Hume	Actor	(1911-)
Davis, Bette	Actress	(1908-1990)
Davis, Sammy Jr.	Actor, singer	(1925-1990)
De Havilland, Olivia	Actress	(1916-)
DeNiro, Robert	Actor	(1943-)
Dietrich, Marlene	Actress	(1901-)
Disney, Walt	Director, cartoonist	(1901-1966)
Domino, Fats	Musician	(1928-)
Donahue, Phil	Talk show host	(1935-)
Dunaway, Faye	Actress	(1941-)
Duvall, Robert	Actor	(1931-)
Dylan, Bob	Rock musician	(1941-)
Ellington, Duke	Composer, pianist, band leader	(1899-1974
Fawcett, Farrah	Actress	(1947-)
Fiedler, Arthur	Conductor	(1894-1979)
Fields, W. C.	Actor, comedian	(1880-1946)
Fitzgerald, Ella	Jazz musician	(1918-)
Flynn, Errol	Actor	(1909-1959)
Fonda, Henry	Actor	(1905-1982)
Fonda, Jane	Actress	(1937-)
Fontaine, Joan	Actress	(1917-)
Ford, Harrison	Actor	(1942-)
Fosse, Bob	Director	(1927-1987)
Foster, Jodie	Actress	(1962-)

Franklin, Aretha	Soul and gospel musician	(1942-)
Funicello, Annette	Actress, mouseketeer	(1942-)
Gable, Clark	Actor	(1901-1960)
Gabor, Zsa Zsa	Actress, cop slapper	(19?-)
Garbo, Greta	Actress	(1905-1990)
Garland, Judy	Actress	(1922-1969)
Gershwin, George	Composer, lyricist	(1898-1937)
Gish, Lillian	Actress	(1896-)
Goldberg, Whoopi	Actress, comedienne	(1949-)
Griffin, Merv	Producer	(1925-)
Griffith, Andy	Actor	(1926-)
Guthrie, Woody	Folk musician	(1912-1967)
Hayworth, Rita	Actress	(1918-1987)
Hendrix, Jimi	Rock musician	(1942-1970)
Henie, Sonja	Actress, skater	(1910-1969)
Hepburn, Audrey	Actress	(1929-)
Hepburn, Katharine	Actress	(1909-)
Herman, Pee-Wee	Actor	(1952-)
Heston, Charlton	Actor	(1923-)
Hines, Gregory	Actor, tap dancer	(1946-)
Hitchcock, Alfred	Director	(1899-1980)
Ho, Don	Singer	(1930-)
Hoffman, Dustin	Actor	(1937-)
Holiday, Billie	Blues singer	(1915-1959)
Hope, Bob	Comedian	(1903-)
Horne, Lena	Singer	(1917-)
Houdini, Harry	Magician	(1874-1926)
Huston, John	Director	(1906-1987)
Iglesias, Julio	Singer	(1943-)
Ives, Burl	Folk singer	(1909-)
Jackson, Michael	Rock musician	(1958-)
Jagger, Mick	Rock musician	(1943-)
Jones, James Earl	Actor	(1931-)
Joplin, Scott	Composer, pianist	(1868-1917)
Keaton, Diane	Actress	(1946-)
Kelly, Grace	Actress	(1929-1982)
King, B. B.	Blues musician	(1925-)
Lancaster, Burt	Actor	(1913-)
Landon, Michael	Actor	(1936-)
Langtry, Lillie	Actress	(1852-1929)
Lansbury, Angela	Actress, singer	(1925-)
Lee, Spike	Director	(1957-)
Leno, Jay	Comedian	(1950-)
Letterman, David	Comedian, TV entertainer	(1947-)
Lewis, Jerry Lee	Actor, comedian, telethoner	(1935-)
Liberace	Pianist	(1919-1987)
Lynch, David	Director	(1946-)
MacLaine, Shirley	Actress	(1934-)
Mancini, Henry	Musician	(1924-)
Marshall, Penny	Director, actress	(1943-)
Martin, Steve	Actor, comedian	(1945-)
Marx, Groucho	Actor, comedian	(1890-1977)
McEntire, Reba	Country musician	(1955-)
Miller, Glenn	Band leader	(1904-1944)

Monroe, Marilyn	Actress	(1926-1962)
Moore, Mary Tyler	Actress	(1937-)
Morrison, Jim	Rock singer	(1943-1971)
Nabors, Jim	Actor, singer	(1933-)
Nelson, Willie	Country singer	(1933-)
Newhart, Bob	Actor, comedian	(1929-)
Newman, Paul	Actor	(1925-)
Nicholson, Jack	Actor	(1937-)
Nimoy, Leonard	Director, actor	(1931-)
Oakley, Annie	Sharp shooter	(1860-1926)
Orbison, Roy	Rock musician	(1936-1988)
Ozawa, Seiji	Conductor	(1935-)
Parton, Dolly	Actress, country musician, singer	(1946-)
Peck, Gregory	Actor	(1916-)
Poitier, Sidney	Actor	(1927-)
Porter, Cole	Composer	(1893-1964)
Presley, Elvis	Actor, rock singer	(1935-1977)
Quinn, Anthony	Actor	(1915-)
Redford, Robert	Actor	(1937-)
Reiner, Rob	Director, actor	(1945-)
Rivers, Joan	Comedienne, TV entertainer	(1933-)
Rogers, Ginger	Actress, dancer, singer	(1911-)
Rooney, Mickey	Actor	(1920-)
Sarandon, Susan	Actress	(1946-)
Schwarzenegger, Arnold	Actor	(1947-)
Scorsese, Martin	Director	(1942-)
Scott, George C.	Actor	(1927-)
Selznick, David O.	Producer	(1902-1965)
Shepard, Sam	Actor, playwright	(1943-)
Simon, Paul	Singer, musician	(1942-)
Sinatra, Frank	Singer	(1915-)
Sousa, John Philip	Composer	(1854-1932)
Springsteen, Bruce	Rock musician	(1949-)
Stallone, Sylvester	Actor	(1946-)
Stanwyck, Barbara	Actress	(1907-1990)
Stewart, James	Actor	(1908-)
Stone, Oliver	Director	(1946-)
Stravinsky, Igor	Composer	(1882-1971)
Streep, Meryl	Actress	(1949-)
Sullivan, Ed	Talk show host	(1901-1974)
Tandy, Jessica	Actress	(1909-)
Taylor, Elizabeth	Actress	(1932-)
Temple, Shirley	Actress	(1928-)
Tracy, Spencer	Actor	(1900-1967)
Turner, Tina	Rock musician, actress	(1939-)
Waller, Fats	Composer	(1904-1943)
Wayne, John	Actor	(1907-1979)
Welk, Lawrence	Band leader	(1903-)
Welles, Orson	Director	(1915-1985)
West, Mae	Actress	(1893-1980)
Williams, Hank	Country musician	(1923-1953)

Source: The World Almanac and Book of Facts 1991, New York © 1990

List 12: Heroes

FOLK HEROES AND CULTURAL ICONS

Horatio Alger
Johnny Appleseed
Billy the Kid
Bonnie and Clyde
Daniel Boone
John Brown
Paul Bunyan
Al Capone
Kit Carson
Davy Crockett
James Dean
Amelia Earhart
Wyatt Earp
Thomas Edison
Benjamin Franklin
Barbara Fritchie
John Henry
Wild Bill Hickock
Jesse James
Casey Jones

Martin Luther King, Jr.
Charles Lindbergh
Malcolm X
Marilyn Monroe
Mickey Mouse
Annie Oakley
Jessie Owens
Rosa Parks
Pecos Bill
Molly Pitcher
Pocahontas
Elvis Presley
Paul Revere
Betsy Ross
Babe Ruth
Tom Swift
Uncle Sam
Rip Van Winkle
Sergeant York

PRESIDENTIAL ICONS

George Washington
Thomas Jefferson
Andrew Jackson
Abraham Lincoln

Teddy Roosevelt
Franklin Roosevelt
John Kennedy

COMIC BOOK HEROES

Alfred E. Newman
Batman and Robin
Betty Boop
Bill the Cat
Buck Rogers
Bugs Bunny
Calvin and Hobbes
Charlie Brown
Daffy Duck
Dagwood and Blondie
Dick Tracy
Donald Duck
Elmer Fudd
Felix the Cat
Fred Flintstone
Garfield

George Jetson
Little Orphan Annie
Mickey Mouse
Mike Doonesbury
Mutt 'n' Jeff
Nancy
Opus
Popeye
Scooby Doo
Snoopy
Spiderman
Superman
Sylvester and Tweety
Wile E. Coyote and the Roadrunner
Wonder Woman
Woody Woodpecker

List 13: Points of Interest

State	Site
Alabama	First capital of the Confederacy in Montgomery
Alaska	Denali National Park, wildlife sanctuary surrounding Mt. McKinley
Arizona	Taliesin West in Scottsdale, home of Frank Lloyd Wright
Arkansas	Eureka Springs, resort since 1880s
California	Disneyland in Anaheim
Colorado	Mesa Verde National Park, cliff-dwelling Indians' cities
Connecticut	Mark Twain House in Hartford
Delaware	John Dickinson home in Dover, residence of "Penman of the Revolution"
Florida	Cape Kennedy, NASA Space Center
	Saint Augustine, oldest city in U.S., est. by Spanish in 1565
Georgia	Chickamauga Battlefield Park, site of decisive 1863 victory for South in Civil War
Hawaii	Iolani Palace in Honolulu, last residence of Hawaiian royalty
Idaho	Hell's Canyon, deepest gorge in North America
Illinois	Lincoln shrines in Springfield, New Salem and Sangamon
Indiana	Fort Vincennes, one of the first white settlements west of the Appalachians
Iowa	Herbert Hoover birthplace and library in West Branch
Kansas	Dodge City, frontier town on Santa Fe Trail
Kentucky	Churchill Downs in Louisville, home of Kentucky Derby since 1875
Louisiana	Mardi Gras in New Orleans
Maine	Ogunquit, Portland, York
Maryland	U.S. Naval Academy in Annapolis
Massachusetts	Plymouth Plantation, pilgrims' first colony
	Old North Church in Boston, beginning of Paul Revere's ride
	Witch trials in Salem in 1692
Michigan	Sault Ste. Marie, French settlement est. 1668
Minnesota	Minnehaha Falls in Minneapolis, inspiration for Longfellow's "Hiawatha"
Mississippi	Vicksburg National Military Park and Cemetery
Missouri	Pony Express Museum in St. Joseph
Montana	Custer Battlefield National Cemetery at Little Bighorn River
Nebraska	Buffalo Bill Ranch State Historical Park in Nebraska City
Nevada	Legalized gambling casinos in Las Vegas, Reno and Tahoe
New Hampshire	Strawbery Banke in Portsmouth, historical buildings dating to 17th century
New Jersey	Miss America Pageant and casinos in Atlantic City
New Mexico	Carlsbad Caverns, a national park with caverns on three levels and the largest natural cave in the world
New York	Ellis Island, immigration station for East Coast
North Carolina	Kitty Hawk, Wright brothers' first flight
	Roanoke Island, first English colony in America
North Dakota	Theodore Roosevelt National Park in Badlands, contains the president's Elkhorn Ranch
Ohio	Mound City National Monuments, group of 24 prehistoric Indian burial mounds
Oklahoma	National Cowboy Hall of Fame, Oklahoma City
Oregon	Columbia River Gorge
Pennsylvania	Valley Forge, encampment grounds for Gen. Washington and troops in 1777
	Gettysburg, site of Civil War battle, turning point in war for Union
Rhode Island	John Brown House in Providence, residence of 18th century merchant
South Carolina	Fort Sumter National Monument, Union troops were overrun by Confederate soldiers to start the Civil War in 1861
South Dakota	Black Hills

State	Site
Tennessee	Graceland in Memphis, home of Elvis Presley
	The Grand Ole Opry in Nashville, country music show est. 1925
Texas	The Alamo in San Antonio, fort settlers were overrun by Santa Anna in 1836
Utah	Temple Square in Salt Lake City, Mormon Church headquarters
Vermont	Bennington Battle Museum
Virginia	Monticello in Charlottesville, Jefferson's home
	Mount Vernon, Washington's home
	Appomattox, site of surrender of Gen. Lee and Confederacy in 1865
	Lexington, birthplace and tomb of Gen. Lee
Washington	Mount St. Helens, volcanic eruption in 1989
West Virginia	Harper's Ferry, John Brown led slave uprising in 1859
Wisconsin	Heritage Hill in Green Bay, museum of historical buildings and artifacts
Wyoming	Yellowstone National Park
District of Columbia	Washington Monument
	Lincoln Monument
	White House
	Jefferson Memorial
	Vietnam War Memorial
	National Archives
	Capitol

Sources: The World Almanac and Book of Facts 1991, New York © 1990
The Encyclopaedia Brittanica, Chicago © 1989

List 14: National Parks

Name	Location	Est.	Features
Acadia	Maine	1916	Mt. Desert Island and adjacent mainland
Arches	Utah	1929	Stone arches and pedestals caused by erosion
Badlands	South Dakota	1929	Arid land inhabited by bison, antelope, deer
Big Bend	Texas	1935	Mountains and desert bordering Rio Grande
Biscayne	Florida	1968	Coral reef south of Miami
Bryce Canyon	Utah	1923	Brilliantly colored eroded rocks
Canyonlands	Utah	1964	Red-rock canyons, spires and arches
Capitol Reef	Utah	1937	Sedimentary rock formations in high narrow gorges
Carlsbad Caverns	New Mexico	1923	World's largest known caves
Channel Islands	California	1938	Marine mammals, endangered species, archaeology
Crater Lake	Oregon	1902	Lake in the heart of an inactive volcano
Denali	Alaska	1917	North America's highest mountain, Mt. McKinley
Everglades	Florida	1934	Subtropical swamp
Gates of the Arctic	Alaska	1978	Diverse wilderness, part of the Brooks Range
Glacier	Montana	1910	Rocky Mountains
Glacier Bay	Alaska	1925	Whales, glaciers
Grand Canyon	Arizona	1908	Mile-deep gorge, 4-18 miles wide, 217 miles long
Grand Teton	Wyoming	1929	High mountain range
Great Basin	Nevada	1922	Biological and geological attractions
Great Smoky Mts.	NC, TN	1926	Highest mountain range east of Black Hills
Guadalupe Mts.	Texas	1966	Highest peak in Texas (8751 ft.)
Haleakala	Hawaii	1916	Dormant Haleakala volcano (10,023 ft.)
Hawaii Volcanoes	Hawaii	1916	Volcanoes, luxuriant vegetation at lower levels
Hot Springs	Arkansas	1832	47 hot springs
Isle Royale	Michigan	1931	Largest wilderness island in Lake Superior
Katmai	Alaska	1918	Dormant volcano, bears
Kenai Fjords	Alaska	1978	Mountain goats, marine mammals, birdlife
Kings Canyon	California	1890	Huge canyons, high mountains, giant sequoias
Kobuk Valley	Alaska	1978	Native culture and anthropology center
Lake Clark	Alaska	1978	Across Cook Inlet from Anchorage
Lassen Volcanic	California	1907	Impressive volcanic phenomena
Mammoth Cave	Kentucky	1926	Limestone labyrinth with underground river
Mesa Verde	Colorado	1906	Best-preserved prehistoric cliff dwellings in U.S.
Mount Rainier	Washington	1899	Single peak glacial system, dense forest
North Cascades	Washington	1968	Alpine landscape, glaciers, mountain lakes
Olympic	Washington	1909	Finest Pacific Northwest rainforest
Petrified Forest	Arizona	1906	Extensive natural exhibit of petrified wood
Redwood	California	1968	Coastal redwood forests, world's tallest known tree
Rocky Mountain	Colorado	1915	107 named Rocky Mountain peaks over 10,000 ft.
Samoa	American Samoa	1988	Two rainforest preserves and a coral reef
Shenandoah	Virginia	1926	Scenic Skyline Drive
Theodore Roosevelt	North Dakota	1947	Roosevelt Ranch, valley of the Little Missouri River
Virgin Islands	U.S. Virgin Islands	1956	Prehistoric Caribbean Indian relics, beaches
Voyageurs	Minnesota	1971	Wildlife, canoeing, fishing, hiking
Wind Cave	South Dakota	1903	Limestone caverns in the Black Hills, buffalo herd
Wrangell-St. Elias	Alaska	1978	Second highest peak in U.S. (Mt. Elias)
Yellowstone	WY, MT, ID	1872	World's greatest geyser area, falls and canyons
Yosemite	California	1890	Giant sequoias, enormous gorges and waterfalls
Zion	Utah	1909	Multicolored gorge in southwestern Utah desert

Source: The 1991 World Alamanac and Book of Facts, New York © 1990

List 15: Natural Features

1. Cape Cod	13. Mississippi Delta	25. Great Salt Lake
2. Erie Canal	14. Mississippi River	26. Death Valley
3. Catskills	15. Arkansas River	27. Mt. Whitney
4. Niagara Falls	16. Ozarks	28. Sierra Nevada
5. Great Lakes	17. Ohio River	29. Big Sur
6. Chesapeake Bay	18. Missouri River	30. San Francisco Bay
7. Cape Hatteras	19. Black Hills	31. Columbia River
8. Appalachian Mountains	20. Rocky Mountains	32. Mt. St. Helens
9. Okefenokee Swamp	21. Pike's Peak	33. Aleutian Islands
10. Lake Okeechobee	22. Rio Grande	34. Bering Strait
11. Everglades	23. Grand Canyon	35. Mt. McKinley
12. Key West	24. Colorado River	36. Kilauea

List 16: Important Dates and Holidays

IMPORTANT DATES IN THE U.S.

Holiday	Date
Confederate Heroes' Day	January 19
Robert E. Lee's Birthday	January 19
Martin Luther King's Birthday	January 15
Chinese New Year	First new moon after the sun enters Aquarius
National Freedom Day	February 1
Groundhog Day	February 2
Boy Scouts' Day	February 8
Lincoln's Birthday	February 12
Saint Valentine's Day	February 14
Susan B. Anthony Day	February 15
Presidents' Day	February 17
Washington's Birthday	February 22
Leap Year Day	February 29
Johnny Appleseed Day	March 11
Girl Scouts' Day	March 12
April Fool's Day	April 1
World Health Day	April 7
Jefferson's Birthday	April 13
Income taxes due	April 15
Patriots' Day	April 19
National Secretaries' Day	April 23
Arbor Day	April 25
Arbor Day	Last Tuesday in April
May Day	May 1
Law Day	May 1
Lei Day (Hawaii)	May 1
Cinco de Mayo	May 5
Mother's Day	Second Sunday in May
Memorial Day	Last Monday in May
Children's Day	June 8
Flag Day	June 14
Emancipation Day	June 19
Fathers' Day	Third Sunday in June
Independence Day	July 4
Leif Erikson Day	October 9
Columbus Day	October 12
Halloween	October 31
Labor Day	September 1
Grandparents' Day	September 7
Citizenship Day	September 17
World Peace Day	September 21
Election Day	First Tuesday after the first Monday in November
Veterans' Day	November 11
Sadie Hawkins Day	First Sunday after November 11
Native American Day	September 26
Thanksgiving	Fourth Thursday in November
Human Rights Day	December 10
Bill of Rights Day	December 15

MAJOR RELIGIOUS HOLIDAYS IN THE U.S.

Holiday	Date	Religion
Epiphany	January 6	Christian
Three King's Day	January 6	Christian
Eastern Orthodox Christmas	January 7	Christian
Shrove Tuesday (Mardi Gras)	Day before Ash Wednesday	Christian
Ash Wednesday	40 days (excluding Sundays) before Easter	Christian
World Day of Prayer	March 7	Inter-faith
Saint Patrick's Day	March 17	Christian
Palm Sunday	Sunday before Easter	Christian
Purim (Feast of Lots)	14th or 15th of Hebrew month of Adar	Jewish
Good Friday	Friday before Easter Sunday	Christian
Easter Sunday	The first Sunday after the full moon occurring on or after March 21	Christian
Passover (Pesach)	15-22 of Hebrew month of Nisan	Christian & Jewish
Ascension Day	Ten days before Pentecost	Christian
Pentecost	50 days after Easter	Christian
Trinity Sunday	Sunday after Pentecost	Christian
Shavuot (Feast of Weeks)	6th or 7th of Hebrew month of Sivan	Jewish
Rosh Hashanah (New Year)	First day of Hebrew month of Tishri	Jewish
Yom Kippur (Day of Atonement)	10th day of Tishri	Jewish
Sukkot (Tabernacles)	15-21 Tishri	Jewish
All Saint's Day	November 1	Christian
Advent	Four-week period before Christmas	Christian
Baha'U'Llah Birthday	November 12	Baha'i
Saint Lucia's Day	December 13	Christian
Christmas	December 25	Christian
Hanukkah	25th of Hebrew month of Kislev	Jewish

ISLAMIC HOLIDAYS

Note: Because the Muslim calendar, containing only 354 days, is shorter than the Gregorian calendar Islamic holidays do not always fall on the same days of the Gregorian calendar and so are listed seperately.

Holiday	Date
Islamic New Year	First day of Islamic month Muharram
Mawlid an-Nabi (Muhammad's Birthday)	12th of Islamic month of Rabi
Fast of Ramadan	9th month of Islamic calendar
Id al-Fitr (Festival of Fast Breaking)	29th or 30th of Ramadan to 3rd of following month of Shawwal
Beiram (The first day of spring)	10th of Islamic month of Zu'lhijjah
Id al-Adhh (The Great Festival)	10th to 13th of the Islamic month of Zu'lhijjah

Sources: The Encyclopaedia Brittanica, Chicago © 1989
The World Almanac and Book of Facts 1991, New York © 1990
Chase's Annual Events, Contemporary Books, Chicago
Customs and Holidays Around the World by Lavinia Dobler. Fleet Publishing Co., New York © 1962

List 17: Major Religions in the U.S.

MAJOR RELIGIONS POPULATIONS

Group	Population	Percent change since 1960
Protestant	79,296,000	+ 88%
Roman Catholic	53,497,000	- 16%
Moslem	1,500,000	unknown
Jewish (Orthodox, Conservative and Reform)	5,947,000	+ 11%
Eastern Orthodox	3,973,000	+ 47%
Old Catholic, Polish National Catholic and Armenian	829,000	+ 40.5%
Buddhist	100,000	+ 400%
Total members of religious groups	145,142,000	

CENSUS OF MAJOR RELIGIOUS GROUPS

Group	Number of Churches	Membership
Protestant		
Adventist	4,458	696,194
Baptist	90,543	26,101,469
Brethren (German, United and River)	888	100,162
Christian and Missionary Alliance	1,785	244,296
Disciples of Christ	4,195	1,086,668
Churches of Christ	19,238	2,706,786
Christian Methodist Episcopal	2,340	718,922
Church of Christ Scientist	3,000	—
Churches of God	2,797	239,058
Church of the Nazarene	5,080	543,762
Episcopal	7,387	2,462,300
Evangelical Churches	3,349	354,085
Friends (Quakers)	1,254	111,311
Independent Fundament Churches	1,019	120,446
Jehovah's Witnesses	8,547	773,219
Latter-day Saints (Mormons)	9,839	4,194,286
Lutheran	18,776	8,404,028
Mennonite	2,307	233,958
Methodist	51,477	12,656,593
Moravian	183	57,156
New Apostolic	487	36,241
Pentacostal	25,941	1,474,353
Presbyterian	13,751	3,184,007
Reformed	1,693	585,121
Unitarian Universalist	956	173,167
United Church of Christ	6,395	1,662,568
The Wesleyan Church	3,217	185,641
Other Protestant groups	3,467	590,196
Protestant totals	**294,369**	**69,217,877**
Roman Catholic	23,552	53,496,862
Moslems	—	6,000,000

177

Jewish organizations	3,416	5,944,000
Old Catholic, Polish National Catholic	305	346,387
Eastern Orthodox, etc.	1,606	4,241,478
Baha'i Faith	1,700	110,000
Buddhist	100	100,000

POLL RESULTS

When adult Americans were asked in 1988 if they attended a church or synagogue weekly, 42% said yes. The highest percentage was 49% in 1949; the lowest was 37% in 1940.

When adults were asked if they are members of a church or synagogue, 65% said yes. This is the lowest percentage since 1937. The highest was 76% in 1947.

Sources: The World Almanac and Book of Facts 1990, New York © 1989
1989 Yearbook of American and Canadian Churches

List 18: A Brief History of the U.S.

c. 1000   Leif Erikson explores North America.

1492-1502   Columbus explores the Caribbean for Spain in four voyages and publicizes the New World.

1497   John Cabot explores the Northeast American coast to Delaware.

1513   Juan Ponce de Leon explores Florida, searches for the Fountain of Youth.

1519   Cortes conquers Mexico.

1539   Hernando de Soto explores Florida past the Mississippi River.

1540   Coronado and other Spanish explorers explore Northern Mexico, the Southwest U.S. and California.

1607   English found Jamestown.

1609   Henry Hudson explores New York Harbor and the Hudson River. Samuel de Champlain explores Lake Champlain. Santa Fe, New Mexico, founded.

1619   First black laborers brought to Jamestown as indentured servants. Slavery legalized in 1650.

1620   Plymouth Plantation, Massachusetts, founded by the Pilgrims, who came on the *Mayflower*.

1626   Peter Minuet buys Manhattan Island for the Dutch; pays the Indians $24 in trinkets.

1634   Frenchman Jean Nicolet explores the Great Lakes to Lake Michigan.

1636   First college, Harvard, founded. Roger Williams founds Rhode Island with democratic rule and religious toleration.

1654   First Jewish settlers come to New Amsterdam.

1664   British seize Dutch colony of New Netherland and rename it New York.

1673   Father Jacques Marquette and Louis Jolliet explore the upper Mississippi, claiming it for France.

1682   Sieur de La Salle explores the Mississippi south to the Gulf of Mexico.

1692   Witchcraft trials in Salem, Massachusetts.

1704   First regular newspaper, *Boston News Letter*, founded.

1741   Capt. Vitus Bering discovers Alaska for Russia.

1744-1763   French lose Canada and Ohio Valley to British after 20 years of war. Indians fight on both sides.

1754-1776   British attempts to tax and control the colonies cause resentment and rebellion.

1773   Boston Tea Party.

1775   Battles of Lexington and Concord—"The shot heard 'round the world." Capture of Fort Ticonderoga, New York, and the Battle of Bunker Hill in Massachusetts are colonial victories. Gen. George Washington takes charge of the colonial army in Boston.

1776   Colonies declare independence from Britain July 4.

1777   First constitution (Articles of the Confederation) adopted.

1781   British lose Revolutionary War

1784   Peace treaty signed with British.

1787   New constitution written and adopted.

1791   Bill of Rights enacted.

1793   Eli Whitney's invention of the cotton gin makes slavery profitable for the Southern states.

1797   Navy started with three ships.

1803   U.S. under President Thomas Jefferson buys Louisiana from Napoleon.

1804-1806   Lewis and Clark, with Sacagawea, an Indian woman guide, explore the Louisiana Purchase.

1808   Slave importation outlawed. Illegal imports continue until 1860.

1812   War with Britain.

1814   New Capitol and White House in Washington, D.C., are burned by British. Peace treaty of Ghent.

1815   British are defeated in Battle of New Orleans.

1818   Troops under Gen. Andrew Jackson invade Florida to attack the Seminole Indians and weaken the Spanish government.

1819   Spain, whose American empire from Chile and Argentina in the south to Mexico and Florida in the north is collapsing, gives Florida to the U.S.

1823   Monroe Doctrine opposes any new colonies or any European intervention in the Americas.

1825   The Erie Canal, stretching from the Great Lakes to the Hudson River, is completed. The settlement of the Middle

West and the growth of its towns and industries is stimulated. New York, New York, the largest city in the U.S. since 1790, expands rapidly.

1828 "Jacksonian Revolution." The new Democratic Party under Andrew Jackson wins the presidency and takes power in Washington. This first major political change, staged without violence, proves the stability of the government.

1836 Mexican-U.S. struggle for Texas. Mexican Gen. Santa Anna takes the Alamo in San Antonio and is then captured by Sam Houston at San Jacinto. First wagon train of settlers travels from Missouri to California.

1848 Gold discovered in California. Development of the West is accelerated.

1853 Commodore Matthew C. Perry opens trade with Japan for U.S. ships.

1860 Abraham Lincoln elected.

1861 Seven Southern states withdraw from the U.S., set up the Confederate States of America and start the Civil War.

1863 Lincoln legally frees the slaves. Battle of Gettysburg. Lincoln's Gettysburg address.

1865 Civil War ends with Northern victory. President Lincoln assassinated. Thirteenth Amendment abolishes slavery.

1866 Reconstruction of the South. Ku Klux Klan formed secretly.

1867 U.S. buys Alaska from Russia.

1869 Transcontinental railroad completed. Knights of Labor founded.

1871 Chicago fire.

1872 Amnesty Act restores civil rights to the South.

1876 Gen. Custer's last stand: 265 soldiers killed by Dakota Indians. Reconstruction ended in the South.

1886 Haymarket riot and other labor unrest. American Federation of Labor (AFL) formed.

1890 "Battle" of Wounded Knee; 200 Indian men, women and children and 29 U.S. soldiers killed in last major conflict of the Indian wars. Sherman Antitrust Act begins to curb monopolies.

1898 U.S. begins to take an aggressive interest in international affairs. Spanish-American War fought to aid independence of Cuba. U.S. annexes Hawaii.

1899 U.S. attempts to save Chinese independence and make China an international market by declaring the Open Door Policy.

1903 U.S. fosters Panama's independence from Colombia to get treaty to build Panama Canal. Wright brothers fly first airplane at Kitty Hawk.

1906 San Francisco earthquake. Pure Food and Drug and Meat Inspection acts.

1911 Supreme Court breaks up Standard Oil Co. monopoly.

1914 Henry Ford raises pay of his workers from $2.40 for a nine-hour day to $5 for an eight-hour day so they can afford to buy a car.

1915 The Great War in Europe. U.S. remains neutral. Clayton Antitrust Act spurs anti-monopoly suits by federal government. U.S. frees Haiti to make it a "protectorate." U.S. actively supports various factions in Mexican Revolution of 1913-1916. U.S. hegemony expands in Carribbean.

1917 U.S. declares war on Germany. Prohibition amendment submitted; enacted 1919-1933.

1918 World War I ends November 11.

1919 First transatlantic flight.

1920 U.S. refuses to join the League of Nations.

1921 Congress curbs immigration and sets national quotas. Ku Klux Klan revives terror against blacks and Jewish Americans.

1924 Indians are made U.S. citizens.

1925 Scopes Monkey Trial dramatizes the changing understanding of evolution, science versus religion, and education in the U.S.

1926 Robert Goddard fires first fuel rocket.

1927 Marines are sent into China to protect U.S. interests during civil war. Charles Lindbergh crosses Atlantic solo.

1929 St. Valentine's Day Massacre dramatizes the power and violence of gangsters. Stock market crash begins the Great Depression.

1923 Roosevelt initiates new federalist approach to solving the crisis in the economy. To give Americans a "New Deal" and try to end the Depression Roosevelt rapidly increases the size and spending of the federal government over the next eight years.

1935   Committee for Industrial Organization (CIO) forms, promoting stronger unions in auto, steel and other heavy industry. Congress passes the Social Security Act.

1939   World War II begins in Europe. U.S. remains neutral but rearms and supports Britain more and more actively through 1941.

1941   Japan attacks Pearl Harbor December 7. U.S. declares war on Axis Powers (Japan, Germany and Italy).

1945   Germany surrenders May 7. First atomic bomb dropped on Hiroshima August 6. Second atomic bomb destroys Nagasaki August 9. Japan surrenders August 15. United Nations founded.

1946   Philippines given independence by U.S. July 4. Labor unrest.

1947   Truman Doctrine combats communism. The Marshall Plan aids reconstruction in Europe. Congress passes the Taft-Hartley Labor Relations Act over President Truman's veto to curb strikes.

1948   U.S.S.R. blockades West Berlin. British and U.S. break blockade with a massive airlift. Organization of American States founded.

1949   NATO founded for mutual protection of West Europe, Canada and U.S. People's Republic of China established under Mao Tse-tung; U.S. refuses recognition and maintains relations with the Nationalist government in exile in Taiwan (Formosa).

1950   Korean War begins; UN (including U.S.) sides with South Korea against Communist China–backed North Korea. U.S. agrees to give economic and military support to South Vietnam.

1951   Senate investigations, led by Estes Kefauver, expose the power of the Mafia and organized crime. Popular Gen. Douglas MacArthur is fired from his command in Korea.

1953   Peace is declared in Korea. U.S. supports anti-communists with massive aid in Indochina War.

1954   Anti-communist investigations by Sen. Joseph McCarthy end in his condemnation by Senate.

1955   AFL-CIO formed. Rosa Parks refuses to give up her bus seat, beginning a city-wide boycott in Birmingham, Alabama, led by Martin Luther King, Jr. Federal court overthrows bus segregation law. Civil Rights movement gains strength.

1956   Supreme Court requires schools to desegregate.

1957   Congress passes the first civil rights bill since Reconstruction on voting rights.

1958   U.S.S.R.'s successful launch of the first man-made satellite, *Sputnik*, spurs U.S. scientific efforts and the space race. U.S. *Explorer I* launched.

1959   Alaska and Hawaii become states. St. Lawrence Seaway opens.

1960   Congress passes a stronger voting rights bill.

1961   Cuban exiles, with help from the CIA, invade Cuba at the Bay of Pigs; they fail to inspire a revolt and withdraw.

1962   Military advisors sent to Vietnam are permitted to "fire if fired upon." John Glenn is the first American in space.

1963   President John F. Kennedy is assassinated.

1964   Major civil rights legislation is proposed. President Johnson and Congress begin a great increase in government spending on social welfare programs to create Johnson's "Great Society."

1965   President Johnson orders continuous bombing in South Vietnam and sends 184,300 troops. Riots in Watts section of Los Angeles, California.

1966   U.S. fights in North Vietnam and Cambodia.

1967   Riots in Newark, New Jersey, and Detroit, Michigan. 475,000 troops in Vietnam.

1968   Vietnam War peace talks begin in Paris. Martin Luther King, Jr., and Robert Kennedy are assassinated.

1969   President Nixon expands the peace talks and begins phased withdrawal of U.S. troops from Vietnam. Neil Armstrong walks on the moon.

1970   U.S. and South Vietnamese fight in Cambodia.

1972   President Nixon reopens relations with China.

1973   Vietnamese peace pacts signed.

1974   President Nixon resigns when threatened with impeachment for covering up evidence on the 1972 break-in at the Democratic National Committee offices in Watergate in Washington.

1975	South Vietnam, without U.S. military support, falls to North Vietnam.
1978	The U.S. agrees to hand the Panama Canal over to Panama in 1999.
1979	90 hostages are taken in Iran as the Shah's U.S.-backed government falls in a popular uprising. The crisis continues for 444 days.
1981	President Reagan's tax cuts are passed by Congress. The economy grows for nine years, but so does the national debt.
1982	The Equal Rights Amendment, guaranteeing women and others equal rights, fails to be ratified by enough states to change the Constitution. The Space Shuttle *Columbia* successfully returns from space.
1983	281 U.S. and French military personnel serving in a UN peacekeeping force in Lebanon are killed by terrorist bombs. President Reagan and six Carribbean nations send troops into Grenada to restore democratic government.
1984	Marines are withdrawn from Lebanon; civil war continues.

1985	President Reagan and Soviet leader Mikhail Gorbachev hold their first summit. Congress passes Gramm-Rudman bill to try to reduce government spending.
1986	Space Shuttle *Challenger* explodes while the world watches on TV. U.S. war planes attack Libya in response to "state-sponsored terrorism." AIDS is acknowledged as an international health emergency.
1989	President Bush sends troops into Panama and ousts Gen. Manuel Noriega. U.S., U.S.S.R. and their allies declare the end of the Cold War.
1990	U.S. sends troops to Saudi Arabia to protect Middle East allies after Iraqi leader Saddam Hussein seizes Kuwait.
1991	U.S. and other UN forces bomb Iraq and reclaim Kuwait.

List 19: Folk Songs

Places
The Banks of the Ohio
Dixie
Down in the Valley
The Eyes of Texas
Home on the Range
My Old Kentucky Home
Red River Valley
The Sidewalks of New York
The Streets of Laredo

Traveling
Five Hundred Miles
Freight Train
The Golden Vanity
Sloop John B.
The Wabash Cannonball

Work
Blow the Man Down
Drill, Ye Tarriers, Drill
The Erie Canal
Git Along Little Dogies
Goodbye, Old Paint
I've Been Working on the Railroad

Children's Songs
Bingo
Hush Little Baby
This Old Man
Pop Goes the Weasel
Rock-a-Bye Baby
Row, Row, Row Your Boat
Skip to My Lou
Old MacDonald
Three Blind Mice

People
Barbara Allen
Casey Jones
Clementine
Dan Tucker
Go Tell Aunt Rhodie
Jeanie with the Light Brown Hair
John Henry
Oh, Susanna
She'll Be Coming 'Round the Mountain
Sweet Betsy from Pike
Tom Dooley

Love
Black Is the Color of My True Love's Hair
Goodnight Irene
House of the Rising Sun
In the Good Old Summertime
My Bonnie Lies over the Ocean
On Top of Old Smokey

Animals
Blue Tail Fly
The Fox
Froggie Went A-Courtin'
The Old Gray Mare

Play
A Bicycle Built for Two
Camptown Races
For He's a Jolly Good Fellow
Happy Birthday
Mountain Dew
Turkey in the Straw
What Shall We Do with the Drunken Sailor?

Spirituals
Amazing Grace
Joshua Fought the Battle of Jericho
Kum Bay Yah
Nearer My God to Thee
Nobody Knows the Trouble I've Seen
Old Folks at Home
Rock of Ages
Rock-a My Soul
Swing Low, Sweet Chariot
When the Saints Go Marching In

Patriotism
The Battle Hymn of the Republic
When Johnny Comes Marching Home Again
Yankee Doodle

Modern
Blowin' in the Wind
Brother, Can You Spare a Dime?
City of New Orleans
If I Had a Hammer
Old Man River
We Shall Overcome

Source: The Folksinger's Wordbook, by Irwin and Fred Silber. Oak Publications, New York © 1973

List 20: Nursery Rhymes

COMMON NURSERY RHYMES

Humpty Dumpty
Humpty Dumpty sat in a wall,
Humpty Dumpty had a great fall.
All the king's horses and all the king's men
Couldn't put Humpty together again.

There Was an Old Woman
There was an old woman
Who lived in a shoe,
She had so many children
She didn't know what to do.
She gave them some broth,
Without any bread,
Whipped them all soundly
And sent them to bed.

The Cat and the Fiddle
Hey diddle diddle,
The cat and the fiddle,
The cow jumped over the moon.
The little dog laughed to see such sport,
And the dish ran away with the spoon.

Old Mother Hubbard
Old Mother Hubbard went to the cupboard
To get her poor dog a bone.
But when she got there, the cupboard was bare,
And so the poor dog had none.

Jack and Jill
Jack and Jill went up the hill
To fetch a pail of water.
Jack fell down and broke his crown
And Jill came tumbling after.

Baa, Baa, Black Sheep
Baa, baa, black sheep, have you any wool?
Yes, sir, yes, sir, three bags full.
One for my master and one for my dame
And one for the little boy who lives down the lane.
Baa, baa, black sheep, have you any wool?
Yes, sir, yes, sir, three bags full.

Hickory Dickory Dock
Hickory dickory dock,
The mouse ran up the clock.
The clock struck one,
The mouse ran down,
Hickory dickory dock.

Mary Had a Little Lamb
Mary had a little lamb,
Little lamb, little lamb,
Mary had a little lamb
Its fleece was white as snow.
And everywhere that Mary went,
Mary went, Mary went,
Everwhere that Mary went
The lamb was sure to go.

Old King Cole
Old King Cole was a merry old soul,
And a merry old soul was he.
He called for his pipe
And he called for his bowl
And he called for his fiddlers three.
Every fiddler had a very fine fiddle
And a very fine fiddle had he.
Oh, there's none so rare as can compare
With King Cole and his fiddlers three.

Rain, Rain, Go Away
Rain, rain, go away,
Come again some other day.

Rock-a-bye Baby
Rock-a-bye, baby, on the treetop
When the wind blows the cradle will rock.
When the bough breaks, the cradle will fall,
And down will come baby, cradle and all.

Thirty Days
Thirty days hath September,
April, June and November.
All the rest have thirty-one,
Save February which alone
Has twenty-eight and one day more
When Leap Year comes one year in four.

Solomon Grundy
Solomon Grundy,
Born on Monday,
Christened on Tuesday,
Married on Wednesday,
Sick on Thursday,
Worse on Friday,
Died on Saturday,
Buried on Sunday.
That was the end
Of Solomon Grundy.

One, Two, Buckle My Shoe
One, two, buckle my shoe,
Three, four, open the door,
Five, six, pick up sticks,
Seven, eight, lay them straight.
Nine, ten, a big fat hen,
Eleven, twelve, dig and delve,
Thirteen, fourteen, maids a-courting,
Fifteen, sixteen, maids in the kitchen,
Seventeen, eighteen, maids a-waiting,
Nineteen, twenty, food's a-plenty,
My plate is empty.

ABCs
A, b, c, d, e, f, g,
H, i, j, k, l, m, n, o, p,
Q, r, s, t, u, v,
W, x, y and z.
Now I know my ABCs,
Next time won't you sing with me.

OTHERS

Bow, Wow, Wow, Whose Dog Art Thou?
Bye, Baby Bunting
Cock-a-doodle Doo
Cock Robin
Diddle, Diddle, Dumpling, My Son John
Doctor Foster Went to Gloucester
Georgie Porgie
Goosey Goosey Gander
Hark, Hark, the Dogs Do Bark
Here We Go Round the Mulberry Bush
Hot Cross Buns
Jack Be Nimble
Jack Sprat
Little Bo Peep
Little Boy Blue
Little Jack Horner
Little Miss Muffet
Mistress Mary, Quite Contrary

Now I Lay Me Down to Sleep
Old Mother Goose
Pat-a-cake, Pat-a-cake, Baker's Man
Pease Porridge Hot
Peter, Peter, Pumpkin Eater
Pussy Cat, Pussy Cat
The Queen of Hearts
Ride A Cock Horse
Ring around the Roses
Simple Simon
Sing a Song of Sixpence
There Was a Crooked Man
This is the House That Jack Built
Three Little Kittens
Tom, Tom, the Piper's Son
To Market, to Market, to Buy a Fat Pig
Wee Willie Winkie
What Are Little Boys Made of?

TONGUE TWISTERS

Peter Piper picked a peck of pickled peppers,
A peck of pickled peppers Peter Piper picked.
If Peter Piper picked a peck of pickled peppers,
Where's the peck of pickled peppers Peter Piper
    picked?

She sells sea shells by the seashore.
The shells she sells are seashore shells.

Round and round the rough and ragged rock the
ragged rascal ran.

Rubber baby buggy bumpers

The sixth sheik's sixth sheep's sick.

Betty bought some butter, "But," she said, "this
butter's bitter, and a bit of better butter would
make a better batter." So she bought a bit of butter
better than the bitter butter, and it made her
batter better—so it was that Betty bought a bit of
better butter!

A tutor who tooted a flute
Tried to teach two tooters to toot.
    Said the two to the tutor,
    "Is it harder to toot or
To tutor two tooters to toot?"

Source: Tongue Twisters by Charles Keller, Simon and Schuster, Inc., New York © 1989

List 21: Light Verse

LIGHT VERSE

The Owl and the Pussy-cat

The Owl and the Pussy-cat went to sea
    In a beautiful pea-green boat.
They took some honey, and plenty of money,
    Wrapped up in a five-pound note.
The Owl looked up to the stars above,
    And sang to a small guitar,
"O lovely Pussy! O Pussy, my love,
      What a beautiful Pussy you are,
        You are,
        You are!
    What a beautiful Pussy you are!

Pussy said to Owl, "You elegant fowl!
    How charmingly sweet you sing!
O let us be married! too long we have tarried:
    But what shall we do for a ring?"
They sailed away, for a year and a day,
    To the land where the Bong-tree grows
And there in a wood a Piggy-wig stood
    With a ring at the end of his nose,
        His nose,
        His nose,
    With a ring at the end of his nose.

"Dear Pig, are you willing to sell for one shilling
    Your ring?" Said the Piggy, "I will."
So they took it away, and were married next day
    By the Turkey who lives on the hill.
They dined on mince, and slices of quince,
    Which they ate with a runcible spoon;
And hand in hand, on the edge of the sand,
    They danced by the light of the moon,
        The moon,
        The moon,
    They danced by the light of the moon.
            —Edward Lear, 1851

Wynken, Blynken, and Nod

Wynken, Blynken, and Nod one night
    Sailed off in a wooden shoe,—
Sailed on a river of crystal light
    Into a sea of dew.
"Where are you going, and what do you wish?"
    The old moon asked the three.

"We have come to fish for the herring-fish
    That live in this beautiful sea;
    Nets of silver and gold have we,"
        Said Wynken,
        Blynken,
        And Nod.

The old moon laughed and sang a song,
    As they rocked in the wooden shoe;
And the wind that sped them all night long
    Ruffled the waves of dew;
The little stars were the herring-fish
    That lived in the beautiful sea.
"Now cast your nets wherever you wish,—
    Never afraid are we!"
    So cried the stars to the fishermen three,
        Wynken,
        Blynken,
        And Nod.

All night long their nets they threw
    To the stars in the twinkling foam,—
Then down from the skies came the wooden shoe,
    Bringing the fishermen home:
'Twas all so pretty a sail, it seemed
    As if it could not be;
And some folk thought 'twas a dream they'd dreamed
    Of sailing that beautiful sea;
    But I shall name you the fishermen three:
        Wynken,
        Blynken,
        And Nod.

Wynken and Blynken are two little eyes,
    And Nod is a little head,
And the wooden shoe that sailed the skies
    Is a wee one's trundle-bed;
So shut your eyes while Mother sings
    Of wonderful sights that be,
And you shall see the beautiful things
    As you rock in the misty sea
    Where the old shoe rocked the fishermen three:—
        Wynken,
        Blynken,
        And Nod.
            —Eugene Field

LIGHT VERSE (CONTINUED)

As I Was Going to Saint Ives
As I was going to Saint Ives
I met a man with seven wives.
Every wife had seven sacks,
Every sack had seven cats,
Every cat had seven kits.
Kits, cats, sacks and wives,
How many were going to Saint Ives?

Paul Revere's Ride
Listen my children, and you shall hear
Of the midnight ride of Paul Revere,
On the eighteenth of April in Seventy-five;
Hardly a man is now alive
Who remembers that famous day and year . . .
                    —Henry Wadsworth Longfellow

NONSENSE VERSE

Jabberwocky
'Twas brillig, and the slithy toves
    Did gyre and gimble in the wabe;
All mimsy were the borogroves,
    And the mome raths outgrabe.

"Beware the Jabberwock, my son!
    The jaws that bite, the claws that catch!
Beware the Jubjub bird, and shun
    The frumious Bandersnatch!"

He took his vorpal sword in hand;
    Long time the manxome foe he sought—
So rested he by the Tumtum tree,
    And stood awhile in thought.

And, as in uffish thought he stood,
    The Jabberwock, with eyes of flame,
Came whiffling through the tulgey wood,
    And burbled as it came!

One, two! One, two! And through and through
    The vorpal blade went snicker-snack!
He left it dead, and with its head,
    He went galumphing back.

"And hast thou slain the Jabberwock?
    Come to my arms, my beamish boy!
O frabjous day! Callooh! Callay!"
    He chortled in his joy.

'Twas brillig, and the slithy toves
    Did gyre and gimble in the wabe;
All mimsy were the borogroves,
    And the mome raths outgrabe.
                    —Lewis Carroll, 1871

The Jumblies
They went to sea in a sieve, they did;
    In a sieve they went to sea;
In spite of all their friends could say,
On a winter's morn, on a stormy day,
    In a sieve they went to sea.
And when the sieve turned round and round,
And everyone cried, "You'll be drowned!"
They called aloud, "Our seive ain't big,
But we don't care a button, we don't care a fig—
    In a seive we'll go to sea!"
       Far and few, far and few,
         Are the lands where the Jumblies live.
       Their heads are green, and their hands are blue;
         And they went to sea in a sieve.
                    —Edward Lear, 1871

Sources: The Norton Anthology of English Literature, W. W. Norton & Company © 1986
Golden Treasury of Poetry, Louis Untermeyer, ed. Golden Press, New York © 1989

List 22: American Literature

1776-1830

Cooper, James Fenimore	(1789-1851)	The Last of the Mohicans
Franklin, Benjamin	(1706-1790)	Poor Richard's Almanack
Irving, Washington	(1783-1859)	"Rip Van Winkle," "Legend of Sleepy Hollow"
Paine, Thomas	(1737-1809)	Common Sense, The Crisis

THE AMERICAN RENAISSANCE (1830-1870)

Alcott, Louisa May	(1832-1888)	Little Women
Emerson, Ralph Waldo	(1803-1882)	Essays, Nature
Fuller, Margaret	(1810-1850)	Woman in the Nineteenth Century
Hawthorne, Nathaniel	(1804-1864)	The Scarlet Letter
Melville, Herman	(1819-1891)	Moby Dick, Billy Budd
Poe, Edgar Allen	(1809-1849)	The Fall of the House of Usher
Stowe, Harriet Beecher	(1811-1896)	Uncle Tom's Cabin
Thoreau, Henry David	(1817-1862)	Walden

MODERN LITERATURE (1870-1940)

Anderson, Sherwood	(1876-1941)	Winesburg, Ohio
Cather, Willa	(1876-1947)	Death Comes for the Archbishop
Chopin, Kate	(1851-1904)	The Awakening
Crane, Stephen	(1871-1900)	The Red Badge of Courage
Dreiser, Theodore	(1871-1945)	Sister Carrie
Faulkner, William	(1897-1962)	The Sound and the Fury
Fitzgerald, F. Scott	(1896-1940)	The Great Gatsby
Hemingway, Ernest	(1899-1961)	The Sun Also Rises
Henry, O.	(1862-1910)	The Gift of the Magi
James, Henry	(1843-1916)	Portrait of a Lady, The Bostonians
Lewis, Sinclair	(1885-1951)	Babbit, Main Street, Arrowsmith
London, Jack	(1876-1916)	The Call of the Wild, Sea Wolf
Mitchell, Margaret	(1900-1949)	Gone with the Wind
Pasternak, Boris	(1890-1960)	Doctor Zhivago
Porter, Katherine Ann	(1890-)	Flowering Judas; Pale Horse, Pale Rider
Sinclair, Upton	(1878-1968)	The Jungle
Stein, Gertrude	(1874-1946)	Three Lives
Steinbeck, John	(1902-1968)	The Grapes of Wrath
Tarkington, Booth	(1869-1946)	Seventeen, Penrod
Twain, Mark	(1835-1910)	Huckleberry Finn, Tom Sawyer
Wharton, Edith	(1862-1937)	Ethan Frome, The Age of Innocence
Williams, William Carlos	(1883-1963)	Tempers
Wodehouse, P.G.	(1881-1975)	Anything Goes
Wolfe, Thomas	(1900-1938)	You Can't Go Home Again
Wright, Richard	(1908-1960)	Native Son, Black Boy

CONTEMPORARY LITERATURE (1940-)

Baldwin, James	(1924-)	The Fire Next Time
Bellow, Saul	(1915-)	Herzog
Bradbury, Ray	(1920-)	Farenheit 451
Capote, Truman	(1924-1984)	In Cold Blood
Cheever, John	(1912-1982)	The Wapshot Chronicle
Doctorow, E. L.	(1931-)	Ragtime
Ellison, Ralph	(1914-)	The Invisible Man
Heller, Joseph	(1923-)	Catch-22
Hersey, John	(1914-)	A Bell for Adano
Lee, Harper	(1926-)	To Kill a Mockingbird
Mailer, Norman	(1923-)	The Naked and the Dead
Malamud, Bernard	(1914-1986)	The Fixer, The Natural
McCullers, Carson	(1917-1967)	The Heart is a Lonely Hunter
McMurtry, Larry	(1936-)	Lonesome Dove, Leaving Cheyenne
Michener, James	(1907-)	Tales of the South Pacific
Nabokov, Vladimir	(1899-1977)	Lolita
Oates, Joyce Carol	(1938-)	Do with Me What You Will
Pynchon, Thomas	(1937-)	Gravity's Rainbow
Rand, Ayn	(1905-1982)	Atlas Shrugged
Roth, Philip	(1933-)	Portnoy's Complaint, Zuckerman Unbound
Salinger, J. D.	(1919-)	Catcher in the Rye
Updike, John	(1932-)	Rabbit, Run
Vonnegut, Kurt	(1922-)	Slaughterhouse Five, Jailbird
Walker, Alice	(1944-)	The Color Purple
Warren, Robert Penn	(1905-1989)	All the King's Men
Welty, Eudora	(1909-)	The Optimist's Daughter

POETS

Benét, Stephen Vincent	(1898-1943)	John Brown's Body
Bradstreet, Anne	(c.1612-1672)	The Tenth Muse Lately Sprung up in America
Brooks, Gwendolyn	(1917-)	The Bean Eaters, "Malcolm X"
cummings, e. e.	(1894-1962)	Tulips and Chimneys
Dickinson, Emily	(1830-1886)	"There's a Certain Slant of Light"
Eliot, T. S.	(1888-1965)	"The Waste Land," "Four Quartets"
Frost, Robert	(1874-1963)	"Birches," "Mending Fence"
Ginsberg, Allen	(1926-)	"Howl"
Jeffers, Robinson	(1887-1966)	"Shine Perishing Republic," "Hurt Hawks"
Longfellow, Henry W.	(1807-1882)	"Evangeline," "Hiawatha"
Nash, Ogden	(1902-1971)	I'm a Stranger Here Myself
Parker, Dorothy	(1893-1967)	Laments for the Living
Plath, Sylvia	(1932-1963)	The Colossus
Poe, Edgar Allen	(1809-1849)	"The Raven"
Pound, Ezra	(1885-1972)	The Cantos
Riley, James Whitcomb	(1849-1916)	"When the Frost is on the Pumpkin"
Robinson, Edward A.	(1869-1935)	"Richard Cory"
Sandberg, Carl	(1878-1967)	Chicago Poems
Teasdale, Sara	(1884-1933)	"Helen of Troy"
Millay, Edna St. Vincent	(1892-1950)	A Few Figs from Thistles
Warren, Robert Penn	(1905-1989)	"Brother to Dragons"
Whitman, Walt	(1819-1892)	"Song of Myself"

PLAYWRIGHTS

Albee, Edward	(1928-)	Who's Afraid of Virginia Woolf?
Baraka, Imamu Amiri	(1934-)	Dutchman, The Slave
Hart, Moss	(1904-1961)	Once in a Lifetime
Hellman, Lillian	(1904-1984)	The Little Foxes
Hughes, Langston	(1902-1967)	Shakespeare in Harlem
Mamet, David	(1947-)	American Buffalo
Miller, Arthur	(1915-)	Death of a Salesman
Odets, Clifford	(1906-1963)	Waiting for Lefty, The Golden Boy
O'Neill, Eugene	(1888-1953)	Long Day's Journey into Night
Saroyan, William	(1980-1981)	The Human Comedy
Shepard, Sam	(1943-)	True West, Buried Child
Sherwood, Robert	(1896-1955)	The Petrified Forest
Simon, Neil	(1927-)	Barefoot in the Park
Wilder, Thornton	(1897-1975)	Our Town
Williams, Tennessee	(1911-1983)	A Streetcar Named Desire

Sources: The World Almanac and Book of Facts 1991, New York © 1990
The 1990 Information Please Almanac, Boston © 1989
The Encyclopaedia Brittanica, Chicago © 1989

List 23: A Few Famous Quotations

Early to bed and early to rise, makes a man healthy, wealthy and wise.
Nothing is certain but death and taxes.
There never was a good war or a bad peace.

Benjamin Franklin, *Poor Richard's Almanack*, 1732–1757

Taxation without representation is tyranny.　　　　**James Otis, 1761**

By uniting we stand, by dividing we fall.　　　　**John Dickinson, 1775**

Give me liberty or give me death.　　　　**Patrick Henry, 1775**

Don't one of you fire until you see the whites of their eyes.　　　　**William Prescott, 1775**

We must all hang together, else we shall all hang seperately.　　　　**Benjamin Franklin, 1776**

I only regret that I have but one life to give for my country.　　　　**Nathan Hale, 1776**

I have just begun to fight.　　　　**John Paul Jones, 1779**

These are the times that try men's souls.　　　　**Thomas Paine, 1785**

To be prepared for war is one of the most effectual means of preserving peace.

George Washington, 1790

There is always room at the top.　　　　**Daniel Webster**

Be sure you are right, then go ahead.　　　　**Davy Crockett, 1812**

Don't give up the ship.　　　　**Capt. James Lawrence, 1813**

Go West, young man.　　　　**John L. B. Soule, 1851**

The mass of men lead lives of quiet desperation.　　　　**Henry David Thoreau, 1854**

It is well that war is so terrible—we would grow too fond of it.　　　　**Robert E. Lee, 1862**

You can fool all of the people some of the time and some of the people all of the time, but you can't fool all
of the people all of the time.　　　　**Abraham Lincoln, 1863**

The true republic—men, their rights and nothing more; women, their rights and nothing less.

Susan B. Anthony, 1868

There's a sucker born every minute.　　　　**P.T. Barnum**

Politics makes strange bedfellows.　　　　**Charles Dudley Warner, 1871**

There's many a boy here today who looks on war as all glory, but, boys, it is all hell.

Gen. William T. Sherman, 1888

Everybody talks about the weather, but nobody does anything about it.　　　　**Charles Warner, 1890**

SOME FAMOUS QUOTATIONS (CONTINUED)

The report of my death was an exaggeration.   **Mark Twain, 1897**

Speak softly and carry a big stick; you will go far.   **Theodore Roosevelt, 1901**

Win one for the Gipper.   **Knute Rockne, 1921**

You are all a lost generation.   **Gertrude Stein, 1926**

What this country really needs is a good five-cent cigar.   **Thomas Riley Marshall**

Never give a sucker an even break.   **W. C. Fields**

I tell you, Folks, all Politics is Apple Sauce.   **Will Rogers, 1932**

I never forget a face, but in your case I'll make an exception.   **Groucho Marx**

The only thing we have to fear is fear itself.   **Franklin D. Roosevelt, 1933**

A radical is a man with both feet firmly in the air.   **Franklin D. Roosevelt, 1939**

Here's looking at you, kid.
Play it, Sam.   **Humphrey Bogart, *Casablanca*, 1943**

You can never be too rich or too thin.   **Wallis Simpson, Duchess of Windsor**

The world is run by C students.
The buck stops here.   **Harry S. Truman, 1945**

Fasten your seatbelts; it's going to be a bumpy night.   **Bette Davis, *All About Eve*, 1950**

Ask not what your country can do for you; ask what you can do for your country.
                                                               John F. Kennedy, 1961

You win some, you lose some, and some get rained out.   **C. E. Wood**

One small step for a man, one giant step for mankind.   **Neil Armstrong, 1969**

I cried all the way to the bank.   **Liberace, 1973**

Nice guys finish last.   **Leo Durocher, 1975**

Sometimes when I look at all my children, I say to myself, "Lillian, you should have stayed a virgin."
                                                               Lillian Carter, 1980

How do I know why there were Nazis? I don't even know how to work the can opener.
                                                               Woody Allen, *Hannah and Her Sisters*, 1986

Sources: The Harper Book of American Quotations, Gordon Carruth and Eugene Ehrlich, eds. Harper &
         Row, New York © 1988
         Wit and Wisdom of Famous American Women, Evelyn Beilenson and Ann Tenenbaum, eds.
         Peter Pauper Press, Inc., White Plains © 1986

List 24: Proverbs

Note: The list of proverbs has been correlated with the list of Topics. Obviously, the assignment of a proverb to a particular semantic category can be done according to several different criteria. We have assigned the proverbs mostly on the basis of their literal, rather than figurative, meaning.

Food
Half a loaf is better than none.
Variety is the spice of life.
The bread is buttered on both sides.

Cooking
Too many cooks spoil the broth.
The pot calls the kettle black.
Out of the frying pan and into the fire.

Eating
Don't bite the hand that feeds you.
You can't eat your cake and have it too.
First come, first served.

Housing/Housekeeping
There's no place like home.
People in glass houses shouldn't throw stones.
Walls have ears.

Clothing
Too big for their britches.
If the shoe fits, wear it.
A stitch in time saves nine.

Relationships
Every man for himself.
A friend in need is a friend indeed.
Familiarity breeds contempt.
Live and let live.
It takes one to know one.
Two is company, three is a crowd.
Spare the rod and spoil the child.

Human Qualities
He who hesitates is lost.
Honesty is the best policy.
Haste makes waste.
Where there's a will, there's a way.
Beauty is only skin deep.
Beggars can't be choosers.

Human Stages
A sucker is born every minute.
Don't throw out the baby with the bath water.
Boys will be boys.
Never say die.
Dead men tell no tales.

Time
Time heals all wounds.
Never put off until tomorrow what you can do
    today.
Rome was not built in a day.
Better late than never.
Here today, gone tomorrow.
Last but not least.

Weather
Save it for a rainy day.
Make hay while the sun shines.

Animals
You can't make a silk purse out of a sow's ear.
Don't throw pearls before swine.
His bark is worse than his bite.
Let sleeping dogs lie.
You can't teach an old dog new tricks.
Curiosity killed the cat.
Let the cat out of the bag.
There are many ways to skin a cat.
When the cat's away the mice will play.
You can lead a horse to water but you can't make
    it drink.
Don't look a gift horse in the mouth.

Birds
The early bird catches the worm.
Kill two birds with one stone.
A bird in the hand is worth two in the bush.
Birds of a feather flock together.
Don't count your chickens before they hatch.

Language
Easier said than done.
No sooner said than done.
Ask me no questions and I'll tell you no lies.
Actions speak louder than words.

Thinking
Seeing is believing.
Out of sight, out of mind.
Necessity is the mother of invention.
Let your conscience be your guide.
Two heads are better than one.

Numbers
Six of one and half-dozen of another.
Give them an inch and they'll take a mile.

Substances and Materials
A rolling stone gathers no moss.
All that glitters is not gold.
Good riddance to bad rubbish.
Every little bit helps.

Containers
Don't put all your eggs in one basket.
One rotten apple spoils the barrel.

Emotions
Love makes the world go 'round.
Absence makes the heart grow fonder.
It's no use crying over spilled milk.
Better safe than sorry.
Misery loves company.
Once bitten, twice shy.
He who laughs last, laughs best.

The Body
In one ear and out the other.
Don't cut off your nose to spite your face.
Blood is thicker than water.
Look before you leap.

Transportation
Don't put the cart before the horse.
Like carrying coals to Newcastle.

Money
Money doesn't grow on trees.
Money talks.
Money is the root of all evil.
A penny saved is a penny earned.
The best things in life are free.
Easy come, easy go.

Recreation
All work and no play makes Jack a dull boy.
The more the merrier.

Sports and Games
Slow and steady wins the race.
Sink or swim.
If you can't beat 'em, join 'em.
Practice makes perfect.

Medicine and health
An apple a day keeps the doctor away.
An ounce of prevention is worth a pound of cure.

Business
Nothing ventured, nothing gained.
Everyone has their price.
Business before pleasure.
The customer is always right.

Shops and Tools
Jack of all trades, master of none.
Hit the nail on the head.

Law
Truth will out.
Two wrongs don't make a right.
The end justifies the means.

Media
Bad news travels fast.
No news is good news.
The pen is mightier than the sword.
Don't judge a book by its cover.

Education
Practice what you preach.
Do as I say, not as I do.

War
Don't give up the ship.
All is fair in love and war.

Energy
Where there's smoke, there's fire.
Burn the candle at both ends.

Source: The Dictionary of American Proverbs, David Kin, ed. Philosophical Library.

List 25: Superstitions

The **ace of spades** is a sign of death.

Getting out of **bed** on the wrong side means you will have a bad day.

Letting a **black cat** cross your path brings bad luck.

The **bride** should not see the **husband** on the morning before the wedding.

Cattle lying down indicate rain.

A four-leaf **clover** brings good luck.

A **cricket** in the house is good luck.

Hanging a **horseshoe** over the door, points up, brings good luck.

Passing under a **ladder** brings bad luck.

Killing a **ladybug** beetle brings bad luck.

Lightning never strikes twice in the same place.

Lighting three cigarettes from one **match** brings bad luck or pregnancy to the third person.

Breaking a **mirror** brings seven years of bad luck.

Finding a **penny** brings good luck ("see a penny, pick it up, all day long you'll have good luck").

Carrying a **rabbit's foot** brings good luck.

Spilling **salt** brings bad luck, but a pinch of the spilled salt thrown over your right shoulder will keep away evil spirits.

Killing a **spider** brings rain.

If you make a wish on a falling **star**, your wish will come true.

The number **thirteen** brings bad luck.

Opening an **umbrella** in the house brings bad luck.

List 26: Curses and Oaths

Note: A word of caution is in order. This list is included for the purpose of comprehension. It is ill-advised to attempt to use these curses and oaths until one is thoroughly acculturated. The words in this list are not all equally offensive, but they are all potentially dangerous if not used properly.

MILD WORDS AND PHRASES

Cripes	Heck
Dang	Holy cow
Dang it	Holy smoke
Darn	I'll be darned
Darn it	Jeez
Fudge	Phooey
Gee	Shoot
Golly	Shucks
Gosh	Son of a gun
Heavens	Sugar

MILD INSULTS

Boob	Good for nothing
Buffoon	Harebrained
Bum	Hopeless
Chicken	Idiot
Clown	Jerk
Cow	Nerd
Crazy	Nincompoop
Creep	Nut
Dog	Pig
Doofus	Scaredy cat
Dork	Silly
Dumb	Stupid
Dumbbell	Turkey
Dummy	Useless
Flake	Weenie
Fool	Witch
'Fraidy cat	Worthless

STRONG WORDS AND PHRASES

Christ	God
Crap	God damn it
Damn	Hell
Damn it	Jesus Christ
Frigging	Jesus H. Christ
Fuck	Shit
Fucking A	Son of a bitch (SOB)

STRONG INSULTS

Ass
Asshole
Bastard
Bitch
Cocksucker
Dick
Dumb fuck
Dumb shit
Eat me
Eat shit
Fuck face
Fucking asshole
Fuck you
Fucker
Go fuck yourself

Go to hell
Mother fucker
Piss off
Prick
Queer
Screw you
Shithead
Shove it up your ass
Slut
Son of a bitch
Suck my dick
Up yours
Whore
Yellow bellied

List 27: Names

Most Common First Names (Given to babies in 1990)*

Rank	Girls			Rank	Boys		
1	Jessica	13	Amber	1	Michael	13	Brandon
2	Ashley	14	Lauren	2	Christopher	14	Jason
3	Amanda	15	Danielle	3	Matthew	15	Justin
4	Jennifer	16	Michelle	4	David	16	Jonathan
5	Sarah	17	Christina	5	Daniel	17	Nicholas
6	Stephanie	18	Crystal	6	Joshua	18	Anthony
7	Nicole	19	Laura	7	Andrew	19	William
8	Brittany	20	Kimberly	8	James	20	Eric
9	Heather	21	Rachel	9	Robert	21	Steven
10	Melissa	22	Amy	10	Ryan	22	Adam
11	Megan	23	Tiffany	11	John	23	Kyle
12	Elizabeth	24	Samanatha	12	Joseph	24	Kevin
		25	Emily			25	Brian

Common Women's Names

Alice	Catherine	Gail	Jean	Linda	Paula
Alison	Claire	Hannah	Jill	Margaret	Patricia
Ann	Deborah	Helen	Joan	Mary	Rebecca
Anita	Diane	Jackie	Judith	Marilyn	Susan
Barbara	Donna	Jane	Karen	Martha	Ruth
Carol	Ellen	Janet	Kathleen	Nancy	Virginia

Common Men's Names

Albert	Dennis	George	Patrick	Roger	Stanley
Alexander	Donald	Gerald	Paul	Ronald	Stewart
Allan	Douglas	Henry	Peter	Roy	Theodore
Arthur	Edward	Lawrence	Ralph	Samuel	Thomas
Benjamin	Frank	Louis	Raymond	Saul	Timothy
Charles	Fredrick	Mark	Richard	Scott	Walter

The Sixty Most Common Surnames (Ranked)**

Smith(son)	Harris(on)	Lewis	Morris(on)	Mitchell	Rivera
Johnson	Thomas(on)	Robinson	King	Philips(on)	Hernandez
Williams(on)	Taylor	Walker	Wright	Campbell	Edwards
Brown	Moore	Gonzalez	Hill	Carter	Murphy
Jones	Jackson	Hall	Nelson	Evans	Rogers
Martin(ez)	White	Lee	Green	Lopez	Cook
Miller	Thompson	Peters(on)	Richards(on)	Turner	Perez
Davis(on)	Rodreguez	Allens(on)	Scott	Stewart	Griffin
Anderson	Clark(son)	Young	Baker	Collins	Christian(son)
Wilson	Roberts(on)	Garcia	Adams(on)	Parker	Morgan

Sources: *The Baby Name Countdown by Janet Schwegel. Paragon House © 1990

   **Social Security Administration, Data and Research. The names of everyone given a S.S. Number from 1936 through September 1984 have been included in the count.

List 28: Place Names

COMMON PLACE NAMES

Washington	Springfield	Stratford
Jefferson	Longmeadow	Portland
Madison	Edgewood	Columbia
Monroe	Elmwood	Lebanon
Jackson	Pleasantville	New Haven
Lincoln	Summerville	Riverdale
Franklin	Bloomington	Troy
Lafayette	Canton	Hanover
Leesburg	Elkton	Salem
Libertyville	Evanston	Richmond
Independence	Hampton	London
Brookfield	Lexington	Dover
Deerfield	Princeton	Plymouth
Fairfield	Wheaton	Highland Park
Greenfield	Guilford	Newport

ENGLISH ELEMENTS OF COMMON PLACE NAMES

Note: Indian, Spanish and French place names are also common, e.g., Massachusetts, Mississippi, Santa Fe, San Francisco, New Orleans, Vermont. However, the practice of building place names from standard elements prefixed and/or suffixed to family names is typically English, e.g., East *Hart*ford Junction.

North	-	-	town	-	City
East	-	-	ton	-	Village
South	-	-	ville	-	Park
West	-	-	apolis	-	Valley
New	-	-	burg	-	Junction
Great	-	-	bury	-	Hills
Little	-	-	boro(ugh)	-	Heights
Fort	-	-	minster	-	Mills
Port	-	-	stead	-	Locks
Brook	-	-	sex	-	Lake
Glen	-	-	ford	-	Beach
Mount	-	-	land	-	Point
Saint	-	-	wood	-	Haven
Oak	-	-	forest	-	Harbor
Elm	-	-	field	-	Shores
Pine	-	-	vale	-	Rock
Maple	-	-	dale	-	Bluffs
Cedar	-	-	crest	-	Falls
		-	port	-	Creek
		-	side	-	Rapids
		-	view	-	Springs
		-	bridge	-	Ferry

List 29: Sports Teams

MAJOR INDOOR SOCCER LEAGUE (1989)

Baltimore	Blast
Dallas	Sidekicks
Kansas City	Comets
Los Angeles	Lazers
San Diego	Sockers
Tacoma	Stars
Wichita	Wings

MAJOR LEAGUE BASEBALL

AMERICAN LEAGUE
Eastern Division

Baltimore	Orioles
Boston	Red Sox
Cleveland	Indians
Detroit	Tigers
Milwaukee	Brewers
New York	Yankees
Toronto	Blue Jays

Western Division

California	Angels
Chicago	White Sox
Kansas City	Royals
Minnesota	Twins
Oakland	Athletics (A's)
Seattle	Mariners
Texas	Rangers

NATIONAL LEAGUE
Eastern Division

Chicago	Cubs
Montreal	Expos
New York	Mets
Philadelphia	Phillies
Pittsburgh	Pirates
Saint Louis	Cardinals

Western Division

Atlanta	Braves
Cincinnati	Reds
Houston	Astros
Los Angeles	Dodgers
San Diego	Padres
San Francisco	Giants

NATIONAL HOCKEY LEAGUE

WALES CONFERENCE
Patrick Division

New Jersey	Devils
New York	Islanders
New York	Rangers
Philadelphia	Flyers
Pittsburgh	Penguins
Washington	Capitals

Adams Division

Boston	Bruins
Buffalo	Sabres
Hartford	Whalers
Montreal	Canadiens
Quebec	Nordiques

CAMPBELL CONFERENCE
Norris Division

Chicago	Black Hawks
Detroit	Red Wings
Minnesota	North Stars
St. Louis	Blues
Toronto	Maple Leafs

Smythe Division

Calgary	Flames
Edmonton	Oilers
Los Angeles	Kings
Vancouver	Canucks
Winnepeg	Jets

NATIONAL BASKETBALL ASSOCIATION

EASTERN CONFERENCE
Atlantic Division

Boston	Celtics
Miami	Heat
New Jersey	Nets
New York	Knickerbockers (Knicks)
Philadelphia	'76ers
Washington	Bullets

Central Division

Atlanta	Hawks
Chicago	Bulls
Cleveland	Cavaliers
Detroit	Pistons
Indiana	Pacers
Milwaukee	Bucks
Orlando	Magic

WESTERN CONFERENCE
Midwest Division

Charlotte	Hornets
Dallas	Mavericks
Denver	Nuggets
Houston	Rockets
Minnesota	Timberwolves
San Antonio	Spurs
Utah	Jazz

Pacific Division

Golden State	Warriors
Los Angeles	Clippers
Los Angeles	Lakers
Phoenix	Suns
Portland	Trail Blazers
Sacramento	Kings
Seattle	SuperSonics

NATIONAL FOOTBALL LEAGUE

NATIONAL CONFERENCE
Eastern Division

Dallas	Cowboys
New York	Giants
Philadelphia	Eagles
Phoenix	Cardinals
Washington	Redskins

Central Division

Chicago	Bears
Detroit	Lions
Green Bay	Packers
Minnesota	Vikings
Tampa Bay	Buccaneers

Western Division

Atlanta	Falcons
Los Angeles	Rams
New Orleans	Saints
San Francisco	'49ers

AMERICAN CONFERENCE
Eastern Division

Buffalo	Bills
Indianapolis	Colts
Miami	Dolphins
New England	Patriots
New York	Jets

Central Division

Cincinnati	Bengals
Cleveland	Browns
Houston	Oilers
Pittsburgh	Steelers

Eastern Division

Denver	Broncos
Kansas City	Chiefs
Los Angeles	Raiders
San Diego	Chargers
Seattle	Seahawks

Sources: The World Almanac and Book of Facts 1991, New York © 1990
The 1990 Information Please Almanac, Boston © 1989

List 30: Sports Personalities

BASEBALL

Aaron, Hank	(1934-)
Bench, Johnny	(1947-)
Berra, Yogi	(1925-)
Boggs, Wade	(1958-)
Brett, George	(1953-)
Carew, Rod	(1945-)
Cobb, Ty	(1886-1961)
Dean, Dizzy	(1911-1974)
DiMaggio, Joe	(1914-)
Durocher, Leo	(1906-)
Gehrig, Lou	(1903-1941)
Gibson, Josh	(1911-1947)
Grove, Lefty	(1900-1975)
Hornsby, Rogers	(1896-1963)
Jackson, Reggie	(1946-)
Koufax, Sandy	(1935-)
Mantle, Mickey	(1931-)
Mays, Willie	(1931-)
Musial, Stan	(1920-)
Ott, Mel	(1909-1958)
Paige, Satchel	(1906-1982)
Ruth, Babe	(1895-1948)
Ryan, Nolan	(1947-)
Schmidt, Mike	(1949-)
Spahn, Warren	(1921-)
Stengel, Casey	(1895-1975)
Wagner, Honus	(1874-1955)
Williams, Ted	(1918-)
Yastrzemski, Carl	(1939-)
Young, Cy	(1867-1955)

BASKETBALL

Abdul-Jabbar, Kareem	(1947-)
Baylor, Elgin	(1934-)
Bird, Larry	(1956-)
Chamberlain, Wilt	(1936-)
Cousy, Bob	(1928-)
Erving, Julius	(1950-)
Havlicek, John	(1940-)
Johnson, Earvin "Magic"	(1959-)
Jordan, Michael	(1963-)
Malone, Moses	(1955-)
Mikan, George	(1924-)
Petit, Bob	(1932-)
Robertson, Oscar	(1938-)
Russell, Bill	(1934-)
West, Jerry	(1938-)

FOOTBALL

Blanda, George	(1927-)
Bradshaw, Terry	(1948-)
Brown, Jim	(1936-)
Bryant, Paul "Bear"	(1913-1983)
Ditka, Mike	(1939-)
Dorsett, Tony	(1954-)
Graham, Otto	(1921-)
Grange, Red	(1903-1991)
Lombardi, Vince	(1913-1970)
Marino, Dan	(1961-)
Montana, Joe	(1956-)
Nagurski, Bronco	(1908-1990)
Namath, Joe	(1943-)
Payton, Walter	(1954-)
Rockne, Knute	(1883-1931)
Simpson, O. J.	(1947-)
Stagg, Amos Alonzo	(1862-1965)
Starr, Bart	(1934-)
Staubach, Roger	(1942-)
Tarkenton, Fran	(1940-)
Unitas, Johnny	(1933-)

GOLF

Berg, Patty	(1918-)
Boros, Julius	(1920-)
Hagen, Walter	(1892-1969)
Hogan, Ben	(1912-)
Jones, Bobby	(1902-1971)
Lopez, Nancy	(1957-)
Nelson, Byron	(1912-)
Nicklaus, Jack	(1940-)
Palmer, Arnold	(1929-)
Snead, Sam	(1912-)
Trevino, Lee	(1934-)
Watson, Tom	(1949-)
Whitworth, Kathy	(1939-)
Wright, Mickey	(1935-)

FIGURE SKATING

Boitano, Brian	
Button, Dick	(1929-)
Fleming, Peggy	(1948-)
Hamill, Dorothy	(1957?-)
Hamilton, Scott	(1958-)
Henie, Sonja	(1912-1969)

BOXING

Ali, Muhammad	(1942-)
Corbett, James J.	(1866-1933)
Dempsey, Jack	(1895-1983)
Frazier, Joe	(1944-)
Leonard, Sugar Ray	(1956-)
Louis, Joe	(1914-1981)
Marciano, Rocky	(1923-1969)
Patterson, Floyd	(1935-)
Robinson, Sugar Ray	(1920-)
Sullivan, John L.	(1858-1918)
Tunney, Gene	(1897-1978)
Tyson, Mike	(1966-)

TRACK AND FIELD

Beamon, Bob	(1946-)
Benoit, Joan	(1957-)
Griffith Joyner, Florence	(1959-)
Jenner, Bruce	(1949-)
Johnson, Rafer	(1935-)
Lewis, Carl	(1961-)
Moses, Edwin	(1956-)
Oerter, Al	(1936-)
Owens, Jesse	(1913-1980)
Rudolph, Wilma	(1940-)
Ryun, Jim	(1947-)
Tyus, Wyomia	(1945-)
Thorpe, Jim	(1888-1953)
Zaharias, Babe Didrikson	(1914-1956)

TENNIS

Ashe, Arthur	(1943-)
Austin, Tracy	(1962-)
Budge, Don	(1915-)
Bueno, Maria	(1939-)
Connelly, Maureen	(1934-1969)
Connors, Jimmy	(1952-)
Evert, Chris	(1954-)
Gonzalez, Pancho	(1928-)
Gibson, Althea	(1927-)
King, Billie Jean	(1943-)
Kramer, Jack	(1921-)
Marble, Alice	(1913-)
McEnroe, John	(1959-)
Navratilova, Martina	(1956-)
Tilden, Bill	(1893-1953)
Wills, Helen	(1906-)

HOCKEY

Clarke, Bobby	(1949-)
Gretzky, Wayne	(1961-)
Howe, Gordie	(1928-)
Hull, Bobby	(1939-)
Lemieux, Mario	(1965-)
Morenz, Howie	(1902-1937)
Orr, Bobby	(1948-)
Richard, Maurice	(1921-)
Robinson, Larry	(1951-)
Shore, Eddie	(1902-1985)

MISCELLANEOUS

Andretti, Mario	(1940-)	Stock car driving
Arcaro, Eddie	(1916-)	Horse racing
Biondi, Matt	(1965-)	Swimming
Butcher, Susan	(195?-)	Dogsled racing
Evans, Janet	(197?-)	Swimming
Foyt, A. J.	(1935-)	Stock car driving
Heiden, Eric	(1954-)	Speed skating
Louganis, Greg	(1960-)	Diving
Meagher, Mary T.	(1964-)	Swimming
Petty, Richard	(1937-)	Stock car driving
Pincay, Laffit	(1946-)	Horse racing
Plante, Jacques	(1929-1986)	Soccer
Retton, Mary Lou	(1968-)	Gymnastics
Shoemaker, Bill	(1931-)	Horse racing
Spitz, Mark	(1950-)	Swimming
Unser, Al	(1939-)	Stock car racing
Unser, Bobby	(1934-)	Stock car racing
Weissmuller, Johnny	(1903-)	Swimming

Source: The 1991 World Almanac and Book of Facts, New York © 1990

List 31: U.S. School System

GRADE SCHOOL

Name of School	Grade	Age of Students	Subjects
Nursery		3–5	Games, songs, creative playing
Kindergarten	K	4–6	Games, drawing, crafts, beginning reading and writing
Elementary Grades 1–5 or 6	1	5–7	Reading, writing, spelling, adding, drawing, music
	2	6–8	Language arts, subtraction, spelling, drawing, music
	3	7–9	Language arts, social studies, multiplication, music
Middle Grades 5 or 6–9	4	8–10	Language arts, social studies, division
	5	9–11	Language arts, social studies, fractions
	6	10–12	Language arts, social studies, decimals, science
Junior High	7	11–13	Language arts, social studies, math, science, foreign language, manual arts, home economics
	8	12–14	Language arts, social studies, math, science, foreign language, manual arts, home economics
High School Freshman	9	13–15	**Core Courses:** English, algebra, civics, biology, foreign language **Electives:** Music, art, typing, bookkeeping, economics, technical education, home economics
Sophmore	10	14–16	**Core Courses:** English, geometry, history, chemistry, foreign language **Electives:** Music, art, typing, bookkeeping, economics, technical education, home economics
Junior	11	15–17	**Core Courses:** English, advanced math, history, physics, foreign language **Electives:** Music, art, typing, bookkeeping, economics, technical education, home economics
Senior	12	16–18	**Core Courses:** English, calculus, history, foreign language **Electives:** Music, art, typing, bookkeeping, economics, technical education, home economics

COLLEGES

College	Age	Degree	Length of time
Junior college	17–		Two-year degree
College	18–	BA, BS	4–5 years
Graduate school	21–	MA, MS	2–3 years plus thesis
		PhD, LHD, Litt. D., DCL	3 years plus thesis
Medical school		MD, DDS	2 years plus residency
Law school		JS	3 years

List 32: Television

TRADITIONAL PROGRAMMING

Morning
Game shows
Daytime talk shows
Cartoons (weekends)
News programs/weather
Religious programs (Sunday)
Children's/educational programs

Afternoon
Movies
Game shows
Daytime talk shows
Afternoon soap operas
Sports events (weekends)
News programs/weather/sports
Children's/educational programs

Evenings
Movies
Documentaries
Special reports
Drama programs
Situation comedies
Evening soap operas
News programs/weather/sports

Late night
Movies
Talk shows
News programs

TELEVISION SETS

	Numbers	Percent
Total TV Households:	92,100,000	98
Homes with:		
Color TV sets	90,100,000	98
B&W only	2,000,000	2
2 or more sets	59,865,000	65
One set	32,235,000	35
Cable	53,970,600	58.6

FAVORITE SHOWS

1950s
A. Godfrey's Talent Scouts
I Love Lucy
You Bet Your Life
Dragnet
The Jack Benny Show
A. Godfrey and Friends
Gunsmoke
The Red Skelton Show
December Bride
I've Got a Secret
$64,000 Question
Disneyland
The Ed Sullivan Show
Have Gun—Will Travel
The Danny Thomas Show

1960s
Bonanza
The Red Skelton Show
The Andy Griffith Show
The Beverly Hillbillies
The Ed Sullivan Show
The Lucy Show/Here's Lucy
The Jackie Gleason Show
Bewitched
Gomer Pyle
Candid Camera
The Dick Van Dyke Show
The Danny Thomas Show
Family Affair
Laugh-in
Rawhide

1970s
All in the Family
M*A*S*H
Hawaii Five-O
Happy Days
The Waltons
The Mary Tyler Moore Show
Sanford & Son
One Day at a Time
Three's Company
60 Minutes
Maude
Gunsmoke
Charlie's Angels
The Jeffersons
Laverne & Shirley

1989
Bill Cosby Show
Cheers
Roseanne
A Different World
America's Funniest Home Videos
Golden Girls
Wonder Years
Empty Nest
60 Minutes
Unsolved Mysteries
L.A. Law
Who's the Boss?
Grand
Murder, She Wrote
NBC Sunday Night Movie

Source: 1991 World Almanac and Book of Facts, New York © 1990

List 33: U.S. Publications

MAGAZINES

Rank	Magazine	Circulation
1	Reader's Digest	16,452,422
2	TV Guide	16,302,705
3	National Geographic Magazine	10,574,562
4	Better Homes and Gardens	8,143,083
5	Family Circle	5,922,530
6	Woman's Day	5,571,573
7	Good Housekeeping	5,217,147
8	McCall's	5,142,460
9	Ladies' Home Journal	5,086,710
10	Time	4,648,450
11	National Enquirer	4,285,700
12	Redbook	3,950,489
13	Star	3,682,796
14	Playboy	3,555,663
15	People Weekly	3,349,401
16	Sports Illustrated	3,329,415
17	Newsweek	3,227,391
18	Prevention	3,136,447
19	Cosmopolitan	2,760,010
20	U.S. News & World Report	2,300,197
21	Southern Living	2,288,695
22	Smithsonian	2,262,015
23	Glamour	2,190,027
24	Penthouse	2,108,256
25	Field & Stream	2,032,020
26	Country Living	1,833,816
27	Money	1,821,625
28	Parents Magazine	1,772,633
29	Ebony	1,764,993
30	Seventeen	1,752,308
31	Life	1,749,936
32	Popular Mechanics	1,668,096
33	1,001 Home Ideas	1,536,706
34	Globe	1,525,745
35	Outdoor Life	1,514,400
36	Sunset, The Magazine of Western Living	1,430,860
37	The Workbasket	1,402,785
38	US Magazine	1,379,602
39	Bon Appetit	1,344,050
40	New Woman	1,332,586
41	Golf Digest	1,314,434
42	True Story	1,300,829
43	Mademoiselle	1,283,242
44	Rolling Stone	1,273,681
45	The Family Handyman	1,260,373

Source: The World Almanac and Book of Facts 1991, New York © 1990

TOP U.S. DAILY NEWSPAPERS

Rank	Newspaper	Circulation
1	New York (NY) *Wall Street Journal*	1,835,713
2	Arlington (VA) *USA Today*	1,325,507
3	New York (NY) *Daily News*	1,194,237
4	Los Angeles (CA) *Times*	1,107,623
5	New York (NY) *Times*	1,068,217
6	Washington (DC) *Post*	772,749
7	Chicago (IL) *Tribune*	720,155
8	Long Island (NY) *Newsday*	700,174
9	Detroit (MI) *News*	690,422
10	Detroit (MI) *Free Press*	626,434
11	San Francisco (CA) *Chronicle*	560,640
12	Chicago (IL) *Sun-Times*	535,864
13	Boston (MA) *Globe*	516,031
14	New York (NY) *Post*	507,568
15	Philadelphia (PA) *Inquirer*	504,903
16	Newark (NJ) *Star-Ledger*	463,738
17	Houston (TX) *Chronicle*	437,481
18	Cleveland (OH) *Plain Dealer*	433,615
19	Miami (FL) *Herald*	427,954
20	Minneapolis (MN) *Star Tribune*	406,292
21	St. Louis (MO) *Post-Dispatch*	376,888
22	Dallas (TX) *Morning News*	371,537
23	Boston (MA) *Herald*	358,218
24	Denver (CO) *Rocky Mountain News*	345,943
25	Orange County-Santa Ana (CA) *Register*	343,899
26	St. Petersburg (FL) *Times*	349,460
27	Houston (TX) *Post*	325,407
28	Phoenix (AZ) *Arizona Republic*	322,534
29	Buffalo (NY) *News*	312,246
30	Portland (OR) *Oregonian*	310,446
31	Atlanta (GA) *Constitution*	284,015
32	New Orleans (LA) *Times-Picayune*	276,195
33	Kansas City (MO) *Times*	275,844
34	Milwaukee (WI) *Journal*	275,632
35	San Jose (CA) *Mercury News*	274,484
36	Tampa (FL) *Tribune*	268,681
37	San Diego (CA) *Union*	268,450
38	Orlando (FL) *Sentinel*	266,549
39	Sacramento (CA) *Bee*	259,497
40	Columbus (OH) *Dispatch*	252,206
41	Denver (CO) *Post*	240,162
42	Baltimore (MD) *Sun*	238,533
43	Charlotte (NC) *Observer*	236,496
44	Indianapolis (IN) *Star*	234,888
45	Seattle (WA) *Times*	233,106
46	Pittsburgh (PA) *Press*	232,282
47	Philadelphia (PA) *Daily News*	232,129
48	Louisville (KY) *Courier-Journal*	231,042
49	Hartford (CT) *Courant*	227,763
50	Dallas (TX) *Times Herald*	225,691

Source: The World Almanac and Book of Facts 1991, New York © 1990

List 34: Leading U.S. Advertisers

Rank	Advertiser	Ad Spending
1	Philip Morris	$ 2,058,200,000
2	Procter & Gamble	1,506,900,000
3	General Motors	1,294,000,000
4	Sears, Roebuck	1,045,200,000
5	RJR Nabisco	814,500,000
6	Grand Metropolitan	773,900,000
7	Eastman Kodak	735,900,000
8	McDonald's	728,300,000
9	PepsiCo	712,300,000
10	Kellogg	683,100,000
11	Anheuser-Busch	634,500,000
12	K mart	632,000,000
13	Werner-Lambert	609,200,000
14	Unilever	607,500,000
15	Nestle	573,800,000
16	Ford Motor	569,800,000
17	American Telephone & Telegraph	547,500,000
18	Chrysler	474,000,000
19	General Mills	470,100,000
20	Johnson & Johnson	468,800,000
21	Bristol-Myers Squibb	430,700,000
22	J. C. Penney	426,600,000
23	Quaker Oats	423,400,000
24	Ralston Purina	421,000,000
25	Time Warner	409,700,000
26	May Department Stores	399,700,000
27	American Home Products	393,200,000
28	Coca-Cola	385,100,000
29	H. J. Heinz	340,100,000
30	Mars	339,700,000
31	Sara Lee	326,900,000
32	Macy	308,900,000
33	Colgate-Polmolive	306,600,000
34	Walt Disney	300,600,000
35	Hershey Foods	298,600,000
36	U.S. Government	295,100,000
37	General Electric	276,600,000
38	Toyota Motor	272,900,000
39	SmithKline Beecham	264,200,000
40	Schering-Plough	262,200,000
41	Campeau	260,500,000
42	American Cyanamid	256,200,000
43	American Stores	250,500,000
44	American Express	247,200,000
45	Honda Motor	243,300,000
46	Tandy	232,000,000
47	Dayton Hudson	230,200,000
48	Pfizer	230,100,000
49	Nissan Motor	224,900,000
50	IBM	214,400,000

Source: The World Almanac and Book of Facts 1991, New York © 1990

List 35: National Documents

DECLARATION OF INDEPENDENCE
Thomas Jefferson, 1776

When in the Course of human Events, it becomes necessary for one People to dissolve the Political Bands which have connected them with another, and to assume among the Powers of the Earth, the separate and equal Station to which the Laws of Nature and of Nature's God entitle them, a decent Respect to the Opinions of Mankind requires that they should declare the causes which impel them to the Separation.

We hold these Truths to be self-evident, that all Men are created equal, that they are endowed by their Creator with certain unalienable Rights, that among these are Life, Liberty and the Pursuit of Happiness— That to secure these Rights, Governments are instituted among Men, driving their just Powers from the Consent of the Governed, that whenever any Form of Government becomes destructive of these Ends, it is the Right of the People to alter or to abolish it, and to institute new Government, laying its Foundation on such Principles, and organizings its Powers in such Form, as to them shall seem most likely to affect their Safety and Happiness. Prudence, indeed, will dictate that Governments long established should not be changed for light and transient Causes; and accordingly all Experience hath shewn, that Mankind are more disposed to suffer while Evils are sufferable, than to right themselves by abolishing the Forms to which they are accustomed. But when a long Train of Abuses and Usurpations, pursuing invariably the same Object, evinces a Design to reduce them under absolute Despotism, it is their Right, it is their Duty, to throw off such Government, and to provide new Guards for their future Security.

THE PREAMBLE OF THE CONSTITUTION, 1787

We the People of the United States, in order to form a more perfect Union, establish Justice, insure domestic Tranquility, provide for the common Defense, promote the general Welfare, and secure the Blessings of Liberty to ourselves and our Posterity, do ordain and establish this Constitution for the United States of America.

THE BILL OF RIGHTS
The Ten Original Constitutional Amendments, 1791

First Amendment
Congress shall make no law respecting an establishment of religion, or prohibiting the free excercise thereof; or abridging the freedom of speech, or of the press; or the right of the people peaceably to assemble, and to petition the Government for a redress of grievances.

Second Amendment
A well-regulated militia, being necessary to the security of a free State, the right of the people to keep and bear arms, shall not be infringed.

Third Amendment
No soldier shall, in time of peace be quartered in any house, without the consent of the owner, nor in time of war, but in a manner to be prescribed by law.

Fourth Amendment
The right of the people to be secure in their persons, houses, papers, and effects, against unreasonable searches and seizures, shall not be violated, and no warrants shall issue, but upon probable cause, supported by oath or affirmation, and particularly describing the place to be searched, and the persons or things to be seized.

210

THE BILL OF RIGHTS (CONTINUED)

Fifth Amendment

No person shall be held to answer for a capital, or otherwise infamous crime, unless on a presentment or indictment of a Grand Jury, except in cases arising in the land or naval forces, or in the militia, when in actual service in time of war or public danger; nor shall any person be subject for the same offense to be twice put in jeopardy of life or limb; nor shall be compelled in any criminal case to be a witness against himself, nor be deprived of life, liberty, or property, without due process of law; nor shall private property be taken for public use without just compensation.

Sixth Amendment

In all criminal prosecutions, the accused shall enjoy the right to a speedy and public trial, by an impartial jury of the State and district wherein the crime shall have been committed, which district shall have been previously ascertained by law, and to be informed of the nature and cause of the accusation; to be confronted with the witnesses against him; to have compulsory process for obtaining witnesses in his favor, and to have the assistance of counsel for his defense.

Seventh Amendment

In suits at common law, where the value in controversy shall exceed twenty dollars, the right of trial by jury shall be preserved, and no fact tried by a jury shall be otherwise reexamined in a court of the United States, than according to the rules of the common law.

Eighth Amendment

Excessive bail shall not be required, nor excessive fines imposed, nor cruel and unusual punishments inflicted.

Ninth Amendment

The enumeration in the Constitution, of certain rights, shall not be construed to deny or disparage others retained by the people.

Tenth Amendment

The powers not delegated to the United States by the Constitution, nor prohibited by it to the States, are reserved to the States respectively, or to the people.

THE NATIONAL ANTHEM
The Star-Spangled Banner
Francis Scott Key, 1814

O say, can you see, by the dawn's early light,
What so proudly we hail'd at the twilight's last gleaming?
Whose broad stripes and bright stars, thro' the perilous fight,
O'er the ramparts we watch'd, were so gallantly streaming?
And the rockets' red glare, the bombs bursting in air,
Gave proof thro' the night that our flag was still there,
O say, does that star-spangled banner yet wave
O'er the land of the free and the home of the brave?

O thus be it ever when free men shall stand
Between their loved homes and the war's desolation;
Blest with victory and peace, may the heaven-rescued land
Praise the power that hath made and preserved us a nation.

THE NATIONAL ANTHEM (CONTINUED)

Then conquer we must, for our cause it is just,
And this be our motto: "In God is our trust!"
And the star spangled banner in triumph shall wave
O'er the land of the free and the home of the brave.

THE GETTYSBURG ADDRESS
Abraham Lincoln, 1863

Fourscore and seven years ago our fathers brought forth on this continent a new nation, conceived in liberty and dedicated to the proposition that all men are created equal.

Now we are engaged in a great civil war, testing whether that nation or any nation so conceived and so dedicated can long endure. We are met on a great battlefield of that war. We have come to dedicate a portion of that field, as a final resting place for those who here gave their lives that that nation might live. It is altogether fitting and proper that we should do this.

But, in a larger sense, we cannot dedicate—we cannot consecrate—we cannot hallow—this ground. The brave men, living and dead, who struggled here, have consecrated it, far above our poor power to add or detract. The world will little note, nor long remember, what we say here, but it can never forget what they did here. It is for us the living, rather, to be here dedicated to the great task remaining before us—that from these honored dead we take increased devotion to that cause for which they gave the last full measure of devotion—that we here highly resolve that these dead shall not have died in vain—that this nation, under God, shall have a new birth of freedom—and that government of the people, by the people, for the people, shall not perish from the earth.

STATUE OF LIBERTY INSCRIPTION
The New Colossus
Emma Lazarus

Not like the brazen giant of Greek fame,
With conquering limbs astride from land to land;
Here at our sea-washed, sunset gates shall stand
A mighty woman with a torch, whose flame
Is the imprisoned lightning, and her name
Mother of Exiles. From her beacon-hand
Glows world-wide welcome; her mild eyes command
The air-bridged harbor that twin cities frame.
"Keep ancient lands, your storied pomp!" cries she
With silent lips. "Give me your tired, your poor,
Your huddled masses yearning to breathe free,
The wretched refuse of your teeming shore.
Send these, the homeless, tempest-tost to me,
I lift my lamp beside the golden door!"

AMERICA THE BEAUTIFUL
Katherine Lee Bates, 1893

O beautiful for spacious skies,
For amber waves of grain,
For purple mountain's majesties
Above the fruited plain.
America! America!
God shed his grace on thee,
And crown thy good with brotherhood
From sea to shining sea.

"I HAVE A DREAM"
Martin Luther King, 1963

Five score years ago, a great American, in whose symbolic shadow we stand, signed the Emancipation Proclamation. This momentous decree came as a great beacon of hope to millions of Negro slaves who had been seared in the flames of withering injustice. It came as a joyous daybreak to end the long night of captivity.

But one hundred years later, we must face the tragic fact that the Negro is still not free.

I say to you today, my friends, that in spite of difficulties and frustrations of the moments, I still have a dream. It is a dream deeply rooted in the American dream.

I have a dream that one day this nation will rise up and live out the true meaning of its creed: "We hold these truths to be self evident; that all men are created equal."

I have a dream that one day on the red hills of Georgia the sons of former slaves and the sons of former slaveowners will be able to sit down together at the table of brotherhood.

I have a dream that one day even the state of Mississippi, a desert state sweltering with the heat of injustice and oppression, will be transformed into an oasis of freedom and justice.

I have a dream that my four little children will one day live in a nation where they will not be judged by the color of their skin but by the content of their character.

I have a dream today.

I have a dream that one day the state of Alabama, whose governor's lips are presently dripping with the words of interposition and nullification, will be transformed into a situation where little black boys and girls will be able to join hands with little white boys and white girls and walk together as sisters and brothers.

I have a dream today.

I have a dream that one day every valley shall be exalted, every hill and mountain shall be made low, the rough places will be made plains, and the crooked places will be made straight, and the glory of the Lord shall be revealed, and all flesh shall see it together.

This is our hope. This is the faith with which I return to the South. With this faith we will be able to hew out of the mountain of despair a stone of hope. With this faith we will be able to transform the jangling discords of our nation into a beautiful symphony of brotherhood. With this faith we will be able to work together, to pray together, to struggle together, to go to jail together, to stand up for freedom together, knowing that we will be free one day.

This will be the day when all God's children will be able to sing with new meaning:

My country, 'tis of thee,
Sweet land of liberty,
Of thee I sing:
Land where my fathers died,
Land of the pilgrims' pride,
From every mountain side
Let freedom ring.

And if America is to be a great nation, this must become true. So let freedom ring from the prodigious hilltops of New Hampshire. Let freedom ring from the mighty mountains of New York. Let freedom ring from the

"I HAVE A DREAM" (CONTINUED)

heightening Alleghenies of Pennsylvania. Let freedom ring from the snowcapped Rockies of Colorado. Let freedom ring from the curvaceous peaks of California. But not only that; let freedom ring from Stone Mountain of Georgia. Let freedom ring from Lookout Mountain of Tennessee. Let freedom ring from every hill and molehill of Mississippi. From every mountainside, let freedom ring.

When we let freedom ring, when we let it ring from every village and every hamlet, from every state and every city, we will be able to speed up that day when all of God's children, black men and white men, Jews and Gentiles, Protestants and Catholics, will be able to join hands and sing in the words of the old Negro spiritual, "Free at last, free at last, thank God almighty, we are free at last!"

PLEDGE OF ALLEGIANCE

I pledge allegiance to the flag of the United States of America and to the republic for which it stands, one nation under God, indivisible, with liberty and justice for all.

The Metalinguistic Aspect and Miscellaneous Materials

Contents

List 1: Glossary of Grammatical Terms

Absolute construction

A word or phrase which modifies the sentence as a whole, not any single element in it.
The game over, the players left the field.
The cattle having been branded, the cowboys saddled up and rode off.

Active

See **Voice**

Adjective

A word which modifies a noun or a pronoun.
The old man walked across the narrow street.

Adjective clause

A dependent clause serving an adjective function. See **Relative clause.**
The woman who performed lives next door to me.

Adjective phrase

A word or group of words that functions as an adjective.
dull, exceedingly dull, so very dull

Adverb

A word which modifies a verb, an adjective, or another adverb.
The car moved slowly in very heavy traffic.

Adverbial

A word or group of words which functions as an adverb.
He works in a large university.
It rained very hard.
He was happy when his friend arrived.

Adverbial clause

A dependent clause serving an adverbial function, Common adverbial clauses include:
Comparison (as...as, as...than)
I can't run as fast as I used to.
Concession (though, although, even if)
Although I had a good time, I was happy to leave.
Condition - See **Conditional sentences.**
Purpose (so as to, in order to, so that, in order that)
We are going to France to learn French.
Reason (because, as, since)
They turned on the lights because it was too dark.
Result (so...that, such ...that)
He spoke so fast that no one understood a thing.
Time (when, as, while, until, as soon as)

As soon as he lit his cigar, people began to leave the room.

Agreement

Correspondence between grammatically related elements. Agreement in number and person between a subject and its verb.
(The children play.   The child plays.)
Agreement in gender, number, and person between a pronoun and its antecedent.
(The girl washed her face.)

Antecedent

The word to which a pronoun refers.
Aunt Mary fainted when she heard the news.

Appositive

A word, phrase, or clause used as a noun and placed next to another noun to modify it.
George Washington, the president, slept here.

Article

A and **an** are indefinite articles. **The** is the definite article.

Auxiliary

Function words which help other verbs indicate tense, mood, or voice (be, do, have). Modal auxiliaries *(can, may, might, must, should, etc.)* serve also as structural signals and have a meaning of their own *(ability, obligation, possibility.)*

Case

English has the remnants of three cases: *subjective, possessive,* and *objective.* Nouns are inflected for case in the possessive *(John's).* Some pronouns and the relative pronoun *who* are inflected.
subjective: *I, he, she, we, they, who.*
possessive: *my (mine), your (yours), his, her (hers), its, our (ours), their (theirs), whose.*
objective: *me, him, her, us, them, whom.*

Clause

A group of words containing a subject and a predicate. See Independent clause and Dependent clause.

Collective noun

A noun singular in appearance which indicates a class or group of persons or things. *(a committe of citizens, an army)*

216

Comparative

The form of adjectives and adverbs which is used to indicate relative superiority

tall	**taller**	*less tall*
important	**more important**	*less important*
slowly	**more slowly**	*less slowly*

Complement

A word or group of words used to complete a predicate. Predicate nominatives, predicate adjectives, direct objects, and indirect objects are complements.

Compound sentence

A sentence which combines two or more independent clauses.

He whistled, and she worked.

Complex sentence

A sentence which contains one or more dependent clauses.

He whistled while she worked.

Compound complex sentence

A sentence which contains two or more independent clauses and one or more dependent clauses.

He whistled and she worked until they both got tired.

Conditional sentences

Conditional sentences have two parts, the conditional clause and the main clause. There are three types:

1. Real condition:

If you bother the cat, it will scratch you.

2. Unreal, contrary-to-fact condition (present):

If I were you, I would keep the money.
If you took a trip, where would you go?

3. Unreal, contrary-to-fact condition (past):

If I had known you were coming, I would have baked you a cake.
If I had been Lincoln, I wouldn't have gone to the theater that night.

Conjunction

A word used to connect sentences or sentence parts. See also **Coordinating conjunctions, Subordinating conjunctions.**

Connective

See **Conjunction.**

Conjunctive adverbs

Adverbs used to relate two independent clauses separated by a semicolon:

then, consequently, however, moreover, therefore, etc.

Coordinating Conjunctions

The simple conjunction that connect sentences and sentence parts of equal rank:

and, but, or, nor, for, yet, so.

Correlative conjunctions

Pairs of conjunctions which join sentence parts:

either...or, neither...nor, not only...but also, but...and.

Count noun

A noun that can be made plural, usually by adding **-s.**

Demonstrative adjectives and pronouns

Words used to point out someone or something: *this, that, these, those.* Also called demonstrative determiners.

Dependent (subordinate clause)

A group of words which contains both a subject and a predicate but which does not stand alone as a sentence. A dependent clause always serves a noun, adverb, or adjective function. See **Noun clause, Adjective clause, Adverbial clause, Relative clause.**

Determiners

A class of modifiers which includes articles *(a, an, the),* possessives *(my, John's, his),* demonstratives *(this, that),* interrogatives *(which, what),* indefinite *(some, any),* numerals, and *each, every.*

Diphthong

Two vowel sounds joined in one syllable to form one speech sound:

out, oil, I.

Direct object

A noun, pronoun, or other substantive which receives the action of the verb.

*Jack climbed the **beanstalk** into the sky.*

Direct speech

Repeats the speaker's exact words, enclosing them in quotation marks.

He said, "I've lost my umbrella."

Elliptical clause

A clause in which one or more words necessary for the full subject-predicate structure are omitted but "understood."

*The manager admired no one else as much as (**he admired**—"understood") her.*

Expletive

The *it* or *there* which serves to fill the subject slot in *it is, there is,* and *there are* sentences.

***It is** easy to understand.*
***There is** a fly in my soup.*

217

Finite verb

A verb in the present or past form, e.g., the finite forms of the verb *be* are *is, am, are, was,* and *were.* The non-finite forms are *be, being,* and *been.*

Function words

Words which establish grammatical relationships within a sentence: articles, auxiliaries, conjunctions, prepositions, pronouns, determiners, intensifiers, and interjections.

Future

I will work, I shall work, I am going to work, I work tomorrow, etc.

Gender

The quality of nouns and pronouns that determines the choice between masculine, female, or neuter *(he, she, it.)*

Gerund

See **Verbal.**

Idiom

An expression that does not conform to general grammatical patterns but is established through usage as the way of conveying a given meaning.

hold up, hold down, be beside oneself, kick the bucket.

Indefinite pronouns

Pronouns not pointing out a particular person, thing, or definite quantity. *Some, any, each, every, everyone, everybody, nobody, anyone, anybody, one, neither* are among the most common.

Independent clause

A group of word which contains a subject and a predicate and which can stand alone as a sentence.

Indirect object

A word which indirectly receives the action of the verb.

*The witch gave **the pretty girl** a poisoned apple.*

Indirect speech

Paraphrases of the speaker's words.

He said he had lost his umbrella.

Infinitive

See **Verbal.**

Inflection

Changes in the form of words to reflect changes in grammatical relationships: *the cabins; he walks; she's talking; quickest.*

Intensifier

Words that modify adjectives or adverbs and express degree: ***very** beautiful, **quite** young, **rather** old.*

Intensive pronoun

A reflexive pronoun ending in ***-self, -selves,*** and used for emphasis.

*I'd rather do it **myself.***

Interjection

A word used to exclaim or to express emotion: *ah, oh, ouch.*

Interrogative pronouns

Who, whose, whom, what, which, when used in questions.

Intonation

The rising and falling of the pitch of the voice in speech.

Intransitive verb

A verb which has no direct object

*The tide **turned** at noon.*

Linking verb

A verb which does not express action but links the subject to another word which names or describes it. *Be, become, seem, appear,* and *look* are common linking verbs.

Mass noun (Non-count noun)

A noun that refers to a quantity and cannot be preceded by a cardinal number, such as *three: sugar, milk, hunger.*

Modifier

A word, phrase, or clause which limits or describes other sentence elements or the sentence as a whole.

Mood

The classification of verb forms as

indicative (plain or factual):

I am ready;

imperative (request or command):

Be ready at six; and

subjunctive (hypothetical or contrary-to-fact):

I wish you were ready.

Nominal

Any structure that functions as a noun.

Nominative case

See **Case, subjunctive.**

Non-restrictive relative clause

A clause which provides further information not essential to identification of the subject or complement and is set off usually with commas.

*John Jones, **who spends a lot of money,** has many friends.*

Noun

A word which names and classifies people, animals, things, ideas.

Thomas Jefferson, lemon, religion, alligator, Paris, worm, justice, school, committee.

Noun clause

A dependent clause serving a nominal function.

*Everyone agrees **that the play was a success.***

Noun phrase

The element in the sentence which functions as subject, object, or complement.

***The pretty girl standing in the corner** is my sister.*

***She and her friends** never dance.*

Number

Choice of appropriate forms to indicate singular or plural.

Object of a preposition

Completes the idea of time, position, direction, etc., begun by a preposition.

*at his **desk,** towards the **door***

Objective complement

A complement after the direct object that provides another name for the object or otherwise amplifies it.

*They elected him **president.***

*The war made many women **widows.***

*Everyone believed him **crazy.***

Participle

See **Verbal.**

Parts of speech

Noun, pronoun, adjective, adverb, conjunction, interjection, preposition, article.

Past

***I worked,** etc.*

Phoneme

A basic unit of sound in a language. (**/i/, /p/, /iy/**)

Perfect

I have worked, I had worked, I will have worked, etc.

Person

Choice of the appropriate forms to express the person speaking:

first person: *I, we*

second person: *you*

third person: *he, she, it, they*

Possessive adjectives

My, your, his, her, its, our, their.

Predicate adjective

An adjective following a linking verb and describing the subject.

*The flowers look **artificial.***

Predicate nominative

A word or group of words which follows a linking verb and identifies the subject.

*The book is **a best-selling science-fiction novel.***

Preposition

A connective which joins a noun or a pronoun to the rest of the sentence. A prepositional phrase may serve either an adverb or an adjective function.

adverb: *The guide led us **into the forest.***

adjective: *Jack is a master **of many trades.***

Present

I work, she/he works, etc.

Progressive (Continuous)

I am working, I was working, I have been working, etc.

Pronouns

Words which stand for nouns, classified as:

personal: *(I, you, he)*

possessive: *(mine, yours, his, hers)*

reflexive or intensive: *(myself, himself, ourselves)*

demonstrative: *(this, that, those)*

relative: *(who, which, what, that, whose)*

interrogative: *(who, which, what)*

indefinite: *(one, anyone, everyone)*

Quantifiers

Words denoting how much *(some, any, most, few, one, two, three)*

Reciprocal pronouns

Each other, one another.

Relative clause

A dependent clause is related to the main clause by a relative pronoun.

*The book **that he recommended** is on sale.*

Restrictive relative clause: A clause that contributes to the identification of the noun it modifies, not separated by a comma from the noun. See Non-restrictive relative clause.

*The man **who called me up** was a complete stranger.*

Sentence

A grammatically complete unit of thought or expression, containing at least a subject and a predicate.

Simple sentence
A sentence consisting of only one independent clause.

Stress
Pronouncing a syllable or a word in such a way that it makes it more prominent in a word or sentence respectivley.
condúctor, Let's gó.

Substantive
See **Nominal.**

Subject
A word or group of words about which the sentence or clause makes a statement.
*The **dog** jumped into the car.*

Subject complement
See **Predicate nominative; Predicate Adjective**

Subjunctive
See **Mood.**

Subordinating conjunctions
Conjunctions which join sentence parts of unequal rank, Usually they begin dependent clauses. Some of the most common ones are:
because, since, though, although, if, when, while, before, after, as, until, so that, as long as, whereas, in order that.

Superlative
The form of adjectives and adverbs used to express absolute superiority.

the tallest	*the least tall*
the most important	*the least important*
the most slowly	*the least slowly*

Syntax
The rules of sentence formation.

Tag questions
Short *yes / no* questions added to statements.
*It's a beautiful day, **isn't it?***
*You haven't seen the film, **have you?***

Tense
The system of verb forms expressing primarily different relationships in time.

Transitive verb
A verb which normally requires an object.
*Monkeys **love** bananas.*

Two-word verbs
A combination of a verb and a preposition or an adverb which forms a new vocabulary item. Two-part verbs are classified as *intransitive, separable,* and *non-separable.*

intransitive:
John **got up** early this morning.
separable:
John **calls up** his wife from the office.
John calls his wife **up** from the office.
John calls her **up** form the office.
non-separable:
Everybody **picks on** fat people.

Verb
A word or group of words expressing action, being, or state of being.
*I **swallowed** a fly.*
*What **is** man?*
*The table **has been** set.*

Verbal
A word or phrase derived from a verb and used as a noun, an adjective, or an adverb. Verbals consist of infinitives, gerunds, or participles.
infinitive: begins with to (sometimes understood) and is used as a noun, an adverb, or an adjective.
noun: To do such a thing would be disastrous.
adverb: Many people jog **to keep physically fit.**
adjective: I'm ready **to testify,** your Honor.
gerund: ends in -ing and is used as a noun.
Playing with matches is a favorite pass-time among children.
participle: ends in -ing, -ed, and is used as an adjective.
I can't live without **running** water.
Accompanied by his faithful dog, Daniel roamed the woods.

Verb phrase
Consists of the main verb and one or more auxiliaries.
*It **is beginning** to rain.*
*It **has been** raining for a long time.*
Modern grammarians use the term **verb phrase** to indicate the verb and all that goes with it (predicate) or the verb and its modifiers.
*The old man and the boy **had quietly taken the book from the library.***

Voice
A distinction in verb forms between *active* (the subject is acting) and *passive* (the subject is acted upon).
active: *Elmer **fed** the chickens.*
passive: *The chickens **were fed** by Elmer.*

220

List 2: A Comparison of Three Phonetic Alphabets

Consonants: (Symbols follow the I.P.A.; exceptions are indicated.)

Sounds   Representations

Sounds	I.P.A.*	T.S.**	Dict.***
may	/ m /		
bay	/ b /		
pay	/ p /		
way	/ w /		
whey	/ ʍ /		/ hw /
vee	/ v /		
fee	/ f /		
thee	/ ð /		/ t̲h̲ /
thigh	/ θ /		/ th /
new	/ n /		
dew	/ d /		
too	/ t /		
Lou	/ l /		
zoo	/ z /		
Sue	/ s /		
you	/ j /	/ y /	/ y /
rue	/ r /		
mea**s**ure	/ ʒ /	/ ž /	/ zh /
show	/ ʃ /	/ š /	/ sh /
joke	/ dʒ /	/ ǰ /	/ j /
choo	/ tʃ /	/ č /	/ ch /
ba**ng**	/ ŋ /		
ba**g**	/ g /		
ba**ck**	/ k /		
hi	/ h /		

*International Phonetic Alphabet
**Trager-Smith System
***Merriam-Webster dictionary

Vowels: (All vowel sounds in each system are represented

Sounds	Representations		
	I.P.A.	**T.S.**	**Dict.**
beat	/ i /	/ iy /	/ ē /
bit	/ ɪ /	/ i /	/ i̇ /
bait	/ e /	/ ey /	/ ā /
bet	/ ɛ /	/ e /	/ e /
bat	/ æ /	/ æ /	/ a /
but	/ ʌ /	/ ə /	/ ə /
alone	/ ə /	/ ə /	/ ə /
boot	/ u /	/ uw /	/ ü /
put	/ ʊ /	/ u /	/ u̇ /
boat	/ o /	/ ow /	/ ō /
bought	/ ɔ /	/ ɔ /	/ ȯ /
father	/ a /	/ a /	/ ä /
how	/ aw /	/ aw / /æw/	/ au̇ /
I	/ aj /	/ ay /	/ ī /
boy	/ ɔi /	/ oy /	/ ȯi /
ear		/ ir /	
air		/ er /	
marry		/ ær /	
father		/ ər /	
fur		/ ər /	/ ər /
poor		/ ur /	
or		/ or /	
are		/ ar /	

List 3: A Brief Guide to Punctuation

Punctuation		Used for	Example(s)
Apostrophe	**'**	to indicate omissions in contractions	doesn't, won't
		to indicate possession	Mary's, the Joneses'
		to indicate plurals of letters and numerals	1870's, p's and q's
Brackets	**[ ]**	to indicate comment or question in quoted material	"He [Lincoln] was assassinated by a mad actor."
		to indicate comment or question within material in parentheses	(Kuwait was liberated [was turned into a desolate battleground] by the U.N. forces in March,1991).
Colon	**:**	in writing clock time	9:15, 2:47, 17:09
		to introduce a list	We need the following items: soap, toothpaste, and hand lotion.
		after the names of speakers in a dialogue	Joe: Will you come, Honey? Sue: Are you nuts? No way!
		before a formal quotation	The tall speaker began: "Four score and seven years ago,....
		after salutations in formal	Dear Sir:
		or business letters	Dear Ms. Landsdowne:
Comma	**,**	after *yes* or *no* in a response	Yes, we have no bananas.
		before the conjunction in a compound sentence	The oldest boy is going to school, and the youngest is going to work.
		except when the clauses are short	He walked and she rode.
		to separate the elements in an address	New Orleans, Louisana, U. S. A. They live at 418 Cedar Street, Winnetka, Illinois
		to separate the elements in a date	He was born on Tuesday, January 25, 1944, in Chicago.
		to separate equivalent elements in a series	Watch the stocks of Kmart, Sears and Roebuck, and Walmart.
		to separate a speaker's words from the introductory statement	John asked, "May I leave?"
		to group large numbers into thousands	9,121; 1,268,421
		to set off the name of a person spoken to in direct speech	Mary, take this ring.

Punctuation		Used for	Example(s)
		to separate an introductory clause from the sentence	When the party was over, I walked home.
		after a mild exclamation	Well, I don't care.
		before and after an appositive	George, a famous poet, spoke next.
		to separate a tag question from the rest of the sentence	It's cold, isn't it?
		before and after a non-restrictive adjective clause	Punctuation, which is essential for writing, seems complicated at first.
Dash	—	to indicate an interruption or an afterthought	We'll be in New York—at last—in an hour! I'll do it—at least, I'll try.
		to indicate special emphasis in place of a comma	Give people what they want—money, fame, and power.
Exclamation Point	!	to indicate strong feeling or emotion or for emphasis	Help! Watch out! She said she'd jump and she did!
Hyphen	-	in certain fixed expressions	person-to-person, matter-of-fact, station-to-station
		in writing out compound numbers	twenty-one, ninety-nine, twenty-first, ninety-ninth
		in expressions of clock time	It's seven-thirty. It's one-fifteen.
		in joining a prefix to a proper name	pre-Columbian, post-Roosevelt, un-Christian
		in joining a prefix to a noun whose first letter is the same as the last letter of the prefix	anti-intellectual, pre-existing, post-temperance
Parenthesis	( )	to enclose remarks, comments, explanations that interrupt the main thought	She invited the two men (they are cousins) to the party. If it rains (it usually doesn't this time of year), we'll postpone the picnic.
Period	.	at the end of a statement	I want to be alone.
		after initials and abbreviations	Mr. P. T. Barnum. It's 7 p.m.
		to indicate cents/decimals	$5.39; 257.0932; .00906
Question Mark	?	at the end of a direct question	Where does it all end?
		after a tag question	You like to talk, don't you?

Punctuation		Used for	Example(s)
Quotation Marks	" "	to enclose direct quotations	"Come here," Jim said.
		around titles of chapters	"The Return to Witchwood"
		articles in magazines or newspapers	"Wood Stove Madness," *Country Journal*
		songs, poems	"Michelle, Ma Belle" "Hurt Hawks"
		radio and TV programs	"Music from the Hearts of Space" "I Love Lucy"
		with other punctuation, as follows:	"Come, " he said. "I'm going." I said, "I will;" I followed. "Can you see?" he asked. Did I answer, "No?"
Semicolon	;	in a compound sentence without a connective	The singular form is "mouse;" the plural form is "mice."
		in a sentence with two main clauses joined by a conjunctive adverb.	The teacher was sick; therefore, the class was called off. Roseanne ran a good race; however, she failed to qualify for the finals.
Underlining and Italics	—	Use underlining in handwritten or typed material and Italics in printed material:	
		for titles of periodicals and books	<u>Newsweek</u> <u>A Farewell to Arms</u>
		foreign phrases and words used in an English context	And then, <u>alors</u>, there she was. "<u>Cuidado</u>," I warned myself, "You're a fool, <u>but que, sera, sera</u>.
		words emphasized	I wanted *three* tickets, not four!
		the names of ships, trains and airplanes	*Titanic, Orient Express, Constellation, Spirit of St. Louis*

List 4: Useful Spelling Rules

A. If a word ends in **y** preceded by a consonant, change the **y** to an **i** before every suffix except **-ing.**

salary	*salaries*	*copy*	*copying*
marry	*married*	*try*	*trying*
lonely	*loneliness*	*fly*	*flying*
worry	*worried*	*worry*	*worrying*

B. Write **i** before **e**, except after **c** or when sounded like **a,** as in *neighbor* and *weigh.*

i before **e:**	*brief, piece, chief, yield*
e before **i:**	*receive, deceive, ceiling, freight, sleigh*

Exceptions: *either, neither, seize, leisure, weird, species, financier*

C. If a word has only one sylable and ends with a single consonant preceded by a single vowel *(hop, bat)* and you add a suffix beginning with a vowel **(-er, -ed, -ing),** double the final consonant.

stop	*stopped*	*trip*	*tripped*
bat	*batter*	*drop*	*dropping*
rub	*rubbing*	*spin*	*spinning*

If the word has more than one syllable and the final syllable is stressed, double the final consonant.

occur	*occurring*	*confer*	*conferred*
admit	*admitted*	*omit*	*omitted*

D. If a word ends with a silent **e** and you add a suffix,

drop the **e** if the suffix begins with a vowel

love	*lovable*	*move*	*moving*
desire	*desirable*	*use*	*usable*

but keep the **e** if the **e** is preceded by **c** or **g** and the suffix begins with **a**, **o**, or **u**

notice	*noticeable*	*manage*	*manageable*
courage	*courageous*	*erase*	*erasure*

Exceptions: words ending in **ee** never drop the final **ee.**

agree	*agreeing*	*flee*	*fleeing*	*see*	*seeing*

keep the **e** if the suffix begins with a consonant

use	*useful*	*engage*	*engagement*
love	*lovely*	*move*	*movement*

Exceptions: words that end in **-ple, -ble** and **-tle,** drop the **-le** before **-ly**

simple	*simply*	*probable*	*probably*
gentle	*gently*		

226

List 5: Differences between British and American Spelling

American		British	
e	*anesthesia* *encyclopedia*	**ae**	*anaesthesia* *encyclopaedia*
-ection	*connection* *reflection*	**-exion**	*connexion* *reflexion*
-ed	*burned* *learned* *spelled*	**-t**	*burnt* *learnt* *spelt*
-ense	*license* *defense*	**-ence**	*licence* *defence*
-er	*center* *meter* *theater*	**re**	*centre* *metre* *theatre*
-ization	*civilization* *naturalization*	**isation**	*civilisation* *naturalisation*
-ize	*criticize* *memorize*	**-ise**	*criticise* *memorise*
-ll	*fulfill* *skillful*	**-l**	*fulfil* *skilful*
-ment	*judgment* *argument*	**-ement**	*judgement* *arguement*
-or	*color* *neighbor*	**-our**	*colour* *neighbour*

Note: **In British usage,** words ending in an **l** preceded by a single vowel usually double the **l.**

quarrel	*quarrelling*	*model*	*modelling*
travel	*travelling*	*signal*	*signalling*

In American usage, the consonant is doubled only if the last syllable is accented.

signal	*signaling*	*excel*	*excellent*
travel	*traveling*	*propel*	*propeller*

British spelling is generally acceptable in the United States, and in some cases it is quite common; *encyclopaedia, centre, colour, traveller, theatre,* for example, are often seen. However, these spellings are considered colourful and amusing, not the normal, preferred spelling.

List 6: Some American – British Vocabulary Differences*

American	British
aisle (theater)	gangway (theatre)
apartment	flat
baby carriage	perambulator, pram
bar	pub
bartender	barman
bathtub	bath
battery (automobile)	accumulator
bill (money)	banknote
broiled (meat)	grilled
can	tin
candy	sweets
store	sweet shop
checkers (game)	draughts
cookie	biscuit
corn	maize
derby (hat)	bowler
detour	diversion
druggist	chemist
elevator	lift
erasers	rubber
faucet	tap
flashlight	torch
French fried	chips
gasoline	petrol
generator	dynamo
groceries	stores
hood (automobile)	bonnet
incorporated (Inc.)	limited (Ltd.)
installment plan	hire-purchase system

*Adapted form H.L.Mencken, *The American Language, Fourth Edition*.
New York: Alfred A. Knopf, 1936.

American	British
internal revenue	inland revenue
janitor	caretaker, porter
kerosene	paraffin
kindergarten	infant's school
lawyer	barrister
line	queue
living-room	sitting-room
liquor	spirits
long distance (telephone)	trunk
mailman	postman
oatmeal	porridge
paste	gum
period(punctuation)	full stop
phonograph	gramophone
private school	public school
raincoat	waterproof, mackintosh
rooster	cock
rubbish collector	dustman
second floor	first floor
sedan	saloon car
sidewalk	path
soccer	football
subway	tube
suspenders (men's)	braces
syrup	treacle
taxes	rates
thermos bottle	flask
truck	lorry
vacation	holiday
windshield	windscreen
wrench	spanner

List 7: 750 High-Frequency Words:
A Basic Vocabulary List

Nouns

A. action, afternoon, age, amount, animal, answer, arm, art, article

B. baby, back, bag, ball, bank, beauty, bed, bird, blood, boat, body, box, boy, brother, building, business

C. car, (in any) case, cause, center, century, chair, chance, child(ren), church, circle, city, class, clothes, cloud, college, color, company, condition, corner, cost, country, (of) course, crowd, cup

D. day, date, daughter, deal, death, difference, dinner, direction, distance, doctor, dog, dollar, door, doubt, dream, dress, drink

E. ear, earth, east, edge, effort, egg, end, evening, eye

F. face, fact, fall, family, farm, father, favor, fellow, field, finger, fire, fish, floor, flower, fly, food, foot (feet), forest, friend, front, fruit, future

G. game, garden, girl, glass, gold, government, grass, guess

H. hair, hall, hand, hat, head, health, heart, hill, history, hole, home, horse, hour, house, husband

I. ice, idea, inch, interest, island

J. job, joy

K. kitchen, knee

L. lady, land, law, leg, letter, life, light, line, lip, (a) lot (of), love

M. man (men), matter, meat, meeting, member, middle, mile, milk, minute, Miss (Ms.), moment, money, month, moon, morning, mother, mountain, mouth, music, Mr., Mrs. (Ms.)

N. name, nation, nature, neck, neighbor, news, night, north, nose, note, number

O. object, ocean, office

P. page, pain, pair, pants, paper, part, pastry, past, peace, people, person, picture, piece, place, plant, pleasure, pound, power, price, president, problem, public, purpose

Q. quarter, question

R. race, rain, reason, report, result, river, road, rock, room, rule

S. salt, school, sea, season, seat, shade, shape, skip, shoe, shop, should, side, sight, sign, sir, size, skin, sky, snow, song, soul, south, space, spirit, spot, spring, star, stone, storm, story, street, subject, success, sugar, summer, supply, surprise, system

T. table, tear, thing, thought, time, today, tomorrow, top, town, tree, trip, trouble, truth

U. uncle

V. view, voice

W. wall, war, watch, water, way, weather, week, west, wind, window, winter, woman (women), wood, word

Y. yard, year

Verbs
Irregular (with past forms)

B. be (was, were), beat (beat), become (became), begin (began), break (broke), bring (brought), build (built), buy (bought)

C. catch (caught), come (came), cost (cost), cut (cut)

D. do (did), draw (drew), drink (drank), drive (drove)

E. eat (ate)

F. fall (fell), feed (fed), feel (felt), fight (fought), find (found), fly (flew), forget (forgot), forgive (forgave)

G. get (got), give (gave), go (went), grow (grew)

H. hang (hung), have (had), hear (heard), hold (held), hurt (hurt)

K. keep (kept), know (knew)

L. lay (laid), lead (led), leave (left), let (let), lie (lay), lose (lost)

M. make (made), mean (meant), meet (met)

P. pay (paid), put (put)

R. read (read), ride (rode), ride (rose), run (run)

S. say (said), see (saw), send (sent), set (set), sing (sang), sleep (slept), speak (spoke), spend (spent), spread (spread), stand (stood)

T. Take (took), teach (taught), tell (told), think (thought)

U. understand (understood)

W. wear (wore), write (wrote)

Regular Verbs

A. accept, act, add, admit, agree, allow, appear, arrive, ask

B. belong, believe, burn

C. call, care, carry, change, close, command, consider, contain, continue, cook, count, cover, cross, cry

D. dance, dare, decide, demand, destroy, discover, doubt, dream, drop

E. enjoy, enter, escape, expect, explain, express

F. fail, fill, finish, force

H. happen, help, hope, hurry

I. increase, include

J. join

K. kill, kiss

L. laugh, learn, like, listen, live, look, love

M. marry, matter, measure, mind, move

N. need, notice

O. offer, open, order

P. pass, pick, pull, plan, plant, play, point, prepare, promise, prove,

R. rain, reach, realize, remain, remember, reply, return, rush

S. save, serve, share, shout, show, smoke, sound, start, stay, step, stop, study, suppose

T. talk, taste, thank, touch, travel, try, turn

U. use

W. wait, walk, want, watch, wish, wonder, work

Conjunctions

A. although, and, as

B. because, both...and, but

E. either...or

H. however

I. if

N. neither...nor

O. or

S. since

T. therefore, though, thus

U. until

W. when, where, whether, while

Y. yet

Adjectives

A. able, alone, afraid

B. bad, beautiful, better, best, big, black, blue, born, bright, brown, bury

C. certain, chief, clean, clear, cold, common, complete, cool

D. dark, dead, deep, different, dry

E. easy

F. fair, famous, fast, fine, foreign, free, fresh, full

G. glad, good, gray, great, green

H. happy, hard, heavy, hot, human, hundred

I. ill, important

L. large, last, late, little, long, low

M. million, modern

N. national, natural, new, next, nice

O. old, only

P. plain, peasant, poor, possible, pretty

Q. quiet

R. ready, real, red, rich, right, round

S. safe, several, short, sick, simple, small, soft, special, square, straight, strong, sure, sweet

T. tall, thin, tired, true

V. various

W. warm, wet, white, whole, wide, wild, wise, wonderful, wrong

Y. yellow, young

Adverbs

A. again, ago, almost, already, also, always, away

B. before, better, best

C. certainly

E. early, else, especially, even, ever

F. far, finally, forward

H. here, how

I. instead

J. just

M. more

N. nearly, necessary, never, no, not, now

O. often, once, out, outside

P. probably

Q. quickly, quietly

R. rather, really

S. so, sometimes, strange, suddenly

T. then, there, today, tomorrow

U. up, usually

V. very

Y. yes, yet

Prepositions

A. above, about, across, after, against, along, among, around, at

D. down, during

E. even

F. for, from

I. in, into

L. less, like

O. of, off, on, over

T. through, to, towards

U. under, until, up, upon

W. with, without, within

Pronouns

E. everything

H. he, her, herself, him, himself, his

I. I, it, itself

M. mine, my, myself,

N. none, nothing

O. one, other, our, ours

S. she

T. their, them, themselves, they

U. us

W. we, who, whom, whose, what, which

Y. you, your, yourself

Auxiliaries

can, could, may, might, must, ought, shall, should, would

Quantifiers

A. all, any

B. (a little) bit (of)

D. (a great) deal (of)

E. eight, either

F. first, five, four

N. neither, nine

O. one

S. second, seven, six

T. third, thirty, thousand, three, twelve, twenty, two

Determiners

A. a, an

E. each, every

T. that, the, these, this, those

W. which, what

List 8: Measurement Terms and Equivalents

Non-Metric

Linear measure

12 inches	=	1 foot
3 feet	=	1 yard
$5\frac{1}{2}$ yards	=	1 rod
40 rods	=	1 furlong
8 furlongs	=	1 mile

Mariner's measure

6 feet	=	1 fathom
1,000 fathoms	=	1 nautical mile
3 nautical miles	=	1 league

Square measure

160 square rods	=	1 acre
640 acres	=	1 square mile

Avoirdupois weight

16 drams	=	1 ounce
16 ounces	=	1 pound
2,000 pounds	=	1 ton

Liquid measure

2 pints	=	1 quart
4 quarts	=	1 gallon

Dry measure

2 pints	=	1 quart
8 quarts	=	1 peck
4 pecks	=	1 bushel

Metric/English Measure Equivalents

Linear and square measure

1 centimeter (cm.)	=	.3937 inch (in.)
1 meter (m.)	=	39.37 in. or
		3.28 feet (ft.)
1 kilometer (km.)	=	.62137 mile (mi.)
1,000 m^2	= 1 hectare (ha.)	
	=	2.471 acres

Liquid measure

1 centiliter (cl.)	=	.338 fluid ounces (fl. oz.)
1 liter (l.)	=	.9081 dry quart (qt.)
	=	1.0567 liquid quarts

Avoirdupois weight

1 centigram (cg.)	=	.1543 gram (gr.)
1 gram (g.)	=	15.432 gram (gr.)
	=	.03527 ounces (oz.)
1 kilogram (kg.)	=	2.2046 pounds (lb.)

English/Metric Measure Equivalents

Linear and square measure

1 inch		=	2.54 centimeters	
12 in.	= 1 foot	=	.3048 meters	
3 ft.	= 1 yard	=	.9144 meters	
$16\frac{1}{2}$ ft.	= 1 rod	=	5.029 meters	
5,280 ft.	= 1 mile	=	1.6093 kilometers	
4,840 yd^2	= 1 acre	=	.4 hectares	

Avoirdupois weight

1 ounce			=	28 grams
16 oz.	=	1 pound	=	.45 kilo (kg.)

Liquid measure

1 teaspoon (tsp.)			=	5 milliliters
3 tsp.	=	1 tbs.	=	15 ml.
2 tablespoon (tbs.)	=	1 fl. ounce	=	30 ml.
8 oz.	=	1 cup (c.)	=	.24 liters (l.)
2 cups	=	1 pint (pt.)	=	.47 l.
2 pints (pt)	=	1 qt.)	=	.95 l.
4 quarts (qt)	=	1 gallon (gal.)	=	3.8 l.

Fahrenheit/Centigrade

$$°F - 32 \times 5 \div 9 = °C$$
$$°C \times 9 \div 5 + 32 = °F$$

Degrees

F   C

100°F = 37.8°C

90°F = 32.2°C

80°F = 26.7°C

70°F = 21.1°C

60°F = 15.6°C

50°F = 10.0°C

40°F = 4.4°C

32°F = 0°C

100°C = 212°F

40°C = 104°F

30°C = 86°F

20°C = 68°F

10°C = 50°F

0°C = 32°F

F	C
212	100
190	90
170	80
150	70
130	60
110	50
90	40
70	30
50	20
32	10
10	0
0	-10
-10	-20
-30	-30

List 9: Common Elements*

Atomic Number	Symbol	Element Name	Atomic Number	Symbol	Element Name
1	H	hydrogen	24	Cr	chromium
2	He	helium	25	Mn	manganese
3	Li	lithium	26	Fe	iron
4	Be	beryllium	27	Co	cobalt
5	B	boron	28	Ni	nickel
6	C	carbon	29	Cu	copper
7	N	nitrogen	30	Zn	zinc
8	O	oxygen	33	As	arsenic
9	F	fluoride	47	Ag	silver
10	Ne	neon	50	Sn	tin
11	Na	sodium	51	Sb	antimony
12	Mg	magnesium	53	I	iodine
13	Al	aluminum	56	Ba	barium
14	Si	silicon	78	Pt	platinum
15	P	phosphorous	79	Au	gold
16	S	sulfur	80	Hg	mercury
17	Cl	chlorine	82	Pb	lead
18	Ar	argon	83	Bi	bismuth
19	K	potassium	88	Ra	radium
20	Ca	calcium	92	U	uranium
			94	Pu	plutonium

* This list contains only the commonly known elements.

List 10: Common Symbols

♂	male		′	foot (6′)
♀	female		″	inch (6′2″)
			×	by (2″ × 4″)
+	plus			
-	minus		$	dollar
×	times		¢	cent
÷	divided by		£	pound (£ 3)
=	equals		/, s	shilling (5/ or 5s)
>	greater than		d	penny, pence (6d)
<	less than			
≠	not equal to		~	tilde (cañon)
√	square root		^	circumflex (fête)
π	pi		₅	cedilla (Français)
∞	infinity		′	acute accent (passé)
			`	grave accent (à la carte)
°	degree (60°)		¨	dieresis (zoölogy)
′	minute (60° 30’)			
″	second (60° 30’ 15″)		©	copyright
@	at (@ 80¢ per quart)		™	trademark
≈	approximately		&	ampersand (and)
O/A	on or about		*	a hypothetical or wrong
%	percent			form (he *drinked)
#	number (#10 nail)		*	asterisk for note
#	pounds (80#)		†	dagger for note
			‡	double dagger for note

List 11: Proofreading and Correction Marks

∧	insert here *a word*		#	insert space *#*
⋏	insert comma		.....	let it stand
⊙	insert period		STET	let it stand *STET*
ℓ	delete this		≡	capitalize (washington) *CAP*
⌣	close up (foot ball)		/	lower case (Capital) *l.c.*
¶	paragraph		Awk	awkward construction
NO ¶	no paragraph		Frag	sentence fragment
∼	transpose (a, b, d, c, e)		Sp	spelling error *here* ~~bear~~

List 12: Roman Numerals

I, i	1	VI, vi	6	XX	20	CD	400
II, ii	2	VII, vii	7	XL	40	D	500
III, iii	3	VIII, viii	8	L	50	CM	900
IV, iv	4	IX, ix	9	XC	90	M	1000
V, v	5	X, x	10	C	100	MMM	3000

MCDXCII	=	1492
MCMXCII	=	1992
MMII	=	2002
MDCXLVIII	=	1,648

List 13: Abbreviations *(abbr., abbrev.)*

A. General (Gen.)

A.A.	Associate of Arts*
A.D.	*anno Domini,* in the year of Our Lord
a.m.	*ante meridiem,* before noon
Amer.	America, American
anon.	anonymous
assn.	association
assoc.	associate(s)
b.	born
B.A., A.B.	Bachelor of Arts
B.C.	before Christ
B.S.	Bachelor of Science
bibliog.	bibliography
biog.	biography
c	hundred (4c = 400)
c., ca.	*circa,* about
C.E.	common era = A.D.
cf.	*confer,* compare
ch., chap.	chapter
Co.	Company
Coll.	college
d.	died
D.D.S.	Doctor of Dental Science (Surgery)
dept.	department
E.	east
E., Eng.,	English
ed.	editor, edited by
e.g.	*exempli gratia,* for example
E.F.L.	English as a foreign language
E.S.L.	English as a second language
E.S.O.L.	English to speakers of other languages
esp.	especially
ESP	extrasensory perception
E.S.P.	English for Special Purposes
et al	*et alii,* and others
etc.	*et cetera,* and so forth
ex.	example
f., ff.	and the following page(s)
Fr.	French
Gr.	German
Gk.	Greek
hist.	history
ibid.	*ibidem,* in the same place
i.e.	*id est,* that is

intro.	introduction
It.	Italian
Jr.	junior
lang.	language
L., Lat.	Latin
LC, L.C.	Library of Congress
Ltd.	Limited
m	thousand ($55m = $55,000)
M.A.	Master of Arts
M.B.A.	Master of Business Administration
M.D.	Doctor of Medicine
misc.	miscellaneous
Mr.	Mister
Mrs.	Mistress
Ms.	Miss, Mrs., Woman
ms.	manuscript
M.S.	Master of Science
N.	north
N.B.	*nota bone,* take note, note well
no.	number
p., pp.	page(s)
par.	paragraph
Ph.D.	Doctor of Philosophy
philos.	philosophy
p.m.	*post meridiem,* afternoon
pub.	published by
q.v.	*quod vide,* which see
rpm	revolutions per minute
S.	south
Sr.	senior
sic	thus
SOS	help!
Sp.	Spanish
sp.	spelling
St.	Saint
St.	Street
T.M.	trademark
TV	television
U., Univ.	university
vol.	volume
W.	west

B. Days and Months (Mos.)

			Nov.	November
Jan.	January		Dec.	December
Feb.	February			
Mar.	March		Mon.	Monday
Apr.	April		Tues.	Tuesday
May	May		Wed.	Wednesday
June	June		Thurs.	Thursday
July	July		Fri.	Friday
Aug.	August		Sat.	Saturday
Sept.	September		Sun.	Sunday
Oct.	October			

Measures

in.	inch		mm.	millimeter
ft.	foot		cm.	centimeter
yd.	yard		m.	meter
mi.	mile		km.	kilometer
gr.	English gram		g.	metric gram
oz.	ounce		c.	centigram
fl. oz.	fluid ounce		kg.	kilo., kilogram
lb.	pound		t.	tonnes
tsp.	teaspoon		ml.	milliliter
tbs.,tbsp.	tablespoon		l.	liter
c.	cup			
pt.	pint			
qt.	quart			
gal.	gallon			

* Acronyms are similar to abbreviations. Organizations are often known not by their long names but by the brief acronyms of their names. AA = American Airlines, Alcoholics Anonymous; AAA = American Automobile Association; WAC = Women's Army Corps; UNESCO = United Nations Educational, Scientific, and Cultural Organization

Postal Abbrs.

State	Traditional	New	State	Traditional	New	State	Traditional	New
Alabama	Ala.	AL	Maine	Me.	ME	Oklahoma	Okla.	OK
Alaska	Alas.	AK	Maryland	Md.	MD	Oregon	Ore.	OR
Arizona	Ariz.	AZ	Massachusetts	Mass.	MA	Pennsylvania	Penn.	PA
Arkansas	Ark.	AR	Michigan	Mich.	MI	Rhode Island	R.I.	RI
California	Cal.	CA	Minnesota	Minn.	MN	South Carolina	S.C.	SC
Colorado	Colo.	CO	Mississippi	Miss.	MS	South Dakota	S.D.	SD
Connecticut	Conn.	CT	Missouri	Mo.	MO	Tennessee	Tenn.	TN
Delaware	Del.	DE	Montana	Mont.	MT	Texas	Tex.	TX
Florida	Fla.	FL	Nebraska	Neb.	NB	Utah	Utah	UT
Georgia	Ga.	GA	Nevada	Nev.	NV	Vermont	Vt.	VT
Hawaii	Ha.	HI	New Hampshire	N.H.	NH	Virginia	Va	VA
Idaho	Ida.	ID	New Jersey	N.J.	NJ	Washington	Wash.	WA
Illinois	Ill.	IL	New Mexico	N.M.	NM	West Virginia	W.V.	WV
Indiana	Ind.	IN	New York	N.Y.	NY	Wisconsin	Wisc.	WI
Iowa	Ia.	IA	North Carolina	N.C.	NC	Wyoming	Wyo.	WY
Kansas	Kan.	KS	North Dakota	N.D.	ND	Puerto Rico	P.R.	PR
Kentucky	Ky.	KY	Ohio	Ohio	OH	Guam	Guam	GU
Louisiana	La.	LA				Virgin Island	V.I.	VI

North American Countries

United States of America	U.S. U.S.A.	Canada	Can.	Central America	C.A.
		Mexico	Mex.		

Cities

District of Columbia	D.C., DC	Miami	MIA	San Francisco	S.F., SF
Los Angeles	L.A., LA	New York City	N.Y.C., NYC	Seattle	SEA

Other Postal Abbrs.

APO	Army and Air Force Post Office	Cir.	Circle	Jct.	Junction
		Ct.	Court	Ln.	Lane
FPO	Naval Post Office	Cres.	Crescent	Pl.	Place
RFD	Rural Free Delivery	Dr.	Drive	Pt.	Point
PO Box	Post Office Box	Expy.	Expressway	Rd.	Road
		Ext.	Extension	Rte.	Route
Ave.	Avenue	Fwy.	Freeway	Sq.	Square
Blvd.	Boulevard	Gdns.	Gardens	St.	Street
Byp.	Bypass	Hts.	Heights	Ter.	Terrace
Cswy.	Causeway	Hwy.	Highway	Tpke.	Turnpike
Ctr.	Center				

STOP

YIELD

DO NOT ENTER

RAILROAD
ADVANCE CROSSING

NO LEFT TURN

NO RIGHT TURN

NO U TURN

NO PARKING

KEEP LEFT

KEEP RIGHT

LEFT ONLY

RIGHT ONLY

TOW AWAY ZONE

TRUCK WEIGHT LIMIT

SPEED LIMIT

HIKING TRAIL

FOOD

GAS

HOSPITAL

REST AREA

Pedagogical
Atlas of the
World

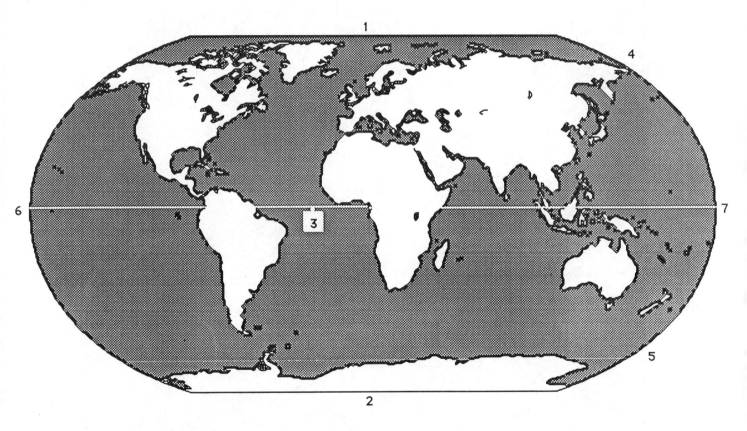

Map 1   World

With Keyed Outine Maps

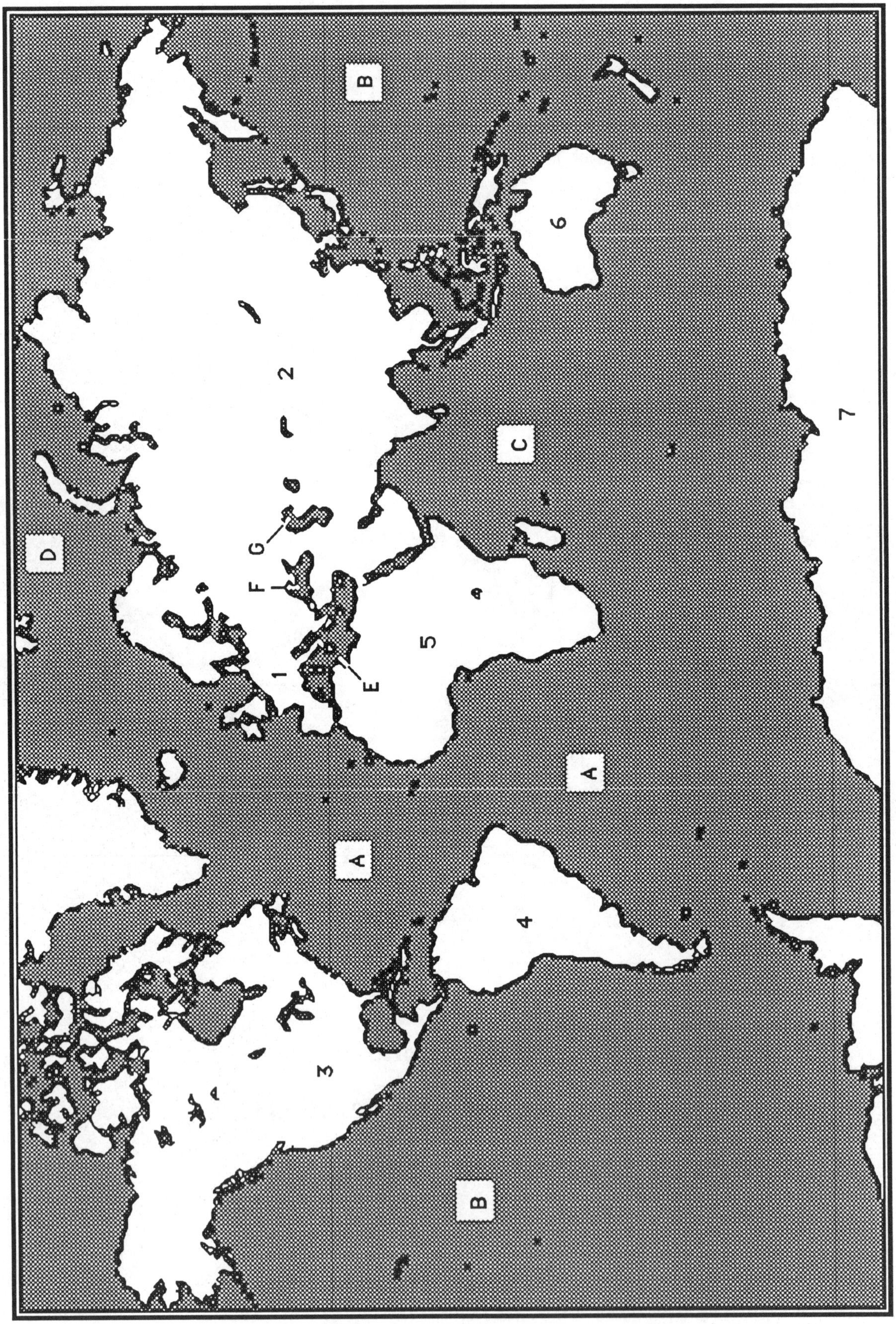

Map 2 Continents and Seas

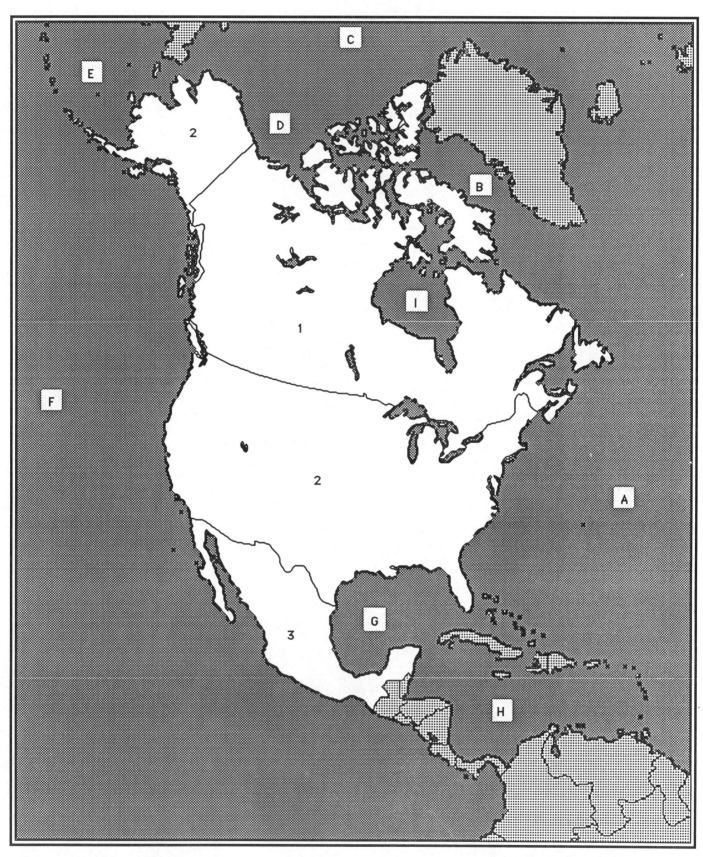

Map 3   North America

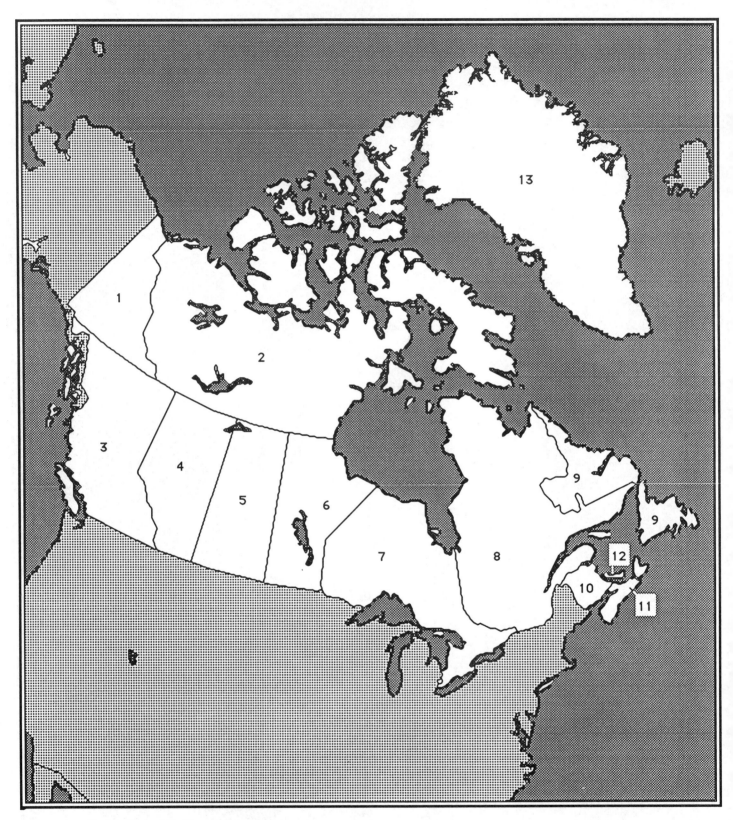

Map 4   Canada and Greenland

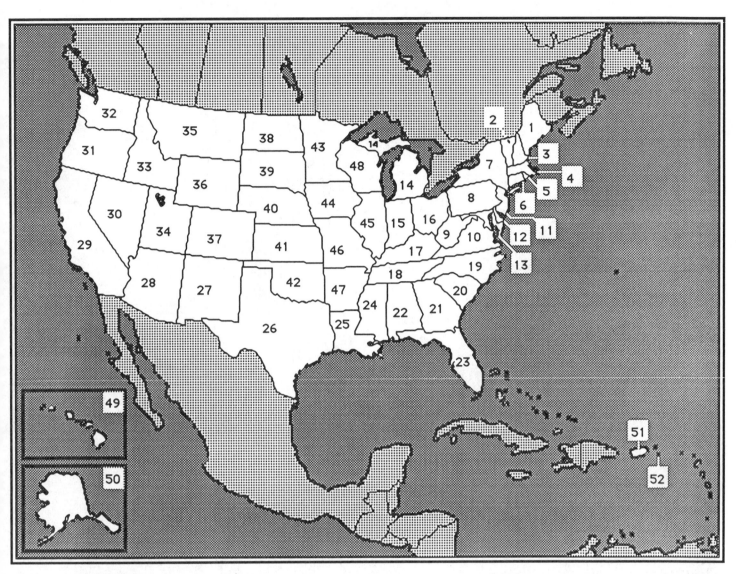

Map 5   United States of America

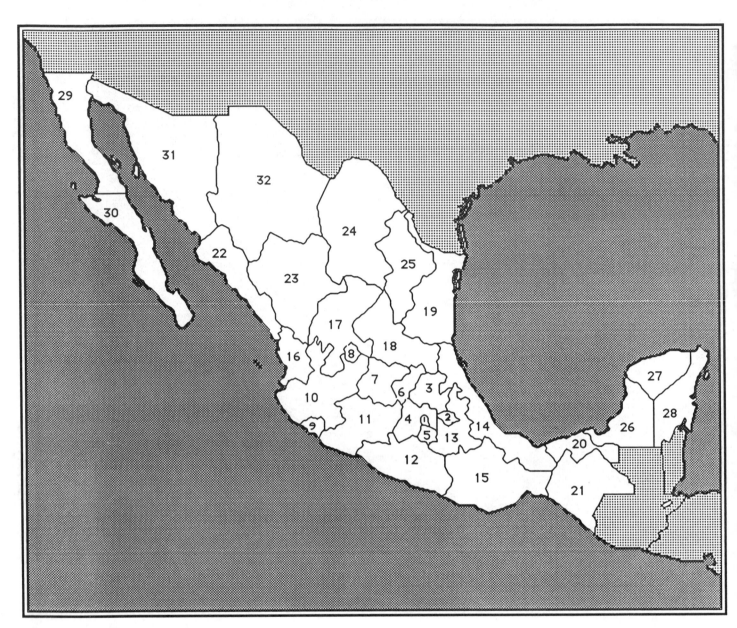

Map 6   Mexico

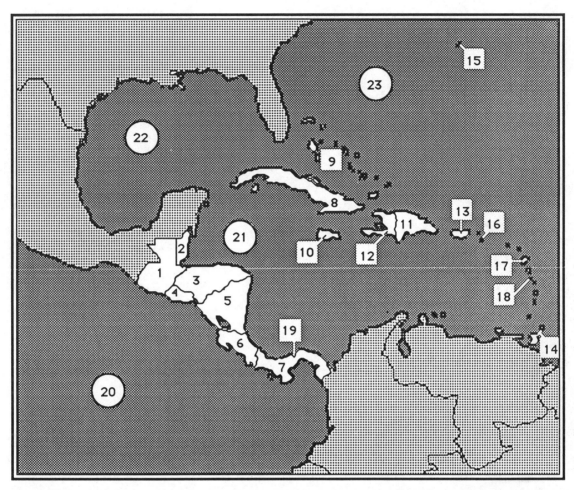

Map 7   Central America and the Caribbean

A PEDAGOGICAL ATLAS OF THE WORLD   **MISCELLANEOUS**

Map 8   South America

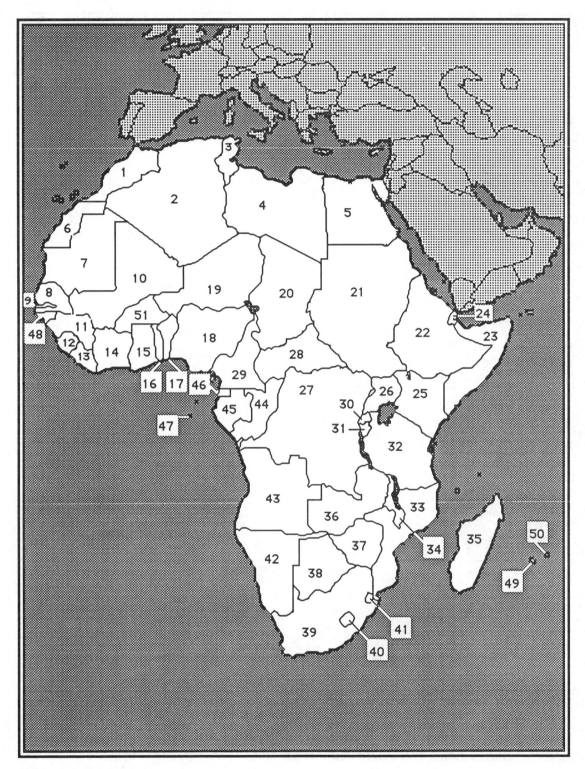

Map 9   Africa

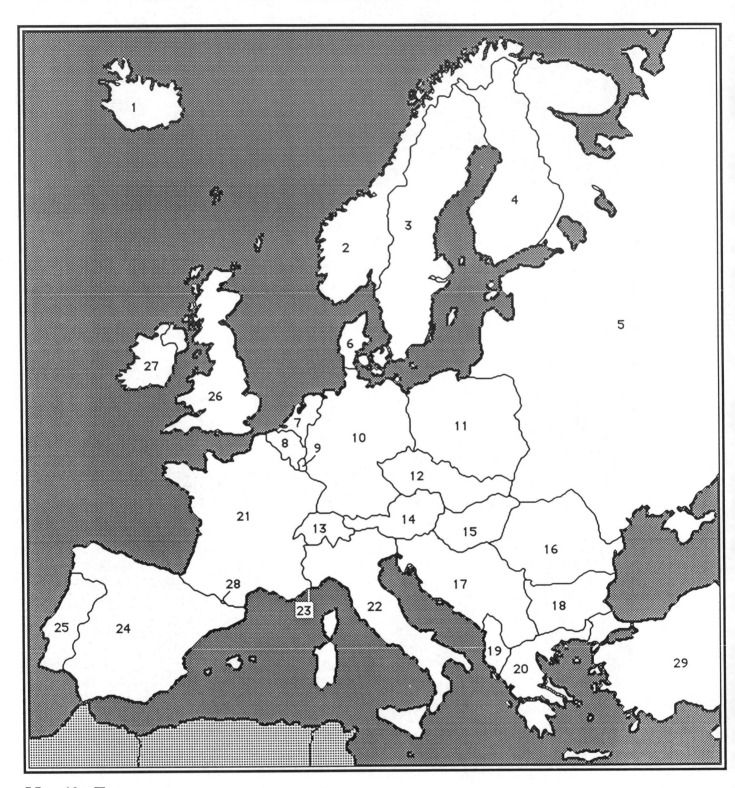

Map 10   Europe

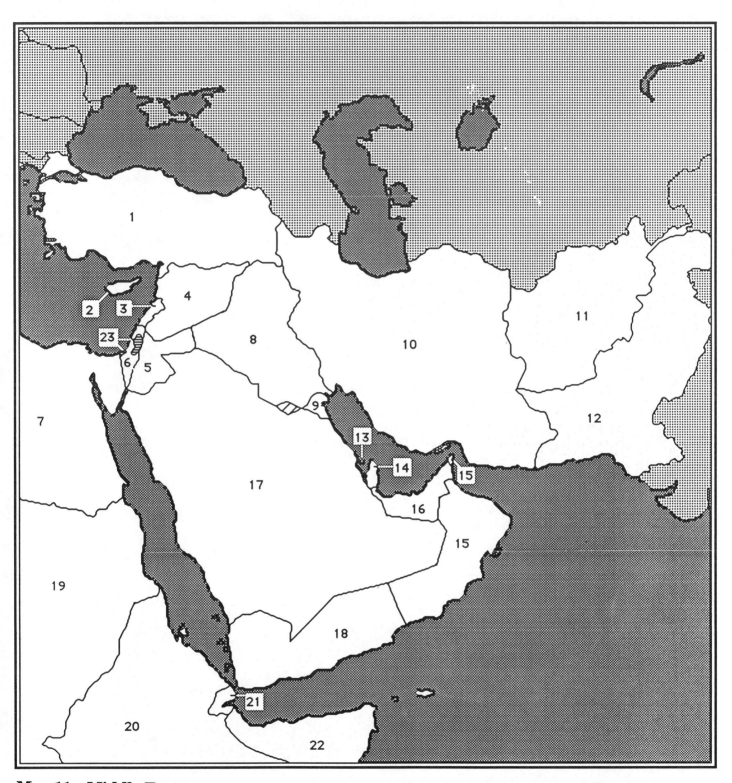

Map 11   Middle East

Map 12   Northern Eurasia - U.S.S.R.

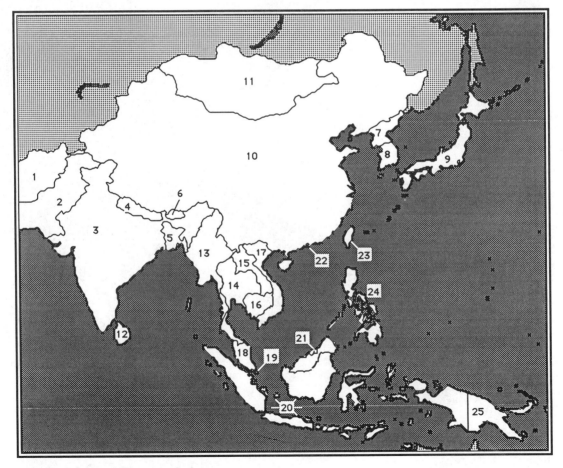

Map 13   Southeast Asia

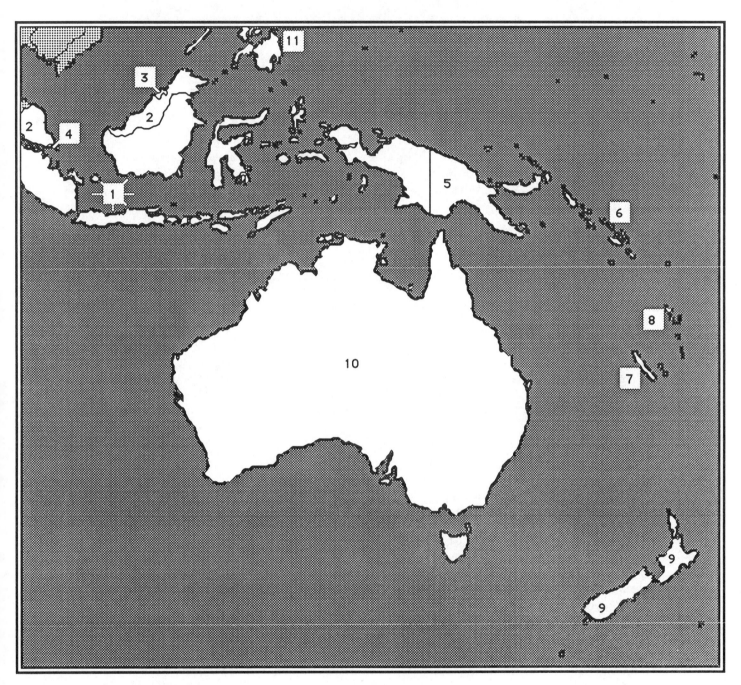

Map 14   South Pacific

Map 1 World

1 North Pole	3 Equator	4 Northern	5 Southern Hemisphere
2 South Pole		Hemisphere	6 East
			7 West

Map 2 Continents and Seas

1 Europe	5 Africa	A Atlantic Ocean	E Mediterranean Sea
2 Asia	6 Australia	B Pacific Ocean	F Black Sea
3 North America	7 Antarctica	C Indian Ocean	G Caspian Sea
4 South America		D Arctic Ocean	

Map 3 North America

1 Canada	A North Atlantic	D Beaufort Sea	G Gulf of Mexico
2 U.S.A.	B Baffin Bay	E Bering Sea	H Caribbean Sea
3 Mexico	C Arctic	F Pacific	I Hudson Bay

Map 4 Canada and Greenland

1 Yukon Territory	4 Alberta	7 Ontario	10 New Brunswick
2 Northwest	5 Saskatchewan	8 Quebec	11 Nova Scotia
Territories	6 Manitoba	9 Newfoundland	12 Prince Edward Island
3 British Columbia			13 Greenland

Map 5 United States of America

1 Maine	14 Michigan	27 New Mexico	40 Nebraska
2 Vermont	15 Indiana	28 Arizona	41 Kansas
3 New Hampshire	16 Ohio	29 California	42 Oklahoma
4 Massachusetts	17 Kentucky	30 Nevada	43 Minnesota
5 Rhode Island	18 Tennessee	31 Oregon	44 Iowa
6 Connecticut	19 North Carolina	32 Washington	45 Illinois
7 New York	20 South Carolina	33 Idaho	46 Missouri
8 Pennsylvania	21 Georgia	34 Utah	47 Arkansas
9 West Virginia	22 Alabama	35 Montana	48 Wisconsin
10 Virginia	23 Florida	36 Wyoming	49 Hawaii
11 New Jersey	24 Mississippi	37 Colorado	50 Alaska
12 Delaware	25 Louisiana	38 North Dakota	51 Puerto Rico
13 Maryland	26 Texas	39 South Dakota	52 Virgin Islands

Map 6 Mexico

	10 Jalisco	19 Tamaulipas	28 Quintana Roo
1 Distrito Federal	11 Michoacan	20 Villahermosa	29 Baja California
2 Tlaxcala	12 Guerrero	21 Chiapas	Norte
3 Hidalgo	13 Puebla	22 Sinaloa	30 Baja California
4 Mexico	14 Veracruz	23 Durango	Sur
5 Morelos	15 Oaxaca	24 Coahuila	31 Sonora
6 Queretaro	16 Nayarit	25 Nuevo Leon	32 Chihuaha
7 Guanajuato	17 Zacatecas	26 Campeche	
8 Aguascalientes	18 San Luis Potosi	27 Yucatan	
9 Colima			

Map 7   Central America and the Caribbean

1 Guatemala	7 Panama	12 Haiti	18 Guadeloupe
2 Belize	8 Cuba	13 Puerto Rico	19 Panama Canal
3 Honduras	9 The Bahamas	14 Trinidad/Tobago	20 Pacific Ocean
4 El Salvador	10 Jamaica	15 Bahamas	21 Caribbean Sea
5 Nicaragua	11 Dominican	16 US Virgin Islands	22 Gulf of Mexico
6 Costa Rica	Republic	17 Martinique	23 Atlantic Ocean

Map 8   South America

1 Colombia	5 French Guiana	8 Bolivia	11 Argentina
2 Venezuela	6 Ecuador	9 Chile	12 Uruguay
3 Guyana	7 Peru	10 Paraguay	13 Brazil
4 Suriname			

Map 9   Africa

1 Morocco	14 Ivory Coast	27 Zaire	39 South Africa
2 Algeria	15 Ghana	28 Central African	40 Lesotho
3 Tunisia	16 Togo	Republic	41 Swaziland
4 Libya	17 Benin	29 Cameroun	42 Namibia
5 Egypt	18 Nigeria	30 Rwanda	43 Angola
6 Western Sahara	19 Niger	31 Burundi	44 Congo
7 Mauritania	20 Chad	32 Tanzania	45 Gabon
8 Senegal	21 Sudan	33 Mozambique	46 Equatorial Guinea
9 Gambia	22 Ethiopia	34 Malawi	47 Sao Tome/Principe
10 Mali	23 Somalia	35 Madagascar	48 Guinea Bissau
11 Guinea	24 Djibouti	36 Zambia	49 Reunion
12 Sierra Leone	25 Kenya	37 Zimbabwe	50 Mauritius
13 Liberia	26 Uganda	38 Botswana	51 Burkina Faso

Map 10   Europe

1 Iceland	9 Luxembourg	16 Romania	23 Monaco
2 Norway	10 Germany	17 Yugoslavia	24 Spain
3 Sweden	11 Poland	18 Bulgaria	25 Portugal
4 Finland	12 Czechoslovakia	19 Albania	26 The United Kingdom
5 U.S.S.R.	13 Switzerland	20 Greece	27 Ireland
6 Denmark	14 Austria	21 France	28 Andorra
7 Netherlands	15 Hungary	22 Italy	29 Turkey
8 Belgium			

Map 11   Middle East

1 Turkey	7 Egypt	13 Bahrain	18 Yemen
2 Cyprus	8 Iraq	14 Qatar	19 Sudan
3 Lebanon	9 Kuwait	15 Oman	20 Ethiopia
4 Syria	10 Iran	16 United Arab	21 Djibouti
5 Jordan	11 Afghanistan	Emirates	22 Somalia
6 Israel	12 Pakistan	17 Saudi Arabia	23 Occupied Territories

Map 12   Northern Eurasia - U.S.S.R.

1 Estonia	5 Belorussia	10 Armenia	14 Kirghiz
2 Latvia	6 Ukraine	11 Turkmen	15 Tajik
3 Lithuania	7 Moldavia	12 Uzbek	16 Russia
4 Kalingrad	8 Georgia	13 Kazakh	(RSFSR)
(RSFSR)	9 Azerbaijan		

Map 13   Southeast Asia

1 Afghanistan	8 South Korea	15 Laos	21 Brunei
2 Pakistan	9 Japan	16 Kampuchea	22 Hong Kong
3 India	10 China	17 Vietnam	23 Taiwan
4 Nepal	11 Mongolia	18 Malaysia	24 The Philippines
5 Bangladesh	12 Sri Lanka	19 Singapore	25 Papua New Guinea
6 Bhutan	13 Burma	20 Indonesia	
7 North Korea	14 Thailand		

Map 14   South Pacific

1 Indonesia	4 Singapore	6 Solomon Islands	9 New Zealand
2 Malaysia	5 Papua New	7 New Caledonia	10 Australia
3 Brunei	Guinea	8 Vanuatu	11 The Philippines

The Paralinguistic Aspect

We are using the term paralinguistic to include a variety of acts that accompany language or are used in place of language to communicate a message. Sometimes sound itself is used, e.g. a "wolf whistle;" sometimes the body is used, e.g. a smile. In short, this Aspect is about non-verbal communication. But let us hasten to say, it is not about all kinds of non-verbal communication. Painting and sculpture, for example, could be considered non-verbal forms of communication, but because they are only very distant cousins of language, they are not of primary interest to the language learner and teacher.

We have not dealt with the entire spectrum of non-verbal communication partly because to do so would make the book overly long and partly because paralinguistic communication does not lend itself to exploration in a book such as this one. Such paralinguistic events as a whistle and a smile are not easily classified or captured and catalogued in print, as are nouns, verbs, and topical vocabulary. Paralinguistic communication is very important, however, and we want to give students and teachers a handle on the subject. To do this we have outlined the field of paralinguistics and non-verbal communication. This outline, in checklist form, as usual, is included as a reminder that at some point in the language program it would be useful to discuss and explore the various sounds and actions suggested by the list. Also, as usual, the outline is far from exhaustive; it is suggestive and is intended only as a start.

Because they do fit into the format of this book, we have chosen to present three forms of paralinguistic communication in some detail: the International Sign Alphabet, Classroom Gestures, and a selection or sampling of common American Gestures.

The International Sign Language Alphabet has been included because we feel it is of potential value to language teachers and learners. For example, it can be used in the classroom in instances where a teacher might want to avoid oral spelling. The signs for the vowels might be especially useful because of the discrepancy between the sounds and the names of English vowels (*A, E,* and *I* give students a lot of trouble). And in general, a sign alphabet might be a useful tool for teachers who try to keep their own verbalizations at a minimum.

The Classroom Gestures are included here only to suggest that there can be a pedagogical use for paralinguistic gestures. To a certain extent, such gestures are idiosyncratic, but our brief page of sketches is, we hope, illustrative of some rather widely used classroom gestures. We would like to suggest that teachers and students might be well advised to establish their own system of classroom gestures at the outset of the language program. Our illustration can be used as a starting point.

The sampling of common American Gestures speaks for itself. These gestures have been collected, photographed, labeled, and categorized by Peg Clement in her thesis *A Handful of English: A Photographic Inventory of Typical American Gestures.* In presenting her pictures, we have used her classification system, with a few minor changes. In the first edition of *The ESL Miscellany,* in keeping with the "just stick to the facts" style of the book, we presented just the raw data, the pictures. However, Michael Jerald brought a problem to our attention. A non-native speaker of English, whether student or teacher, can look up any of the verbal raw data we have included. He or she cannot do so with the gestures.

Ideally, in using this section, the students will look at the pictures and discuss the meanings and implications of the gestures among themselves and with their teacher or a native speaking informant. This is particularly useful because so much of the meaning of any gesture is derived from the context in which it is used, any noises or verbalizations made with it, and related facial gestures and body language. In other words, the meanings and intentions of any of these gestures will vary considerably depending on when and how it is used. For those teaching situations in which a native "speaker" of American gestures is not available as an informant to help explore this kind of communication, Professor Jerald proposed a chart giving the general meaning of the gesture, what it is called, and what is said with it. As usual, this chart is presented in the form of a checklist.

Contents

List 1: An Outline of Paralinguistic Communication

A. Sounds

☐ 1. Individual sounds
   a. Fricatives—Shh!
   b. Nasals—Mmmm.
   c. Trills—Brrr.
   d. Clicks and stops—Tsk, tsk; Pst.

☐ 2. Emotional Intonation
   a. Surprise
   b. Fear
   c. Anger
   d. Irony
   e. Sarcasm
   f. Teasing
   g. Mockery
   h. Complaint
   i. Persuasion
   j. Pleading
   k. Flirtation
   l. Intimacy
   m. Pleasure

☐ 3. Exclamations and Interjections

☐ 4. Voice qualities and styles
   a. Whisper
   b. Baby talk
   c. Falsetto
   d. Command, stern and calm
   e. Command, gruff

☐ 5. Whistling

☐ 6. Humming

☐ 7. Yelling

☐ 8. Laughing

☐ 9. Crying

☐ 10. Coughing and throat clearing

B. Body Language (Kinesics)

☐ 1. Facial expressions

☐ 2. Eye contact

☐ 3. Gestures

☐ 4. Touching (Haptics)

C. Other Areas of Paralinguistic Communication

☐ 1. Silence

☐ 2. Time

☐ 3. Space and distance (Proxemics)

List 2: International Sign Alphabet

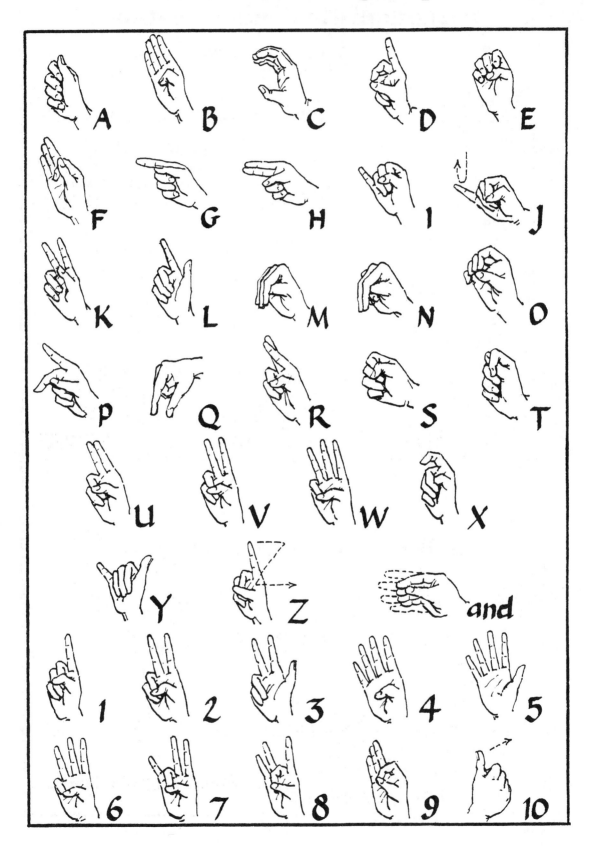

List 3: Classroom Gestures

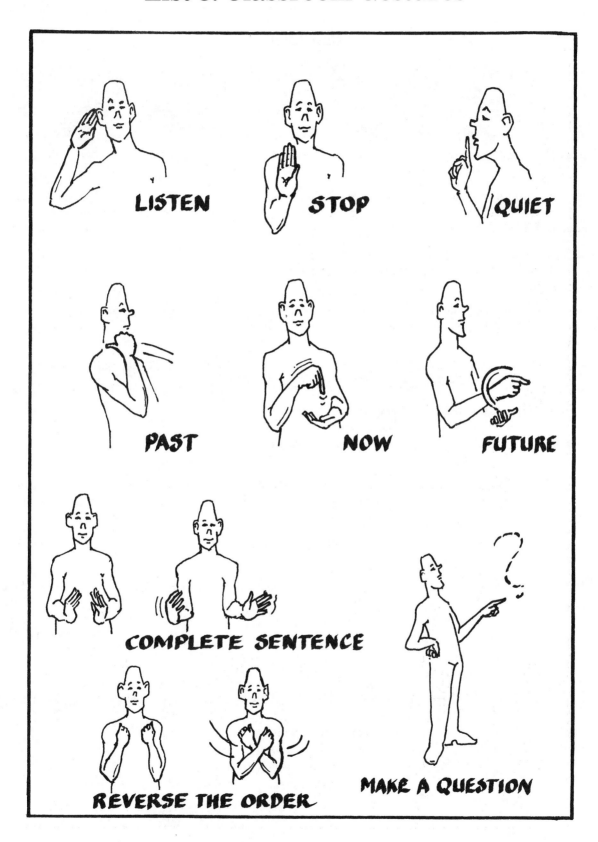

LISTEN

STOP

QUIET

PAST

NOW

FUTURE

COMPLETE SENTENCE

REVERSE THE ORDER

MAKE A QUESTION

List 4: Selected American Gestures

Checklist

Classification: Children's Gestures

Number	What it means	What it's called, if anything	What sounds or words are used with it
☐ 1.	An act of defiance often teasing to someone giving orders	* * *	"Nnn Nnnn!"
☐ 2.	Secretly giving a person who is having his or her picture taken "devil's horns" as a teasing joke or trick. This is very common childish behavior before a camera.	* * *	No noise, because the joke is secret; giggling is typical.
☐ 3.	Teasing ridicule meaning: "Ha ha! you got caught (and I didn't). It serves you right. You made a mistake. I'm right and you're wrong."	* * *	"Naa naa!" "Yaa yaa!"
☐ 4.	Teasing ridicule meaning, literally, something or someone smells bad. It implies, "I don't like him/her. That is awful!"	Holding your nose.	"PU!" "Yuck!" "That stinks!"

Parental Gestures

☐ 5.	Beckoning by wiggling the index finger means: "Come here. I want you here, now!" It is not always imperative and not always done to a child, although the person beckoned is usually of inferior status.	* * *	"Come here." "Come on."- said encouragingly.
☐ 6.	A reprimand or scolding gesture, often teasing, usually done to a child or inferior. The index/forefinger is pointed at the child.	Shaking your finger at someone.	"Naughty, Naughty!" "Bad girl! (or boy) "Tsk, tsk!"
☐ 7.	Scraping your index fingers together at someone usually a child or inferior.	* * *	The same as 6
☐ 8.	A signal to be quiet.	Shushing someone.	Sometimes done silently to avoid noise or with whispered "Shh" "Be quiet!"

Societal Gestures

☐ 9.	A civilian style salute most commonly used when pledging allegiance to the national flag or singing the national anthem. *See National Documents at the end of the Topics section.*	Holding your hand over your heart.	* * *

☐10. A military salute, a gesture of respect given to a superior or during the pledge of allegiance or the national anthem by military personnel and others in uniform (such as scouts) usually while standing stiffly at formal attention.

Saluting ____. (the flag, an officer, etc.)

* * *

☐11. The formal stance assumed while taking an oath. This is sometimes done (by those who reject the Bible) by putting a hand over their heart.

Putting your hand on the Bible.

"I swear (on the Bible/on my honor) that I will...."

☐12. A gesture with several meanings. Here it is shown as a "peace sign" which became popular during the 1960's. It can also mean "victory", either military or political. The gesture must be done carefully with the palm forward, since it resembles an older, traditional vulgar gesture, similar to #22 which is common in other cultures. The context and facial expression are important.

The peace sign.
A V for victory.

"Peace!"
Nothing is usually said with a victory sign.

Gestures of Greeting

☐13. A hand shake is commonly exchanged as a form of greeting, particularly between friends and during introductions. There are many variations. In general, a firm hand shake is appreciated. Most people attempt to express their feelings through the touch of the handshake, at least sometimes; they may feel confident, enthusiastic, friendly, gracious, seductive, "in charge," etc. Shaking hands with both hands suggests warmth of feeling. People will sometimes shake hands when parting or as a gesture of having completed an agreement. Hand shakes are most common between men, then between women or between men and women, then between adults and children of all ages. People even train their pet dog's to shake hands by offering a paw, a very common trick which amuses animal lovers.

Shaking hands.

"Hi."
"Hi there."
"Good to see you."
For introductions:
"Hello."
"How do you do."
"It's nice to meet you."

☐14. Between two members of some cultural and ethnic groups, elaborate special hand shakes are popular. Groups which have typically invented and used such rituals include children, athletes, members of secret societies, and people who identify themselves with both a specific ethnic group and a specific social or political philosophy. Knowing and using the ritual gesture is a way of identifying oneself and celebrating one's beliefs or success. Such rituals change constantly.
Pictured is a very common hand shake ritual, slap me five, of which there have been thousands of variations. One, a "high five" (simply slapping palms with arms and fingers extended upward - not shown), is the most common gesture of congratulations between successful athletes.

* * *

"Slap me five, Brother!"

☐15. A wave of the hand with fingers extended is the common form of greeting or saying goodbye from a distance or of getting someone's attention. Emotions or strength of feeling are indicated by the vigor of the gesture.

A wave.

"Hi." "Hello." "Bye."
"Yoo hoo."
"Here I am."

Gestures of Complicity, Duplicity, Fraternity

☐16.	A wink is a friendly facial gesture. It may mean many different things depending on the context and the people communicating. It may mean that you are taking someone into your confidence and that you agree with them: Don't let on, but I agree with you. Don't really believe me; I was only kidding. A wink may also be a gesture on quiet congratulations: I won't make a fuss, but, between us, you did a great job! Or it may be a gesture of greeting or invitation. A politician may wink to say: I see you are with me and I like you! Others may wink to say: You're attractive to me, Handsome (or Beautiful). Come over and get to know me! People are generally careful who they wink at.	Winking.	Nothing is usually said. Winks are often combined with a slight nod of agreement or encouragement. There is an old saying: "A wink's as good as a nod."
☐17.	Pointing with one's thumb, while extending the lower lip, and rolling one's eyes upwards, is a gesture of mockery and disapproval shared with someone who will agree with the opinion expressed. It is a common comic gesture.	* * *	"Get a load of this!" This expession is generally thought, not said out loud.
☐18.	A raised fist is a defiant and often threatening gesture. It typically suggests anger and a willingness to fight. With the palm outward, it is usually a salute of greeting between members of a group or a statement of political solidarity. In the U.S. since the 1960's, it has most often and widely been associated with the "black power" movement among black Americans, although other ethnic and political groups use it as well.	Often called the "black power salute."	Encouraging expressions such as "OK!" "Right on, Brother!" "Stand firm!" "Give it to 'em." "I'm with you!"
☐19.	Hitting someone in the ribs with your elbow (usually gently) means that you think what that person or someone else is saying is funny (and is probably meant to be.) The gesture is related to the expression, "He's ribbing you,," which means he is teasing or misleading you (usually for the fun of it.)	Poking someone in the ribs.	"Aw, come on." "You're ribbing me." "Ha! You can't fool me!" or "He's kidding!" "Don't believe a word of it!
☐20.	Tapping your temple with your forefinger or making a circular motion around your ear, usually while rolling your eyes towards someone and then pointing at them, means that you disapprove (good naturedly) of that person's behavior or opinions as being abnormal.	* * *	"He's crazy." "...nuts." "...got a screw loose." "...batty." "...loco." "... out of his mind." and other such comic overstatements.

Vulgar and Insulting Gestures

The following gestures should be understood, but non-native "speakers" of American English should avoid either using them or taking serious offense if they are used. "Vulgar" people will often use these gestures and related expressions lightheartedly, being offensive without really intending to give offense. Although these gestures may be expressions of real anger and aggressiveness, they may also be somewhat playful expressions of dramatic humor which may actually be intended to be friendly—children often experiment with such vulgarities among their friends "just for the fun of it." Even native "speakers" generally avoid using such gestures and expressions when they are out of their own cultural and ethnic contexts.

☐21. There are several insulting gestures involving the nose. They come from many different cultures, and some have been used for thousands of years. In most of the U.S., the one pictured (touching your nose with your thumb while wiggling your outstretched fingers) is taunting, a comic gesture of defiance and mockery. Flicking the side or bottom of your nose with your index finger is a much stronger, more vulgar insult. Both imply anger and rejection of the person insulted.

Thumbing your nose at someone.

Often done silently, or with provocative noises such as "Yaaa!" "Psss!" "Pppppft!" or almost any vulgar insult.

☐22. Jabbing upwards with hand extended, palm inward, and the middle finger extended is the ultimate vulgar gesture in most of the U.S. It is an angry and aggressive gesture, often made with such strongly vulgar expressions as "fuck you!" Although both the gesture and the expressions are commonly sexual in nature, only belligerent anger (real or caricatured for amusement) are intended. In some ethnic groups, this gesture is made with the index and little fingers or the middle and index fingers extended and spread in a V like a pair of raised legs. The intent is the same.

Giving someone "the finger."

Hisses, grunts, or any strongly vulgar expression.

Gestures of Hope or Good Luck

The following gestures were originally magic rituals addressed to the powers of Fate or the goddess Fortune. To unbelievers, they are gestures of pagan superstition. Although most people practice them or at least refer to them as good-natured jokes, some strongly religious people and same true believers take such rituals very seriously. Some hotels do not have thirteenth floors, and many people will not walk under ladders and avoid black cats. Magic or superstition, such rituals may amuse people, but they often make them slightly nervous as well.

☐23. A gesture expressing the hope that some specific good thing will happen. This gesture is also sometimes used with arms crossed over the chest (heart), particularly by children, as a pledge of truthfulness: "It's true! Cross my fingers, hope to die, if it's not!"

Crossing your fingers.

"Oh, I hope so!" "I hope, I hope, I hope."

☐24. This gesture is done to avoid tempting fate, to avoid bad luck, when someone says something very positive about you or when you or someone else has just predicted some good luck or fortune. Traditionally, the believer looks for something made of wood to knock on. A common joke is to knock on your head, making gentle fun of the ritual and ridiculing yourself as having a wooden head - a block head - stupid enough to go through with the ritual, which, of course, you always do, religiously.

Knocking on wood.

"I hope so — knock on wood."

269

Gestures of Jubilation and Approval

☐ 25.	Gestures of approval and disapproval, dating back to ancient Rome, when "thumbs up" meant "let the gladiator up; let him live."	* * *	"Thumbs up." "OK!" "Good work!" "Thumbs down." "That's awful!"
☐ 26.	Shaking your hands enthusiastically above your head, like pumping a person's hand enthusiastically, is a gesture of enthusiastic approval.	* * *	"You won!" "You're wonderful!" "Congratulations!" "Yea! We did it!"
☐ 27.	Shaking your hand with the palm out, thumb and index finger touching, and the rest of the fingers extended is a quiet, happy sign of approval and encouragement. *It should be noted that Americans from some non-U.S. cultural backgrounds may mistake the meaning of this gesture; elsewhere it is a vulgar gesture with strongly sexual implications.*	* * *	"All right!" *"That'a way!"* *"That's A OK!"* *"Right on!" said with a smile.*

Gestures of Congratulations and Self-Congratulation

☐ 28.	A gesture meaning that you or someone else has scored a point, either literally, in a game, or figuratively, in a discussion, argument, or some other competitive situation.	Chalking one up.	"OK, that's one for me (you, him, her, them, etc.)
☐ 29.	A comic gesture of self-congratulation. Rubbing your nails on your chest is interpreted variously as polishing an apple, a prize, or a medal.	* * *	The gesture speaks for itself.
☐ 30.	Another comic gesture of self-congratulation. You hook your fingers under your suspenders (imaginary or otherwise) and puff out your chest, looking mighty proud! Sometimes you snap your suspenders, particularly if they are real.	* * *	"Well?" "Don't shout all at once!" "I'm looking good!"

Gestures of Nervousness, Impatience, and Boredom

☐ 31.	Americans from many ethnic groups chew their fingernails when they are anxious or nervous. This gesture refers to the habit meaning that you are, or should be, nervous. It is often done dramatically for comic effect.	Biting your nails.	"Oh, oh." "Oh, my gosh!" "Uuuw!" "Ouch!"
☐ 32.	A gesture of impatience. When it is done openly while someone is talking, it is rude. It is often done covertly to tell someone that you are bored with what someone else is saying or with the situation you are in. Although it can show real annoyance, it is generally a comic or mocking expression.	Twiddling your thumbs.	"Ho hum!" "Really!" "I'm just bored to death!"
☐ 33.	A gesture of resignation or non-involvement meaning: So, what can I do? It's not my problem. I don't know what to do? I don't know anything about it. Don't ask me.	Shrugging your shoulders.	"Don't ask!" "Damned if I know!" "I haven't any idea!"

☐34. A dramatic stance, leaning back with arms crossed, expressing frustrated boredom and inaction. You are immobile. You have been kept from "going" either because you have been kept waiting or because you disapprove of the direction you are being asked to go in.

* * *

"Where the *** have you been?" This situation is impossible!"

Miscellaneous Gestures Showing Emotion

☐35. A gesture of anticipation meaning: that looks good! It is usually made when looking at food, either to show excitement or approval.

Licking your lips. Licking your chops.

"Mmmm!" "Yummm!" "That looks good!"

☐36. A gesture meaning "stop" or "slow down." It can be a command or an expression of concern, depending on your facial expression and the authority of your movement.

* * *

"Whoa!" "Just a minute!" "Hold it right there!"

☐37. A dramatic gesture showing shock or disappointment, particularly with oneself. Variations are clutching your forehead, covering your eyes, or slapping yourself on the forehead. It is often used when you have made a costly mistake.

* * *

"Oh, no!" "Stupid me!" "How could I?" "I don't want to look!"

☐38. The gesture of covering your mouth, gasping, and staring is one of horror.

A quick gasp or sucking sound.

☐39. The gesture of snapping your fingers along with an expression of delight and surprise means that you have just thought of or remembered something you have been trying to think of. Snapping your fingers with a stern, impatient, or angry expression generally means that you want someone to do something immediately. Snapping your fingers to get someone's attention (a waiter in a crowded restaurant, for example) is often effective but is considered to be very offensive; it will often get the waiter's attention but bad service as well.

Snapping your fingers.

"I've got it!" "That's it!" "Ah, ha!" "Eureka!"

☐40. This comic gesture suggests that you have a good and clever idea for some action. It is sometimes done simply to show anticipation, but when it is exaggerated (often with a grin of evil delight and a low chuckling sound), it suggests that you are being crafty.

Rubbing your hands (in glee).

"Oh, boy!" "Hee, hee, hee!" "Oh, just wait 'til I ..."

☐41. An expression of puzzlement or bewilderment.

Scratching your head.

"What?" "I don't get it!" "Huh?" "What's that supposed to mean?"

☐42. A gesture of relief after avoiding a serious misfortune. The same gesture is also used to complain about the heat.

Wiping your forehead. Wiping your brow.

"Phew!" "That was a close call!" "Oh, that was too close for comfort."

271

☐43. A comic gesture meaning: stop doing that, end it, or I disapprove! | Slitting your throat. | "That's it!" "Kill it!" "Wrap it up!" "Cut!" or a sound like "QuekkkkK!"

Miscellaneous Gestured Signals

☐44. Holding your hand out to the side (palm forward, fingers closed in, and thumb extended up) is the signal that you want to be picked up by a passing driver and given a ride. Hitchhikers usually smile and look hopefully at each car while raising their hands slightly or moving them backward and forward as if to get the driver's attention. Long distant hitchhikers often carry a sign announcing their destination. Although the picture shows a lone woman hitching a ride, many women choose not to expose themselves unnecessarily to possible danger or sexual harassment in this way. It is more common to see a woman hitchhiking with a man or another woman for safety and company. | Thumbing a ride. Hitching a ride | Expressions of thanks are reserved until after the driver has stopped and offered a ride.

☐45. This is a "literary" gesture used while a person is speaking before and after expressions which would be in quotation marks were the person's speech to be printed. It may be done in a serious, pedantic way or lightly, for fun. In either case it is a comical, somewhat self-conscious gesture. | * * * | Done either silently, with double funny noises such as "Qurk, qurk" or with the explicit "Quote; Unquote."

☐46. Measurement gestures are common to most languages and cultures. The one shown means the object or person was about as high or tall as the woman's hand. Length is shown by holding the thumb and forefinger apart the right distance or by holding the two hands apart with the fingers extended and the palms held inward. | * * * | "Oh, it was about this high (tall, deep)."

☐47. Gesturing to get the attention of a waiter is extremely difficult in American English, unless the waiter is attentive. You may wave discreetly or lift your index finger as shown here. You may even say "Excuse me," very softly and politely, as he passes close by. However, these gestures often go unseen in a busy restaurant, and snapping your fingers, clapping your hands, whistling, and shouting out for service are all considered to be very objectionable. They are outdoor behavior, suitable for hailing taxicabs in heavy traffic, an art which may also look like the gesture pictured when practiced by a master. | Catching the waiter's eye. | "um." "oh." "Excuse me, please." "ah. could we please..."

2

1

3

4

5

6

7

8

9

10

11

12

13

14

15

16

17

18

19

20

21

22

23

24

25

26

27

28

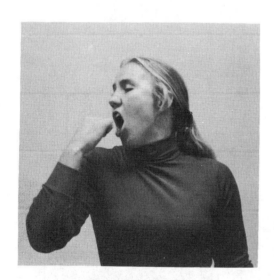

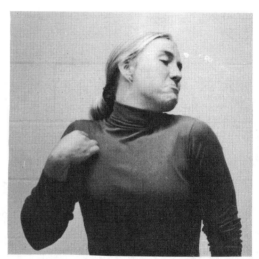

29

30

31

32

33

34

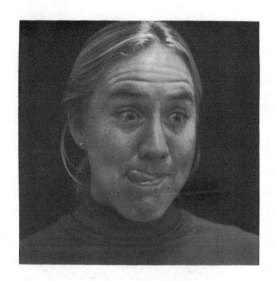

35

36

37

38

39

40

41

42

43

44

45

46

47

SOURCES

Allison, Alexander W., Herbert Barrows, et al. *The Norton Anthology of Poetry,* Third Edition. New York, N.Y.: W. W. Norton & Co., 1986

Boone, Eleanor; Rick Gildea, and Pat Moran. *Resources for TESOL Teaching* (Program and Training Journal 26). Washington, D.C.: ACTION/Peace Corps, 1978

Beilenson, Evelyn, and Ann Tenenbaum, eds. *Wit and Wisdom of Famous American Women.* White Plains, N.Y.: Peter Pauper Press, Inc., 1986

Carruth, Gordon, and Eugene Ehrlich, eds. *The Harper Book of American Quotations.* New York, N.Y.: Harper & Row, 1988

Chase, William D., and Helen M. Chase. *Chase's Annual Events: Special Days, Weeks, and Months.* Chicago, Ill.: Contemporary Books, Inc.

Clement, Margaret A. *A Handful of English.* Unpublished MAT Thesis, School for International Training, 1978

The Concise Columbia Encyclopedia., New York, N.Y.: Avon Books (Columbia University Press), Hearst Corp., 1983

Dobler, Lavinia. Customs and Holidays Around the World. New York, N.Y.: Fleet Publishing Co., 1962

The Encyclopaedia Brittanica. Chicago, Ill., 1990

Evans, Bergan. *Dictionary of Quotations.* New York, N.Y.: Delacorte Press, 1968

Frank, Marcella. *Modern English: A Practical Reference Guide.* Englewood Cliffs, N.J.: Prentice-Hall, 1972

Gunterman, Gail. "Purposeful Communication Practice: Developing Functional Proficiency in a Foreign Language." *FL Annals* (XII No. 3), 1979

Hacker, Andrew. *U/S: A Statistical Portrait of the American People.* New York, N.Y.: Viking Press, 1983

The Hammond Almanac. Maplewood, N.J.: Hammond Almanac, Inc., 1981

Hayden, Rebecca E.; Dorothy Pilgrim and Aurora Quiros Haggard. *Mastering American English.* Englewood Cliffs, N.J.: Prentice-Hall, 1956

The Information Please Almanac, 1990. Boston, Mass.: Houghton, Mifflin Co., 1989

Jacquet, Constant H., ed. *Yearbook of American and Canadian Churches, 1987,* Nashville, Tenn.: Abington Press, 1989

Kehoe, Alice B. *North American Indians: A Comprehensive Account.* Englewood Cliffs, N.J.: Prentice-Hall, 1981

Keller, Charles. *Tongue Twisters.* New York, N.Y.: Simon and Schuster, 1989

Key, Mary Ritchie. *Paralanguage and Kinesics.* Metuchen, N.J.: The Scarecrow Press, 1975

Kin, David. ed. *Dictionary of American Proverbs. New York, N.Y.: Philosophical Library*

Krohn, Robert et al. *English Sentence Structure.* Ann Arbor: University of Michigan Press, 1971

Menken, H.L. *The American Language,* Fourth Edition. New York, N.Y.: Alfred E. Knopf, 1936

Murdock, George P. "The Common Denominators of Culture" in *The Science of Man in the World Crisis,* Ralph Linton, ed. New York, N.Y.: Columbia University Press, 1945

The New American Desk Encyclopedia. New York, N.Y.: New American Library (A Signet Book), 1989

Parnell, E. C. *Oxford Picture Dictionary of American English.* New York: Oxford University Press, 1978

Praninskas, Jean. *Rapid Review of English Grammar* (Second Edition). Englewood Cliffs, N.J.: Prentice-Hall, 1975

Quirk, Randolph. *A Concise Grammar of Contemporary English.* New York: Harcourt, Brace, 1973

Radford, E. and M.A. *Encyclopaedia of Superstitions.* New York: Philosophical Library, 1949

Reader's Digest Almanac, 1987. Pleasantville, N.Y.: The Reader's Digest Association, Inc., 1986

Rutherford, William E. *Modern English.* New York: Harcourt, Brace and World, 1968

Schwegel, Janet. *The Baby Name Countdown.* New York, N.Y.: Paragon House, 1990

Silber, Irwin and Fred. *The Folksinger's Wordbook. New York: Oak Publications, 1973*

U. S. Department of State. *Background Notes, -1991*

Untermeyer, Louis, ed. *Golden Treasury of Poetry.* New York, N.Y.: Golden Press, 1989

Wallechinsky, David, and Irving Wallace. *The People's Almanac.* Garden City, N.J.: Doubleday & Company, Inc., 1975

Wilkins, D. A. *Notional Syllabuses.* Oxford: Oxford University Press, 1976

Whitford, Harold C. and Robert J. Dixon. *Handbook of American Idioms and Idiomatic Usage.* New York: Regents, 1953

The World Almanac and Book of Facts, 1980-1991. New York, N.Y.: World Almanac, Pharos Books, Scripps Howard, 1979-1990

INDEX

Other books from PRO LINGUA ASSOCIATES:

LISTENING MATERIALS

★ **People at Work.** Three-and-a-half hours of taped interviews with 10 varied and interesting Americans working successfully in ten different jobs from waiter and bank teller to medical intern and industrial engineer. Starting with the interviews and listening exercises, the students go on to reading and community exploration projects. Vocabulary building is stressed. Three tapes, student workbook and teacher's book with transcripts.

★ **Stranger in Town.** A "radio play" for building listening and reading skills and cultural awareness. Student script/text and tape.

★ **Biographical Sketches for Listening and Reading.** A workbook with two tapes and readings on 18 Nobel prize winners.

TEACHER'S RESOURCE HANDBOOKS

★ **Language Teaching Techniques.** 35 basic in-class techniques with variations.

★ **Experiential Language Teaching Techniques.** 30 out-of-class activities for learning language and culture.

★ **Cultural Awareness Teaching Techniques.** 20 discussion techniques for language classes and other training and orientation programs.

★ **Technology Assisted Teaching Techniques.** 40 Student-centered techniques for using 14 of the most common types of equipment from brown paper and slide projectors to PCs and VCRs.

★ **Taking Students Abroad.** A complete guide for teachers.

SUPPLEMENTARY MATERIALS

★ **Lexicarry:** An illustrated vocabulary builder for second languages. There is an English word list with over 3,500 words keyed to pictures given at the back of the book.

★ **Lexicarry Posters:** 25 wall charts

★ **54 Function Flashcards from Lexicarry.** Easy-to-handle strips illustrate situations requiring functional language.

★ **Index Card Games for ESL, French** and **Spanish.** The six card games explained in each of these handbooks are easy to prepare and play using 3x5 index cards. These are student-centered, group activities which provide practice with vocabulary, structure, spelling, questioning, and conversation. Sample games are given in the target language.

★ **Families.** Ten card games for language learners. Forty colorful playing cards are included.

★ **Conversation Inspirations for ESL.** Over 1,200 conversation topics and six distinctive conversation activities.

★ **Getting a Fix on Vocabulary.** Using words in the news. A vocabulary builder focused on the affix system in English, with exercises and words in the context of news articles.

Other books from PRO LINGUA ASSOCIATES:

INTERMEDIATE READERS

The following books are called vocabureaders. The readings are brief. Each one is followed by vocabulary-building exercises focused on key words highlighted in the texts. Supplementary material, suggestions for the teacher, and the answers are given at the back of the books.

★ **American Holidays.** Exploring the traditions, customs, and backgrounds of our national holidays.

★ **Summer Olympic Games.** Exploring the individual athletic events in international competition.

★ **The Zodiac.** Exploring human qualities and characteristics. Excellent conversation starters.

★ **Potluck.** Exploring American foods and meals.

★ **Money.** Exploring the ways we use it.

INTERPLAY ESL

★ **Max in America, Book 1, Book 2, Teacher's Handbook,** and **Narrative Picture Poster Cards.** A basic communicative skills text for adults of all ages. Book 1 is a high-beginning text for the "false beginner." Book 2 is for low intermediates. The Teacher's Handbook provides important material not given in the texts.

★ **The Grammar Handbook: Part 1** and **Part 2.** The books, designed for in-class use, provide a simple grammar explanation, a work sheet for use with in-class activities, and a choice of several techniques for teaching the grammar points of the lesson. Part 1 is for "false beginners" and Part 2 for intermediate students.

★ **Grammar Exercises: Part 1** and **Part 2.** These two books cover the same grammar as the Grammar Handbooks, but they are designed for out-of-class use, for homework or self-study, for use with or without the Handbooks. All the exercises are contextualized for high-interest and motivation, and the answers are provided at the back of the book.

★ **Smalltown Daily.** A multilevel reader (elementary, intermediate, and advanced) based on 288 authentic newspaper articles. Six teaching techniques are suggested. A topical index sorts out 25 fields of interest.

For further information or to order please write to

Pro Lingua Associates

15 Elm Street

Brattleboro, Vermont 05301

or call us at (800) 366-4775

We accept VISA and MasterCard orders by phone.